OVER 1000 FANTASTIC HISTORY FACTS

OVER 1000 FANTASTIC HISTORY FACTS

Miles Kelly

First published in 2012 by Miles Kelly Publishing Ltd
Harding's Barn, Bardfield End Green, Thaxted, Essex, CM6 3PX, UK

Copyright © Miles Kelly Publishing Ltd 2012

This edition printed 2016

6 8 10 9 7 5

Publishing Director Belinda Gallagher
Creative Director Jo Cowan
Editorial Director Rosie Neave
Editors Carly Blake, Sarah Parkin, Claire Philip
Editorial Assistant Amy Johnson
Cover Designer Kayleigh Allen
Designers Kayleigh Allen, Angela Ashton, Michelle Cannatella, Jo Cowan,
Joe Jones, Sally Lace, Simon Lee, Louisa Leitao, Andrea Slane, Elaine Wilkinson
Image Manager Liberty Newton
Indexer Gill Lee
Production Elizabeth Collins, Caroline Kelly
Reprographics Stephan Davis, Jennifer Cozens, Thom Allaway
Assets Lorraine King

ISBN 978-1-84810-661-1

Printed in China

British Library Cataloguing-in-Publication Data
A catalogue record for this book is available from the British Library

Made with paper from a sustainable forest

www.mileskelly.net

Contents

ANCIENT EGYPT

PYRAMIDS

MUMMIES

ANCIENT GREECE

ANCIENT ROME

GLADIATORS

VIKINGS

KNIGHTS AND CASTLES

EXPLORERS

ARMS AND ARMOUR

WARRIORS

SAMURAI

Ancient Egypt

Be pharaoh for a day and visit the amazing civilization of ancient Egypt.

Temples • Tombs • Gods and goddesses • Pyramids
Trade • Dynasties • Great Sphinx • Hieroglyphs
Pharaohs • Markets • River Nile • Warfare
Houses • Clothing • Farming

The heart of ancient Egypt

1 Without the waters of the river Nile, the amazing civilization of ancient Egypt might never have existed. The Nile provided water for drinking and watering crops. Every year its floods left a strip of rich dark soil on both sides of the river. Farmers grew their crops in these fertile strips. The Egyptians called their country Kemet, which means 'black land', after this dark soil. The Nile was also important for transport – it was a trade route for the Egyptians.

▼ The Nile supported many activities of ancient Egypt such as trade and farming. It was also an important water source.

Royal news

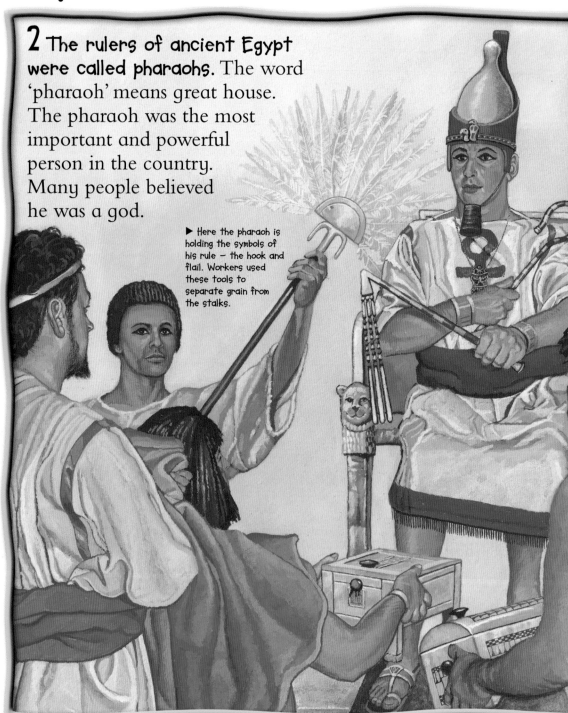

2 **The rulers of ancient Egypt were called pharaohs.** The word 'pharaoh' means great house. The pharaoh was the most important and powerful person in the country. Many people believed he was a god.

▶ Here the pharaoh is holding the symbols of his rule — the hook and flail. Workers used these tools to separate grain from the stalks.

3 Ramses II ruled for over 60 years. He was the only pharaoh to carry the title 'the Great' after his name. Ramses was a great builder and brave soldier. He was also the father of a large number of children: 96 boys and 60 girls.

Ramses II

◀ These people are paying tribute to the pharaoh. They have come from the surrounding countries to give him presents and tell him how great he is!

▲ On her wedding day, the bride wore a long linen dress or tunic.

4 The pharaoh often married a close female relative, such as his sister or half-sister. In this way the blood of the royal family remained pure. The title of 'pharaoh' was usually passed on to the eldest son of the pharaoh's most important wife.

I DON'T BELIEVE IT!

On special occasions, women courtiers wore hair cones made of animal fat scented with spices and herbs. The melting fat trickled down their heads, making their hair sweet smelling — and greasy!

Powerful people

5 Over 30 different dynasties ruled ancient Egypt. A dynasty is a line of rulers from the same family.

Crown of Lower Egypt

Crown of Upper Egypt

6 More than 7000 years ago, people from central Africa began to arrive in Egypt. They settled in villages along the banks of the Nile and around the Nile Delta. These villages formed the two kingdoms of Upper Egypt (Nile Valley) and Lower Egypt (Nile Delta).

► The double crown of Egypt was made up of two crowns, the bucket-shaped red crown of Lower Egypt and the bottle-shaped white crown of Upper Egypt.

▼ This timeline shows the dates of the dynasties of ancient Egypt.

Egypt's first pyramid, the Step Pyramid, was built in 2650 BC.

2750–2250 BC
OLD KINGDOM
(Dynasties III–VI)

The Hyksos people invaded in 1670 BC and introduced the chariot.

2025–1627 BC
MIDDLE KINGDOM
(Dynasties XI–XIII)

The tomb of the New Kingdom pharaoh Tutankhamun was discovered in 1922.

1539–1070 BC
NEW KINGDOM
(Dynasties XVIII–XX)

3100–2750 BC
EARLY DYNASTIC PERIOD
(Dynasties I and II)

King Narmer, also called Menes, unites Egypt and records his deeds on what we call the Narmer palette.

2250–2025 BC
FIRST INTERMEDIATE PERIOD
(Dynasties VII–X)

As the civilization of Egypt progressed people introduced gods for all different areas of life.

1648–1539 BC
SECOND INTERMEDIATE PERIOD
(Dynasties XIV–XVII)

Nilometers were invented to keep track of the height of the river, which was very important for the crops.

1070–653 BC
THIRD INTERMEDIATE PERIOD
(Dynasties XXI–XXV)

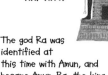

The god Ra was identified at this time with Amun, and became Amun-Ra, the king of the gods.

7 The history of ancient Egypt began more than 5000 years ago. The first period was called the Old Kingdom, when the Egyptians built the Great Pyramids. Next came the Middle Kingdom and finally the New Kingdom.

◄ Pharaoh Pepi II (2246–2152 BC), had the longest reign in history – 94 years. He became king when he was 6 years old.

Queen Cleopatra was the last ruler of the Ptolemaic period.

**332–30 BC
PTOLEMAIC PERIOD**

**664–332 BC
LATE PERIOD
(Dynasties
XXVI–XXXI)**

In 332 BC Alexander the Great conquered Egypt and founded the famous city of Alexandria.

**30 BC–AD 395
ROMAN PERIOD**

The Roman Emperor Octavian conquered Egypt in 30 BC.

▲ This vizier is checking sacks of grain that have been brought in from the harvest while a criminal awaits his punishment. Viziers were among the most important people in the country.

8 Officials called viziers helped the pharaoh to govern Egypt. Each ruler appointed two viziers – one each for Upper and Lower Egypt. Each vizier was in charge of a number of royal overseers. Each overseer was responsible for a particular area of government, for example the army or granaries where the grain was stored.

I DON'T BELIEVE IT!
Farmers tried to bribe tax collectors by offering them gifts of goats or ducks in exchange for a smaller tax charge.

Magnificent monuments

9 The three pyramids at the town of Giza are more than 4500 years old. They were built for three kings: Khufu, Khafre and Menkaure. The biggest, the Great Pyramid, took more than 20 years to build. Around 4000 stonemasons and thousands of other workers were needed to complete the job.

10 The Great Pyramid, the biggest of the three pyramids, was built as a burial place for King Khufu. He ordered three smaller pyramids to be built beside it – for his three main wives. The boat which probably carried Khufu's body to his tomb was buried in a special pit alongside the pyramid.

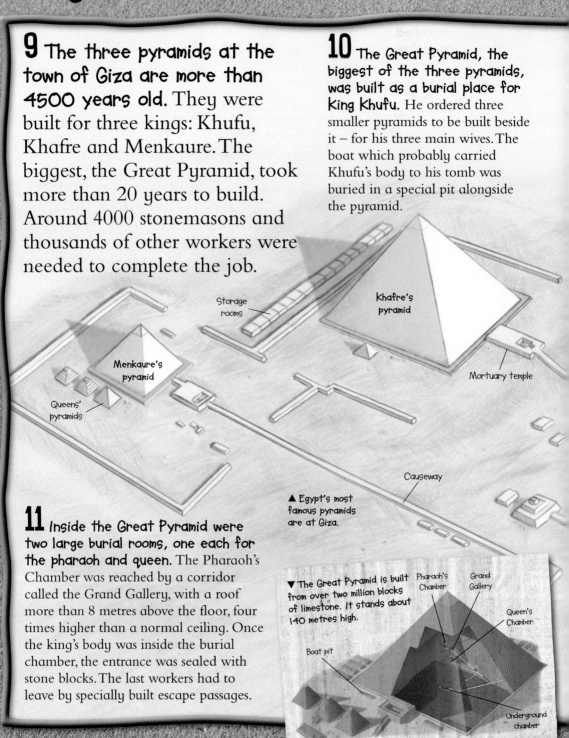

Storage rooms

Khafre's pyramid

Menkaure's pyramid

Queens' pyramids

Mortuary temple

Causeway

▲ Egypt's most famous pyramids are at Giza.

11 Inside the Great Pyramid were two large burial rooms, one each for the pharaoh and queen. The Pharaoh's Chamber was reached by a corridor called the Grand Gallery, with a roof more than 8 metres above the floor, four times higher than a normal ceiling. Once the king's body was inside the burial chamber, the entrance was sealed with stone blocks. The last workers had to leave by specially built escape passages.

▼ The Great Pyramid is built from over two million blocks of limestone. It stands about 140 metres high.

Pharaoh's Chamber

Grand Gallery

Queen's Chamber

Boat pit

Underground chamber

I DON'T BELIEVE IT!

A special handbook for tomb robbers called 'The Book of Buried Pearls' gave details of hidden treasures and tips for sneaking past the spirits that guarded the dead!

Mastabas of Khufu's officials

Khufu's pyramid

Queens' pyramids

Mastabas of Khufu's relatives

Sphinx

Valley temple

12 **The Great Sphinx at Giza guards the way to Khafre's pyramid.** It is a huge stone statue with the body of a lion and the head of a human. The features on the face were carved to look like the pharaoh Khafre.

14 **The earliest pyramids had stepped sides.** The steps were like a giant staircase, which the pharaoh could climb to reach the gods. The first step pyramid was built in the desert at Saqqara in about 2650 BC.

13 **Tomb robbers broke into the pyramids to steal the fabulous treasures inside.** To make things difficult for the robbers, pyramid builders added heavy doors of granite and built false corridors.

▼ The Step Pyramid was built on the orders of a pharaoh called Djoser. It is the world's oldest pyramid.

Supreme beings

15 **The ancient Egyptians worshipped more than 1000 different gods and goddesses.** The most important god of all was Ra, the sun god. People believed that he was swallowed up each evening by the sky goddess Nut. During the night Ra travelled through the underworld and was born again each morning.

◄ The sun god Ra later became Amun-Ra. He was combined with another god to make a new king of the gods.

16 **A god was often shown as an animal, or as half-human, half-animal.** Sobek was a god of the river Nile. Crocodiles were kept in pools next to Sobek's temples. Bastet was the goddess of cats, musicians and dancers. The cat was a sacred animal in ancient Egypt. When a pet cat died, the body would be wrapped and laid in a cat-shaped coffin before burial in the city's cat cemetery. The moon god Thoth usually had the head of an ibis, but he was sometimes shown as a baboon. The ancient Egyptians believed that hieroglyphic writing came from Thoth.

▼ Some of the well-known gods that were represented by animals.

Sobek   Bastet   Thoth

17 As god of the dead, Osiris was in charge of the underworld. Ancient Egyptians believed that dead people travelled to the kingdom of the underworld below the Earth. Osiris and his wife Isis were the parents of the god Horus, protector of the pharaoh.

Isis   Osiris   Horus

QUIZ

1. Who was buried inside the Great Pyramid?

2. Describe the crown of Upper Egypt.

3. What was a vizier?

4. Which pharaoh ruled for more than 90 years?

5. What is the Great Sphinx?

Answers:
1. King Khufu 2. A bottle-shaped white crown 3. An important governor 4. Pepi II 5. An animal with the body of a lion and the head of a human

18 Anubis was in charge of preparing bodies to be mummified. This work was known as embalming. Because jackals were often found near cemeteries, Anubis, who watched over the dead, was given the form of a jackal. Egyptian priests often wore Anubis masks.

▶ Anubis preparing a body for mummification.

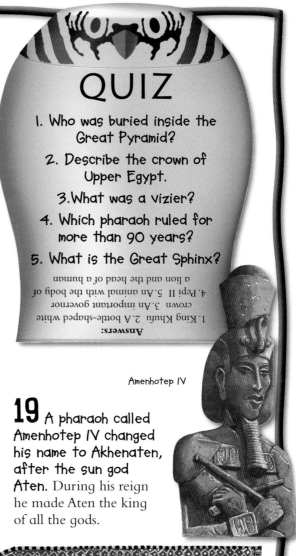

Amenhotep IV

19 A pharaoh called Amenhotep IV changed his name to Akhenaten, after the sun god Aten. During his reign he made Aten the king of all the gods.

23

In tombs and temples

20 From about 2150 BC pharaohs were not buried in pyramids, but in tombs in the Valley of the Kings. At that time it was a fairly remote place, surrounded by steep cliffs lying on the west bank of the Nile opposite the city of Thebes. Some of the tombs were cut into the sides of the cliffs, others were built deep underground.

▲ Robbers looted everything from the royal tombs – gold, silver, precious stones, furniture, clothing, pots – sometimes they even stole the dead ruler's body!

21 Like the pyramids, the riches in the royal tombs attracted robbers. The entrance to the Valley of the Kings was guarded, but robbers had broken into every tomb except one within 1000 years. The only one they missed was the tomb of the boy king Tutankhamun, and even this had been partially robbed and re-sealed.

▲ The solid gold death mask of Tutankhamun found in the Valley of the Kings. The young king's tomb was discovered, with its contents untouched, about 90 years ago.

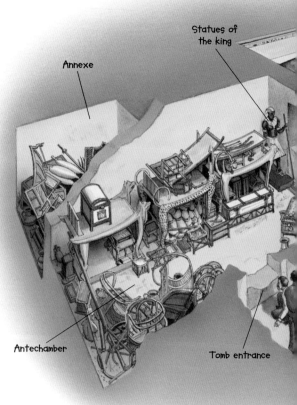

Annexe

Statues of the king

Antechamber

Tomb entrance

22 Archaeologist Howard Carter discovered the tomb of Tutankhamun in 1922. An archaeologist is someone who searches for historical objects. Tutankhamun's body was found inside a nest of three mummy cases in a sarcophagus (stone coffin). The sarcophagus was inside a set of four wooden shrines big enough to contain a modern car.

23 The ancient Egyptians built fabulous temples to worship their gods. Powerful priests ruled over the temples, and the riches and lands attached to them. Many of the finest temples were dedicated to Amun-Ra, king of the gods.

24 The temple at Abu Simbel, in the south of Egypt, is carved out of sandstone rock. It was built on the orders of Ramses II. The temple was built in such a way that on two days each year (22 February and 22 October) the Sun's first rays shine on the back of the inner room, lighting up statues of the gods.

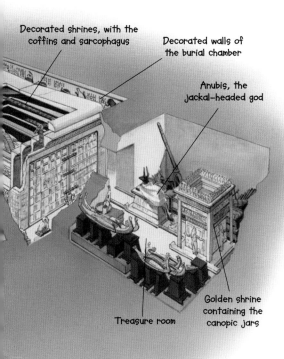

Decorated shrines, with the coffins and sarcophagus

Decorated walls of the burial chamber

Anubis, the jackal-headed god

Golden shrine containing the canopic jars

Treasure room

▲ Carter, and his sponsor Lord Carnarvon, finally found Tutankhamun's tomb after five years of exploration. Carnarvon died just four months after he first entered the tomb. Some people said he was the victim of Tutankhamun's 'curse' because he had disturbed the pharaoh's body. In fact Carnarvon died from an infected mosquito bite.

▲ Four enormous statues of Ramses II, each over 20 metres high, guard the temple entrance at Abu Simbel.

Big building blocks!

25 Each block used to build the Great Pyramid weighed as much as two and a half adult elephants! Labourers used copper chisels and saws to cut and shape the stones before dragging them on wooden sledges to the base of the pyramid.

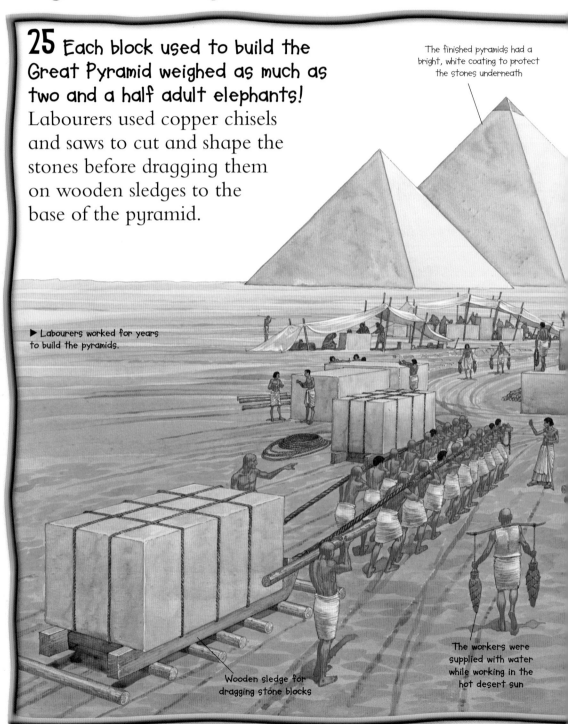

The finished pyramids had a bright, white coating to protect the stones underneath

▶ Labourers worked for years to build the pyramids.

Wooden sledge for dragging stone blocks

The workers were supplied with water while working in the hot desert sun

The huge stones had to be levered into exactly the right position

Up to two million of these blocks could be used to make one pyramid. It could take as long as 20 years

Teams of workers had to drag the stones up the slopes

26 Steep ramps of earth and mud brick were built to raise the stones onto the pyramid structure. As each new layer of stones was laid in position, the ramps were lengthened to allow workers to build the next layer.

I DON'T BELIEVE IT!

Imhotep, the architect of the Step Pyramid at Saqqara, was a busy man — he was also a vizier, a doctor, a scribe, a high priest and a poet! He served under a total of four different kings.

War and enemies

27 Foot soldiers carried metal swords and spears, with shields made of wood or ox hide. Later, soldiers were protected by body armour made from strips of leather.

28 Specially trained soldiers fired arrows from their bows while riding in horse-drawn chariots. Each chariot carried two soldiers and was pulled by a pair of horses. During the time of the New Kingdom (around 3500 years ago), this new kind of war weapon helped the Egyptians to defeat several invading armies.

▶ During the New Kingdom, Egypt formed a professional army of trained soldiers. They had strong shields and long, deadly spears.

▼ The Egyptians were gradually taken over by the Hyksos people from the east. The Hyksos introduced the horse-drawn chariot into Egypt. The Egyptians copied the chariot and eventually used it to defeat the Hyksos and drive them out.

29 The Sea People attacked Egypt during the reign of Ramses III. These raiders came from the northeastern corner of the Mediterranean. Ramses sent a fleet of warships to defeat them.

▼ The Hyksos invaders conquered Lower Egypt during the 1700s BC. They did not reach Thebes, but made their capital at Avaris.

▼ Ramses III fought off three separate lots of invaders. Warships were used by Ramses to defeat the Sea People.

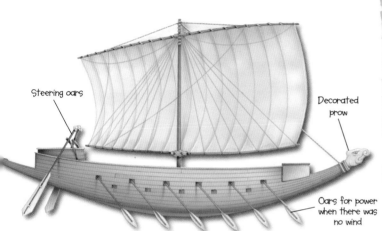

Steering oars

Decorated prow

Oars for power when there was no wind

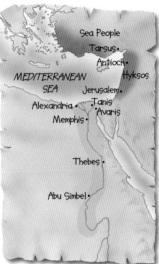

30 A general called Ptolemy won control of Egypt in 323 BC. He was the first of several rulers who made up the Ptolemaic dynasty. Under the Ptolemies, the city of Alexandria, on the Mediterranean Sea, became the new Egyptian capital and an important city for art and culture.

▶ The great harbours at Alexandria were guarded by the huge Pharos, the first lighthouse in the world and one of the Seven Wonders of the Ancient World.

31 The Hyksos people conquered Egypt in about 1700 BC. They ruled the Egyptians for 200 years. They introduced the horse, the chariot and other new weapons which the Egyptians eventually used to conquer an empire.

I DON'T BELIEVE IT!

Soldiers who fought bravely in battle were awarded golden fly medals — for 'buzzing' the enemy so successfully!

Bartering and buying

32 Egyptian traders did not use
money to buy and sell goods.
Instead they bartered (exchanged
goods) with other traders.
Merchants visited the countries
bordering the Mediterranean Sea as
well as those lands to the south. The
Egyptians offered goods such as
gold, a kind of paper called
papyrus, and cattle.

▲ These Egyptian workers are carrying
their oil to market. They can exchange
oil for anything they need, such as food
or clothes.

33 Merchants brought back exotic goods
from the land of Nubia, to the south of Egypt.
These included leopard skins, elephant tusks, ostrich
feathers – and slaves. One of the main trading posts
where goods were exchanged was the town of
Kerma, on the river Nile beyond Egypt.

34 Egyptians traded with a large number of countries in the Middle East and Africa. Traders brought back silver from Syria, cedar wood, oils and horses from Lebanon, copper from Cyprus, a gem called lapis lazuli from Afghanistan, and ebony wood and ivory from central Africa.

I DON'T BELIEVE IT!

Fly swatters made from giraffe tails were a popular fashion item in ancient Egypt.

▲ A busy Egyptian trading market with people bartering for goods.

35 When goods were sold they were weighed using a balance and special copper weights called deben. An item could be exchanged for its equivalent weight in copper. A bed, for example, had a value of 25 deben. Pieces of gold and silver were also weighed and used as payment.

The farmer's year

36 **The farming year was divided into three seasons: the flood, the growing period and the harvest.** Most people worked on the land, but farmers could not work between July and November because the land was covered by flood waters. Instead, they went off to help build the pyramids and royal palaces.

▲ Water was lifted from the Nile using a shaduf. It was a long pole with a wooden bucket hanging from a rope at one end, and a weight at the other.

37 **The river Nile used to flood its banks in July each year.** The flood waters left a strip of rich black soil, about 10 kilometres wide, along each bank. Apart from these fertile strips and a few scattered oases, pools of water in the desert, the rest of the land was mainly just sand.

▼ Almost no rain fell on the dry, dusty farmland of ancient Egypt. No crops could grow properly without the water from the Nile.

◀ Tax collectors would often decide how rich a person was by counting how many cattle he owned.

38 **Egyptian farmers had to water their crops because of the hot, dry climate with no rain.** They dug special channels around their fields along which the waters of the Nile could flow. In this way farmers could water their crops all year round. This was called irrigation.

39 Farmers used wooden ploughs pulled by oxen to prepare the soil for planting. They also had wooden hoes. The seeds were mainly planted by hand. At harvest time, wooden sickles edged with stone teeth were used to cut the crops.

40 Harvesting the grain was only the start of the process. In the threshing room people would beat the grain to separate it from the chaff, the shell, of the grain. It was then winnowed. Men would throw the grain and chaff up into the air and fan away the chaff. The heavier grain dropped straight to the floor. The grain was then gathered up and taken to the granary to be stored.

41 Wheat and barley (for bread and beer) were the two main crops grown by the ancient Egyptians. They also grew grapes (for wine) and flax (to make linen). A huge variety of fruits and vegetables grew in the fertile soil, including dates, figs, cucumbers, melons, onions, peas, leeks and lettuces.

I DON'T BELIEVE IT!

Instead of using scarecrows, Egyptian farmers hired young boys to scare away the birds — they had to have a loud voice and a good aim with a slingshot!

◀ Farmers had to hand over part of their harvest each year as a tax payment. It was usually given to the local temple in exchange for use of the temple's land.

42 Egyptian farmers kept cattle as well as goats, sheep, ducks and geese. Some farmers kept bees to produce honey, which was used for sweetening cakes and other foods.

▲ Winnowers separate the grain from the chaff.

Getting around

43 **The main method of transport in ancient Egypt was by boat along the river Nile.** The Nile is the world's longest river. It flows across the entire length of the desert lands of Egypt.

44 **The earliest kinds of boat were made from papyrus reeds.** They were propelled by a long pole and, later on, by oars. Gradually, wooden boats replaced the reed ones, and sails were added.

Alexandria·
·Tanis
·Avaris
Giza·
Saqqara·Memphis

El-Amarna·

Valley of the Kings
Thebes· ·Karnak
·Luxor

LOWER
NUBIA ·Aswan

Abu Simbel·

UPPER
NUBIA

Kerma·KUSH

RED
SEA

Blue Nile

White Nile

▲ The total length of the river Nile is around 6670 kilometres. To the south of Egypt, the Nile has two main branches — the White Nile and the Blue Nile.

▲ Early boats were made from bundles of reeds tied together.

45 A magnificent carved boat was built to carry the body of King Khufu at his funeral. More than 43 metres long, it was built from planks of cedar wood. The boat was buried in a special pit next to the Great Pyramid.

▼ The cabin on board Khufu's funerary boat was decorated with carved flowers. Other traditional designs were carved into the boat.

46 Wooden barges carried blocks of limestone across the river Nile for the pyramids and temples. The stone came from quarries on the opposite bank to the site of the pyramids. The granite used to build the insides of the pyramids came from much farther away – from quarries at Aswan 800 kilometres upstream.

▼ Simple wooden barges carried materials across the river Nile, so they were essential for building work.

▶ Wooden-built trading ships were propelled by a combination of sail and oar power.

QUIZ

How well do you know your gods and goddesses? Can you name these:

1. This god has a jackal's head and hangs around dead bodies.
2. This god's magic eye will protect you from evil.
3. Cats are fond of this goddess.
4. This god is a bit of a snappy character!

Answers:
1. Anubis 2. Horus 3. Bastet 4. Sobek

47 Transporting cattle across the Nile could be difficult. Wide-bodied cargo boats were used to ferry cattle across the Nile. The animals stood on the deck during the crossing.

Who's who in ancient Egypt

48 **The people of ancient Egypt were organized into three classes: upper, middle and lower.** The royal family, government officials, senior priests and priestesses, scribes and doctors made up the upper class. Traders, merchants and craftworkers were middle class. The biggest group of people – the unskilled workers – made up the lower class.

49 **The man was the head of any Egyptian household.** On his father's death, the eldest son inherited the family's land and riches. Egyptian women had rights and privileges too. They could own property and carry out businesses deals, and women from wealthy families could become doctors or priestesses.

◄ The arrangement of Egyptian society can be shown as a pyramid shape. The pharaoh sits at the top of the pyramid, with the unskilled labourers at the bottom.

Viziers and priests

Scribes and noblemen

Craftworkers and dancers

Peasant workers

50 **Most ancient Egyptians lived along the banks of the river Nile or in the river valley.** As Egypt became more powerful they spread out, up along the river Nile and around the Mediterranean Sea. Others lived by oases, pools of water in the desert.

Egypt, Old Kingdom

Egypt, Middle Kingdom

Egypt, New Kingdom

▲ These maps show the extent of the Egyptian empire in the three kingdoms.

51 Rich families had several servants, who worked as maids, cooks and gardeners. In large houses the servants had their own quarters separate from those of the family.

▼ Family life played an important role in ancient Egypt. Couples could adopt children if they were unable to have their own.

52 Dogs and cats were the main family pets. Egyptians also kept pet monkeys and sometimes flocks of tame doves. Some people trained their pet baboons to climb fig trees and pick the ripe fruits.

53 Young children played with wooden and clay toys. Popular toys were carved animals – often with moving parts – spinning tops, toy horses, dolls and clay balls. Children also played games that are still played today, such as leapfrog and tug-o'-war.

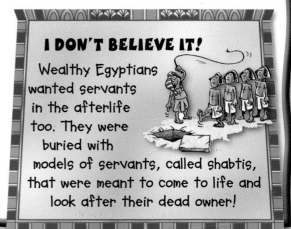

I DON'T BELIEVE IT!

Wealthy Egyptians wanted servants in the afterlife too. They were buried with models of servants, called shabtis, that were meant to come to life and look after their dead owner!

Home sweet home

54 Egyptian houses were made from mud bricks dried in the sun. Mud was taken from the river Nile, and straw and pebbles were added to make it stronger. The trunks of palm trees supported the flat roofs. The inside walls of houses were covered with plaster, and often painted. Wealthy Egyptians lived in large houses with several storeys. A poorer family might live in a crowded single room.

◄ A mixture of mud, straw and stones was poured into wooden frames, or shaped into bricks and left to harden in the sun.

55 In most Egyptian homes there was a small shrine. Here, members of the family worshipped their household god.

◄ The dwarf god, Bes, was the god of children and the home.

56 Egyptians furnished their homes with wooden stools, chairs, tables, storage chests and carved beds. A low three- or four-legged footstool was one of the most popular items of furniture. Mats of woven reeds covered the floors.

57 Rich families lived in spacious villas in the countryside. A typical villa had a pond filled with fish, a walled garden and an orchard of fruit trees.

▼ Here, two family members are playing a popular board game called senet.

58 **Families cooked their food in a clay oven or over an open fire.** Most kitchens were equipped with a cylinder-shaped oven made from bricks of baked clay. They burned either charcoal or wood as fuel, and cooked food in two-handled pottery saucepans.

QUIZ

1. Why did the Egyptians bury a boat next to their pharaoh?

2. Which part of the body was left inside a mummy?

3. Who was Howard Carter?

4. Why did farmworkers have nothing to do between July and November each year?

Answers:
1. So he can use it in the next life
2. The heart 3. The man who discovered the tomb of Tutankhamun 4. The river Nile had flooded the farmland

59 **Pottery lamps provided the lighting in Egyptian homes.** The container was filled with oil and a wick made of cotton or flax was burned. Houses had very small windows, and sometimes none at all, so there was often little natural light. Small windows kept out the strong sunlight, helping to keep houses cool.

60 **In Egypt it was good to eat with your fingers!** In rich households, servants would even bring jugs of water between courses so that people could rinse their hands.

Dressing up

61 Egyptians wore lucky charms called amulets. The charms were meant to protect the wearer from evil spirits and to bring good luck. One of the most popular ones was the eye of the god Horus. Children wore amulets shaped like fish to protect them from drowning in the river Nile.

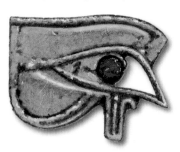

▼ The eye of Horus was thought to protect everything behind it. The god Horus had his eye torn out while defending the throne of Egypt. Later, the eye was magically repaired.

62 In Egypt, men and women both wore eye make-up. A special black eye make-up, called kohl, was made from ground-up raw metals mixed with oil. The Egyptians believed it had magical healing powers and could restore bad eyesight and fight eye infections. Egyptians also used face rouge for the cheeks and lips, face powder, paint for fingernails and hair dyes.

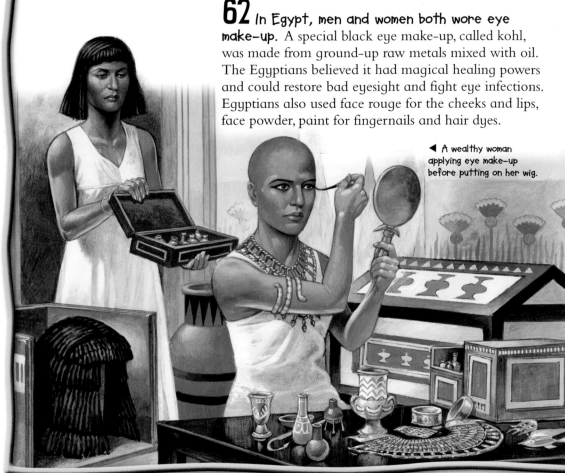

◄ A wealthy woman applying eye make-up before putting on her wig.

63 Most clothes were made from light-coloured linen. Women wore long dresses, often with pleated cloaks. Noblewomen's dresses were made of the best cloth with beads sewn onto it. Men wore either robes or kilt-like skirts, a piece of linen wrapped around the waist and tied in a decorative knot.

▶ This long dress is worn with a see-through cloak. Clothes like this kept people cool in the hot weather.

64 Wealthy people wore wigs made from human hair or sheep's wool, which they kept in special boxes on stands at home. Girls wore their hair in pigtails, while boys mostly had shaved heads, sometimes with a plaited lock on one side.

Comb

Hair pins

Comb

Wigs

▲ Wigs were often long and elaborate and needed a lot of attention. Egyptians cared for their wigs with combs made of wood and ivory.

MAKE A MAGIC EYE CHARM

You will need:

self-hardening modelling clay
length of leather strip or thick cord
pencil   poster paints
paintbrush   varnish

1. Knead the clay until soft and then shape into the charm.
2. Add extra clay for the pupil of the eye and at the top of the charm. Use the pencil to make the top piece into a loop.
3. Leave the clay to harden. Paint in bright colours and leave to dry.
4. Varnish, then thread the leather strip or cord through the loop and wear your charm for extra luck.

65 Sandals were made from papyrus and other reeds. Rich people, courtiers and kings and queens wore padded leather ones. Footwear was a luxury item, and most ordinary people walked around barefoot. Colourful pictures of sandals were even painted onto the feet of mummies!

Leather sandals

Reed sandals

Baking and brewing

66 **Bread was the most important food in ancient Egypt.** Harvested grain was stored in huge granaries until needed. The Egyptians' favourite drink was beer. It was very thick and had to be strained before drinking. Models of brewers were even left in tombs to make sure the dead person had a plentiful supply of beer in the next world!

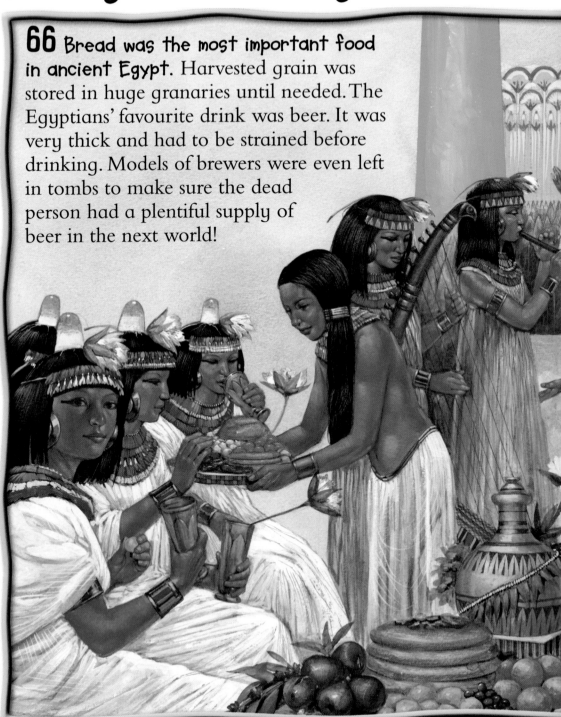

▼ An Egyptian banquet was a real occasion! Rich people could afford the best food and drink, but they would also have servants, as well as musicians and dancers.

67 A rough kind of bread was baked from either wheat or barley. The bread often contained gritty pieces that wore down the teeth of the Egyptians. Historians have discovered this by studying the teeth of mummies.

DESIGN A BANQUET MENU

A huge choice of food was served at banquets for wealthy Egyptians. Meats such as duck, goose, gazelle and heron, fresh fruits and vegetables, sweet pastries and cakes, with lots of beer and grape or date wine to drink.

Choose the food for a banquet and design a decorative menu for your guests.

Hard day's work

68 Scribes were very important people in ancient Egypt. These highly skilled men kept records of everything that happened from day to day. They recorded all the materials used for building work, the numbers of cattle, and the crops that had been gathered for the royal family, the government and the temples.

▼ Craftworkers produced statues and furniture for the pharaoh. Workers such as these often had their own areas within a town. The village of Deir el-Medina was built specially for those who worked on tombs in the Valley of the Kings.

◄ Only the sons of scribes could undergo the strict scribe training, which began as early as the age of nine.

69 The libraries of ancient Egypt held thousands of papyrus scrolls. They covered subjects such as astronomy, medicine, geography and law. Most ordinary Egyptians could not read or write, so the libraries were used only by educated people such as scribes and doctors.

70 Imagine if there were 700 letters in the alphabet! That was how many hieroglyphs Egyptian school children had to learn. Hieroglyphs were symbols that the Egyptians used for writing. Some symbols stood for words and some for sounds. Children went to schools for scribes where they first learned how to read and write hieroglyphs.

71 Most people worked as craftworkers or farm labourers. Craftworkers included carpenters, potters, weavers, jewellers, shoemakers, glassblowers and perfume makers. Many sold their goods from small shops in the towns. They were kept busy making items for the pharaoh and wealthy people.

72 A typical lunch for a worker consisted of bread and onions. They may also have had a cucumber, washed down with a drink of beer.

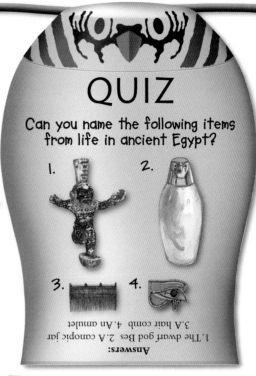

QUIZ

Can you name the following items from life in ancient Egypt?

1.

2.

3.

4.

Answers:
1. The dwarf god Bes 2. A canopic jar
3. A hair comb 4. An amulet

73 The base of the Great Pyramid takes up almost as much space as five football pitches! Huge quantities of stone were needed to build these monuments. The Egyptians quarried limestone, sandstone and granite for their buildings. In the surrounding desert they mined gold for decorations.

74 Slaves were often prisoners who had been captured from Egypt's enemies. They also came from the neighbouring countries of Kush and Nubia. Life as a slave was not all bad. A slave could own land and buy goods – he could even buy his freedom!

Clever Egyptians

75 **The insides of many Egyptian tombs were decorated with brightly coloured wall paintings.** They often depicted scenes from the dead person's life, showing him or her as a healthy young person. The Egyptians believed that these scenes would come to life in the next world.

Sunken relief

▶ The Egyptians produced raised reliefs by cutting away the background, and sunken reliefs by cutting stone from inside the outline.

Raised relief

76 **Egyptian sculptors carved enormous stone statues of their pharaohs and gods.** These were often placed outside a tomb or temple to guard the entrance. Scenes, called reliefs, were carved into the walls of temples and tombs. These often showed the person as they were when they were young, enjoying scenes from daily life. This was so that when the god Osiris brought the dead person back to life, the tomb owners would have a good time in the afterlife.

77 **The ancient Egyptians had three different calendars: an everyday farming one, an astronomical one, and a lunar (Moon) calendar.** The 365-day farming calendar was made up of three seasons of four months. The astronomical calendar was based on observations of the star Sirius, which reappeared each year at the start of the flood season. Priests kept a calendar based on the movements of the Moon which told them when to perform ceremonies for the moon god Khonsu.

▲ The days on this calendar are written in black and red. Black days are ordinary, but the red days are unlucky.

◄ Several artists worked on the tomb paintings. A junior artist drew the outlines of the scene, which were then checked and corrected by a senior artist. Next, painters filled in the outlines in colour.

78 Astronomers recorded their observations of the night skies. The Egyptian calendar was based on the movement of Sirius, the brightest star in the sky. The Egyptians used their knowledge of astronomy to build temples that lined up with certain stars.

79 Egyptian doctors knew how to set broken bones and treat illnesses such as fevers. They used medicines made from plants such as garlic and juniper to treat sick people. The Egyptians had a good knowledge of the basic workings of the human body.

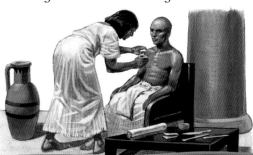

I DON'T BELIEVE IT!

Bulbs of garlic were used to ward off snakes and to get rid of tapeworms from people's bodies.

Nilometer

80 The Egyptians used a nilometer to measure the depth of the river Nile. They inserted measuring posts into the riverbed at intervals along the bank so they could check the water levels at the start of each flood season.

From pictures to words

81 The Egyptians had no paper — they wrote on papyrus. It was made from the tall papyrus reeds that grew on the banks of the Nile. At first papyrus was sold as long strips, or scrolls, tied with string. Later the Egyptians put the papyrus sheets into books. Papyrus is very long lasting — sheets of papyrus have survived 3000 years to the present day.

Reed brush

Papyrus scroll

Ink

82 Ink was made by mixing water with soot, charcoal or coloured minerals. Scribes wrote in ink on papyrus scrolls, using reed brushes with specially shaped ends.

① Cutting

▼ This is the process of making a papyrus sheet.

1. Papyrus was expensive because it took a long time to make. First people had to cut down the papyrus stems, and cut them up into lots of thin strips.

② Laying

2. Then someone laid these strips in rows on a frame to form layers.

3. The papyrus strips were then pressed under weights. This squeezed out the water and squashed the layers together.

③ Pressing

4. Finally, when the papyrus was dry, a man with a stone rubbed the surface smooth for writing.

④ Rubbing

83 The Rosetta Stone was found in 1799 by a French soldier in Egypt. It is a large slab of stone onto which three different kinds of writing have been carved: hieroglyphics, a simpler form of hieroglyphics called demotic, and Greek. All three sets of writing give an account of the coronation of King Ptolemy V. By translating the Greek, scholars could understand the Egyptian writing for the first time.

Rosetta Stone

84 In the 5th century BC a Greek historian called Herodotus wrote about life in ancient Egypt. As he travelled across the country he observed and wrote about people's daily lives, and their religion and customs such as embalming and mummification – he even wrote about cats!

85 The ancient Egyptians used a system of picture writing called hieroglyphics. Each hieroglyph represented an object or a sound. For example, the picture of a lion represented the sound 'l' and a basket represented the word 'lord'. Altogether there were about 700 different hieroglyphs. Scribes wrote them on papyrus scrolls or carved them into stone.

WRITE YOUR NAME IN HIEROGLYPHICS

Below you will see the hieroglyphic alphabet. I have written my name in hieroglyphs. Can you write yours?

J A N E

A B C D E F G H

I J K L M N O P

Q R S T U V W X Y Z

◀ A junior artist's work was checked by a senior artist, who then painted over the work in black paint.

86 The hieroglyphs of a ruler's name were written inside an oval-shaped frame called a cartouche. The pharaoh's cartouche was carved on pillars and temple walls, painted on tomb walls and mummy cases, and written on official documents.

Heroes and heroines

87 **Ramses II built more temples than any other Egyptian ruler.** Two of his greatest achievements are the huge rock-cut temple at Abu Simbel and the Great Hall at Karnak. He also finished building the mortuary temple of Seti I at Luxor. After his death a further nine pharaohs were given the name Ramses.

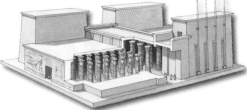

The Great Hall at Karnak

88 **Queen Hatshepsut was often depicted wearing men's clothing and a false beard.** She was the wife of Thutmose II. On his death Hatshepsut took the title of pharaoh and adopted the royal symbols of the double crown, the crook, the flail (whip) – and also the ceremonial beard!

▶ During her 20-year-reign Hatshepsut sent an expedition of five ships to Punt on the coast of the Red Sea. The ships brought back incense, copper and ivory.

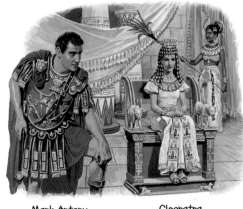

Mark Antony   Cleopatra

89 **Queen Cleopatra VII was one of the last rulers of ancient Egypt.** She fell in love with the Roman emperor Julius Caesar, and later married the Roman general Mark Antony. Cleopatra killed herself in 30 BC when the Romans conquered Egypt.

◄ Tutankhamun was buried in three separate coffins. Each coffin was specially made to fit around the one inside. This is the middle coffin. It is made of gold and inlaid with a gem called lapis lazuli.

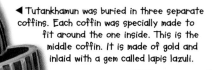

Narmer Palette

90 Tutankhamun is probably the most famous pharaoh of all. His tomb, with its fabulous treasure of over 5000 objects, was discovered complete in 1922. Tutankhamun was only nine years old when he became ruler, and he died at the young age of about 17. He was buried in the Valley of the Kings.

92 King Menes was the first ruler of a united Egypt. He joined together the kingdoms of Upper and Lower Egypt, under one government, in around 3100 BC. Menes was also called Narmer. Archaeologists have found a slate tablet, called the Narmer Palette, that shows him beating his enemies in battle.

Thutmose's giant granite obelisk

91 Thutmose III was a clever general who added new lands to ancient Egypt. Under his leadership, Egypt's armies seized territory in Syria to the north and Palestine to the east. During his reign Thutmose ordered a giant obelisk made of granite to be placed at Heliopolis – it now stands on the bank of the river Thames in London.

QUIZ

1. Name two popular drinks in ancient Egypt.
2. What is a cartouche?
3. What is the Rosetta Stone?
4. What is senet?

Answers:
1. Beer and wine 2. An oval plaque on which the pharaoh's name was written 3. The stone that enabled historians to read hieroglyphs 4. An ancient Egyptian game

Pyramids

Uncover the secrets of the pyramids and
find out how and why they were built.

Workers • Tomb robbers • Tools • Afterlife
Ancient Egyptians • Great Pyramid • Sphinx • Kings
Ziggurats • Aztec pyramids • Mummies • Religion
Maya pyramids • Temples • Pharaohs

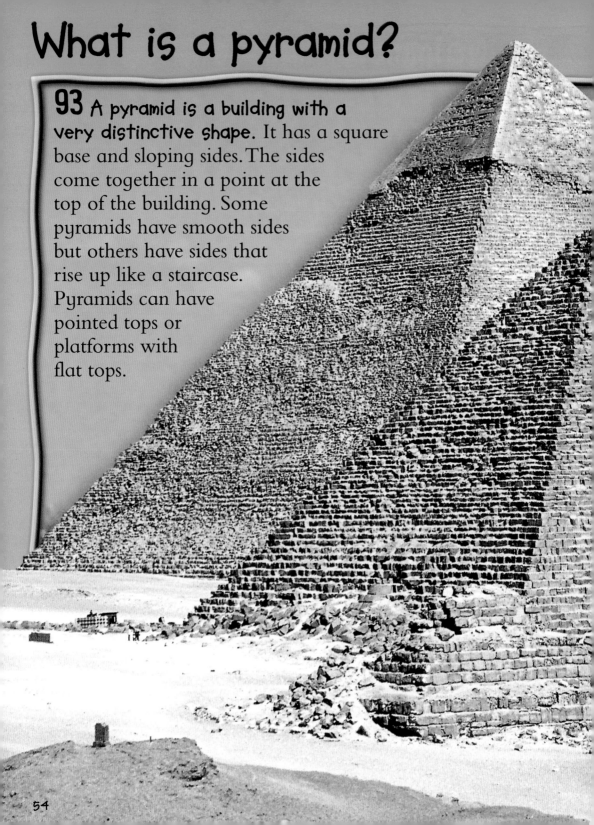

What is a pyramid?

93 **A pyramid is a building with a very distinctive shape.** It has a square base and sloping sides. The sides come together in a point at the top of the building. Some pyramids have smooth sides but others have sides that rise up like a staircase. Pyramids can have pointed tops or platforms with flat tops.

◄ The pyramids of Giza in Egypt are the best-known pyramids in the world. They were built about 4500 years ago. The three biggest pyramids were tombs for ancient Egyptian kings. In front of them are three small pyramids, which were tombs for other members of the royal family.

▶ The pyramid sites of ancient Egypt are all situated along the river Nile.

KEY
1. Giza
2. Saqqara
3. Dahshur
4. Meidum
5. Valley of the kings

SYRIA

LIBYA

Nile Delta

NUBIA

River Nile

55

Egypt, land of pyramids

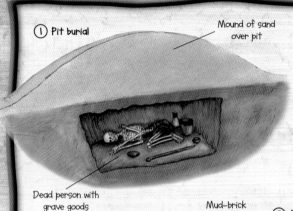

① Pit burial

Mound of sand over pit

Dead person with grave goods

95 The ancient Egyptians didn't suddenly decide to start building pyramids. Around 3100 BC there was a change in the way important people were buried. Instead of burying them in holes in the desert, they were buried in underground tombs carved into the rock. A low platform of mud-brick was built over the tomb, called a mastaba.

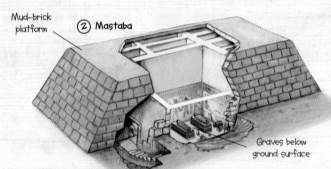

Mud-brick platform

② Mastaba

Graves below ground surface

▲ ▶ At first, bodies were buried in pits (1). Later on, the pits were covered with mud-brick platforms, or mastabas (2). Finally, several platforms were put on top of each other to make the first pyramid — the Step Pyramid (3).

94 The word 'pyramid' was introduced to the English language by the ancient Greeks. They saw that Egyptian loaves were a similar shape to Egypt's huge buildings. The Greeks called Egyptian loaves 'pyramides', meaning 'wheat cakes'. In time, this word changed into the English word 'pyramid'.

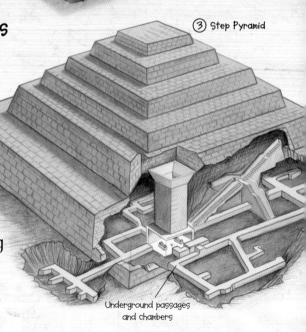

③ Step Pyramid

Underground passages and chambers

96 Pyramids developed from mastabas.
The first pyramid was built for Djoser, one of
the first Egyptian pharaohs (kings). It began
as a mastaba, but was built from stone
instead of mud-brick. A second platform was
added on top of the mastaba, followed by a
smaller one on top of that. The mound grew
until it had six platforms. It looked like an
enormous staircase, which is why it is known
as the Step Pyramid.

97 The architect Imhotep built
the Step Pyramid.
He was Djoser's vizier, or
chief minister, and was in
charge of all building
projects. It was his idea to
build Djoser's tomb from
stone, and to create a pyramid.
Imhotep was also a poet, a
priest and a doctor. Many years
after his death he was made into
a god, responsible for wisdom,
writing and medicine.

98 The Step Pyramid is at Saqqara
– an ancient Egyptian cemetery.
The pyramid was built around 2650 BC.
It is about 60 metres high and its sides are
more than 100 metres in length. King
Djoser was buried inside one of the
chambers that were carved into the solid
rock beneath the pyramid.

▶ The Step Pyramid was a series of
platforms on top of each other. It was
an experiment in building a tall
structure, and it led the way
to later pyramids with
smooth sides.

Sneferu, the pyramid king

99 **Kings who came after Djoser also wanted to be buried in pyramids.** King Sneferu (2613–2589 BC) had a step pyramid built at Meidum rising to 92 metres in height. Later his builders added an outer layer of stone, to create a smooth-sided pyramid. Then, for an unknown reason, the pyramid was abandoned. The stone was stripped away, probably for other buildings, leaving a tower surrounded by rubble.

▶ The pyramid at Meidum is an odd shape because it has lost its outer layer of stone. Some experts think the pyramid may have been started before Sneferu's reign.

100 **Sneferu had a second pyramid built, this time at Dashur.** He wanted a pyramid with smooth sides, but the builders made a mistake. Part-way through building they realized they'd made the sides too steep, so they changed the angle of the slope. This gave the pyramid an odd shape, which is why it is known as the Bent Pyramid.

I DON'T BELIEVE IT!

If you could talk to an ancient Egyptian, he wouldn't know what a pyramid was! In his language a pyramid was a 'mr' (say: 'mer'), and pyramids were 'mrw' (say: 'meroo').

101 The Bent Pyramid is 105 metres high, but it would have been at least 20 metres taller if the angle of the sides hadn't been changed. It is an unusual pyramid as it has two entrances and two burial chambers. Both of these burial chambers are now empty.

▲ King Sneferu's workers began building the Bent Pyramid in about 2600 BC. It has more of its fine stone facing left than any other pyramid.

102 Sneferu was the 'pyramid king' who learned from his mistakes. The Bent Pyramid wasn't good enough for him, so he planned another pyramid, also at Dashur. This is the Red Pyramid (also known as the North Pyramid). The builders got the angle right this time, and the sides slope gently to a point. It was the first 'true' pyramid.

103 Sneferu's Red Pyramid is 104 metres high, and its sides are 220 metres long. Today, it is named for the red limestone it is built from, but when it was finished it would have actually been white. This is because the sides were finished with slabs of gleaming, white limestone. A passage leads inside the pyramid to three chambers.

▶ The Red Pyramid was the third and last pyramid built by King Sneferu. He was probably buried in this pyramid in about 2589 BC.

Why build pyramids?

▲ Every day, Ra, the sun god, travelled across the sky in his sun-boat. He brought light and warmth to the people of Egypt.

104 **The ancient Egyptians believed in many different gods.** The most important was Ra, the sun god, who was said to be the very first pharaoh. Pharaohs who ruled Egypt after Ra were thought of as representatives of the gods. They were god-like kings, who had come to Egypt in human form to do the gods' work.

105 **One purpose of a pyramid was to be a tomb for a dead pharaoh.** It was where his body was buried, and where it was meant to forever rest in peace. His pyramid was also a storehouse, and was filled with all the food, personal belongings, gifts and magical spells he would need in the afterlife.

▶ After a person died, their personality left their body. The ancient Egyptians called it the Ba and thought it looked like a bird with a human head. The Ba made the dangerous journey to the underworld, where the dead were judged.

106 In the 1990s, Robert Bauval and Adrian Gilbert wrote *The Orion Mystery*. They pointed out that the Giza pyramids match the arrangement of the three main stars in the 'belt' of the Orion constellation (a pattern of stars). However, when the pyramids were built the stars in Orion's belt were in different positions in relation to the Earth – so the Egyptians could not have used the stars to help them work out where to place the pyramids.

I DON'T BELIEVE IT!

Pyramids were built with narrow shafts that pointed to the stars. The Egyptians believed that the pharaoh's soul used these to travel between the world of the living and the afterlife.

107 A pyramid was a 'living link' between the dead pharaoh and his country. Everyone in ancient Egypt knew that a pyramid was the last resting place of one of their kings, and as long as the pyramid was there, the pharaoh was there, too. While he was alive, it was a pharaoh's job to protect his people and his country. Once he died, a pyramid acted as a constant reminder of the role the pharaoh had played in people's lives.

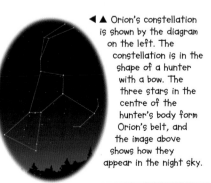

◀▲ Orion's constellation is shown by the diagram on the left. The constellation is in the shape of a hunter with a bow. The three stars in the centre of the hunter's body form Orion's belt, and the image above shows how they appear in the night sky.

Building a pyramid

108 The ancient Egyptians built their pyramids on the west bank of the river Nile. This was because the Egyptians linked the west with death, as this was where the sun set. The site had to be far enough away from the river to avoid flooding, but close enough for building materials to be transported to it.

▼ Builders made slots in the bedrock that were filled with water. The water was at the same level in every slot, showing the builders how much rock to remove in order to make the site flat.

109 After a site was chosen, the position of the pyramid was decided. Egyptian pyramids have sides that face north, south, east and west, but it is not clear how this was worked out. People may have used the stars to work out the position of north. Once they knew where north was, it was easy to work out the positions of south, east and west.

110 The site had to be flat, so the pyramid would rise straight up. One idea is that the builders flooded the site with water, and measured down from the surface. By keeping the measurement the same across the site, it showed them how much bedrock had to be cut away to make the site level.

▶ At the stone quarries, teams of men had specific jobs to do. Some split and levered rough blocks away from the bedrock. Others smoothed the sides of the blocks, and then they were ready to transport to the building site.

111 Pyramid workers used simple tools. Mattocks (digging tools) were used to clear the building site, and the rubble was carried away in woven reed baskets. In the stone quarries, stone was cut using mauls (stone hammers), copper chisels, and wedges. Woodworkers cut and shaped wood using copper saws and chisels, drills, hammers and planes.

112 Hundreds of men usually worked in the stone quarries. At busy times there may have been a few thousand. They worked in teams, cutting blocks of limestone and granite. The bedrock was marked with the outlines of blocks, and then the outlines were chiselled away to leave a grid of grooves. Copper wedges were knocked into the grooves to make the bedrock split. Last of all, wooden levers prised the blocks free.

Pyramid people

113 **Building a pyramid was a huge project.** It needed planning, and a large workforce. An architect was in charge of the whole project. He updated the pharaoh with its progress, and instructed the workers.

114 **Historians used to think that the pyramids of ancient Egypt were built by slaves.** We now know that slaves did not build the pyramids. Instead, they were built by hard-working, ordinary men who came from villages across Egypt.

▼ The pyramid builders lived in small towns near the pyramids on the west 'dead' side of the river Nile, where people did not usually live.

116 **The workers were well treated.** They were given lodgings in a specially built 'pyramid city'. It was a small town, with mud-brick houses set along narrow streets. There were bakeries, grain stores and shops for meat, other foods and tools. Workers were given free food and drink three times a day. They worked nine days in a row, then had the tenth day off to rest.

117 **The workforce was split into two big teams of around 1000 men.** The teams that built the pyramid of Menkaure were called 'Friends of Menkaure' and 'Drunkards of Menkaure'. Each team was split into five smaller teams of 200 men, who were called the 'Great', the 'Asiatic', the 'Green', the 'Little' and the 'Last'. In turn, these teams were made up of 20 groups of ten men.

▲ Metal-workers blew through tubes to increase the heat of a fire until it was hot enough to melt copper ore. Copper was used to make tools.

115 Building a pyramid was dangerous work, and accidents happened. The skeletons of pyramid builders show that they suffered from broken and crushed bones, and from worn out joints. In many cases workers' broken bones healed, but if an arm or leg was badly crushed, it was amputated (cut off). Worn joints could not be repaired, so workers had to live with the pain.

▶ This wall painting from a tomb shows workers shaping pieces of wood and making mud-bricks.

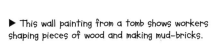

The Great Pyramid

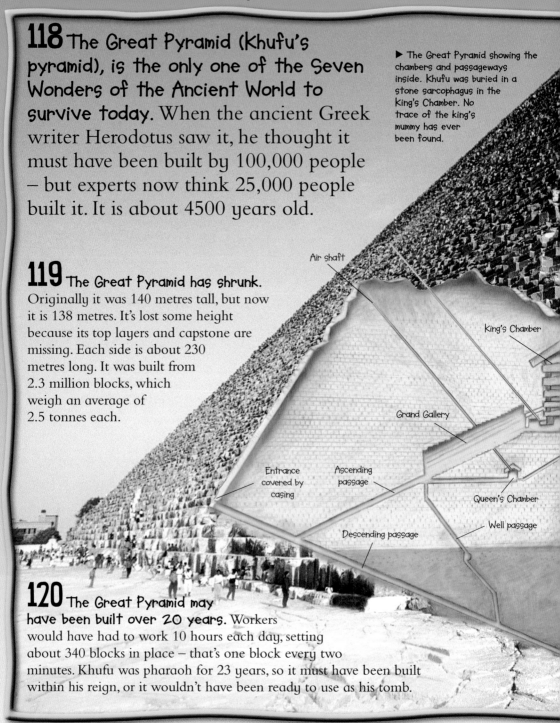

118 The Great Pyramid (Khufu's pyramid), is the only one of the Seven Wonders of the Ancient World to survive today. When the ancient Greek writer Herodotus saw it, he thought it must have been built by 100,000 people – but experts now think 25,000 people built it. It is about 4500 years old.

► The Great Pyramid showing the chambers and passageways inside. Khufu was buried in a stone sarcophagus in the King's Chamber. No trace of the king's mummy has ever been found.

119 The Great Pyramid has shrunk. Originally it was 140 metres tall, but now it is 138 metres. It's lost some height because its top layers and capstone are missing. Each side is about 230 metres long. It was built from 2.3 million blocks, which weigh an average of 2.5 tonnes each.

Air shaft

King's Chamber

Grand Gallery

Entrance covered by casing

Ascending passage

Queen's Chamber

Well passage

Descending passage

120 The Great Pyramid may have been built over 20 years. Workers would have had to work 10 hours each day, setting about 340 blocks in place – that's one block every two minutes. Khufu was pharaoh for 23 years, so it must have been built within his reign, or it wouldn't have been ready to use as his tomb.

121 The builders took a lot of care on the inside of the Great Pyramid, too. A narrow, sloping passage leads up to the Grand Gallery, which is a high, open space in the heart of the pyramid. Beyond that are three huge granite slabs that block the way. They were designed to stop tomb robbers from getting into the King's Chamber, where Khufu was buried.

122 Today, the King's Chamber holds an empty sarcophagus. Originally this stone box held Khufu's coffin and mummified body, and the room was full of his belongings. However, robbers broke in and stole the coffin and burial goods.

QUIZ

1. How many blocks of stone are in the Great Pyramid?
2. How long did it take to build the Great Pyramid?
3. What is the high, open space inside the Great Pyramid called?

Answers:
1. 2.3 million 2. About 20 years 3. The Grand Gallery

Around the Great Pyramid

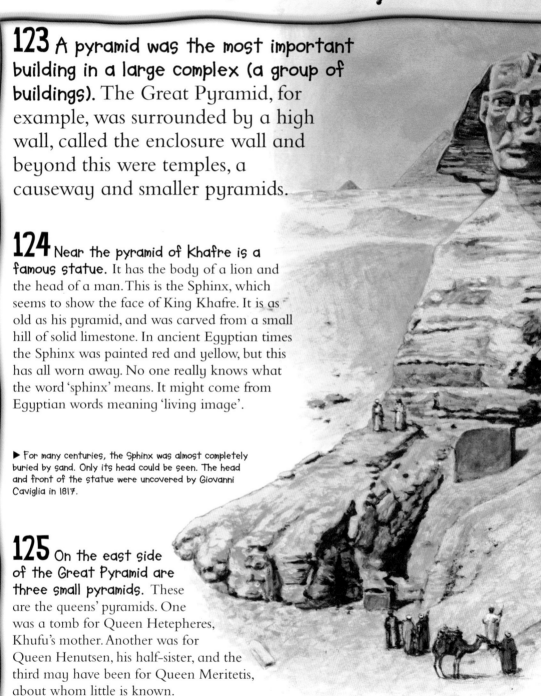

123 **A pyramid was the most important building in a large complex (a group of buildings).** The Great Pyramid, for example, was surrounded by a high wall, called the enclosure wall and beyond this were temples, a causeway and smaller pyramids.

124 **Near the pyramid of Khafre is a famous statue.** It has the body of a lion and the head of a man. This is the Sphinx, which seems to show the face of King Khafre. It is as old as his pyramid, and was carved from a small hill of solid limestone. In ancient Egyptian times the Sphinx was painted red and yellow, but this has all worn away. No one really knows what the word 'sphinx' means. It might come from Egyptian words meaning 'living image'.

▶ For many centuries, the Sphinx was almost completely buried by sand. Only its head could be seen. The head and front of the statue were uncovered by Giovanni Caviglia in 1817.

125 **On the east side of the Great Pyramid are three small pyramids.** These are the queens' pyramids. One was a tomb for Queen Hetepheres, Khufu's mother. Another was for Queen Henutsen, his half-sister, and the third may have been for Queen Meritetis, about whom little is known.

126 A fourth pyramid stood near the Great Pyramid. It was small, and only its base remains today. Khufu may have used it as a changing room when he took part in the sed festival, during which he told the gods that he had done all they had asked.

▼ This is one of the boats found buried at the foot of the Great Pyramid. All the pieces were put back together, and the boat is now in a museum.

127 When archaeologists dug along the south side of the Great Pyramid, they found two boat-shaped pits. They opened one, and out came a jumble of 1224 pieces of wood. It took years to join the pieces together, but eventually a boat measuring 43 metres in length was rebuilt. It may have been used to transport the king's mummy to the pyramid.

I DON'T BELIEVE IT!

Outside the Great Pyramid archaeologists found two pits. The first contained a boat. The second pit has not been opened but a tiny camera has been sent inside – its photos show another boat.

Resting in peace

128 **After a pharaoh died, his body was mummified.** This stopped it from rotting. The ancient Egyptians mummified their dead because they believed a person could only have a life after death if their body was preserved. It took 70 days to mummify a body and it was then ready to be buried.

129 **Once the mummy was ready, it could be buried in its pyramid tomb.** It was pulled over land on a sled, then taken by boat across the river Nile. There were many mourners – some were relatives, others were professional mourners who beat their chests, pulled their hair, and wailed aloud. Priests sprinkled milk on the ground, and burned incense.

130 **When the procession reached the pyramid complex, sacred rites were performed.** The mummy was taken from temple to temple, until it entered the burial chamber. It was then taken from its coffin and a priest touched its mouth, eyes, ears and nose with a Y-shaped stone. This was the Opening of the Mouth ceremony, and was believed to restore the pharaoh's ability to breathe, see and hear.

▼ The mummified body of an Egyptian pharaoh was transported across the river Nile to the west bank – the side of the river where his pyramid tomb had been built for him.

131 The priests placed the mummy back inside its coffin, which was put into a stone sarcophagus. Grave goods were stacked inside the burial chamber for the pharaoh to use in the next life. These included clothes, furniture, food and hundreds of everyday items. Then the priests left, and workers sealed the tomb so that no one would be able to get inside (or so they hoped).

132 After the pyramid was sealed, the pharaoh was believed to travel to the afterlife. On the way he met 42 judges, who accused him of crimes. He denied them all. After this, his heart was weighed against a feather, to see if he had led a good and truthful life. If he had, the scales balanced, and he was allowed to enter the afterlife.

End of the pyramid age

133 Most of the pyramids in ancient Egypt were built during a period called the Old Kingdom (around 2686–2181 BC). During this time pharaohs from Djoser to Pepi II demanded to be buried inside these awe-inspiring buildings.

134 It took much time and effort to build a pyramid. Towards the end of the Old Kingdom there were droughts when crops and animals died, and people struggled to live. They began to question the king's authority. If he was so powerful then why was he letting them starve?

135 The Old Kingdom, and the Pyramid Age, ended with the death of Pepi II. He died around 2184 BC, and after him, weak kings came to the throne. They lacked the power needed to organize pyramid projects. However, some kings did build pyramids, but from mud-brick instead of stone. They were smaller and not as well built as the massive stone pyramids made during the Pyramid Age.

136 Pyramids were supposed to be sealed forever — but every one of them was broken into. For tomb robbers, pyramids were very tempting places. It was impossible to hide a pyramid, so robbers knew exactly where to look. Despite all the blocked passageways and hidden entrances, thieves got in and stole the contents. If a robber was caught, he was put to death, usually by impaling on a sharp wooden stake.

▲ Even small objects such as amulets (lucky charms) were taken by tomb robbers. This is a scarab charm made of green jasper, taken from the tomb of the pharaoh Sobekemsat.

137 The last thing the kings of ancient Egypt wanted was for their tombs to be broken into. Pyramids weren't perfect resting places after all, and for this reason a new type of tomb was needed. Pharaohs of the New Kingdom (around 1550 to 1070 BC) were buried in tombs cut into the side of a remote valley instead. It's called the Valley of the Kings.

I DON'T BELIEVE IT!

The Valley of the Kings is overlooked by a large hill in the natural shape of a pyramid. Maybe this is why the valley was chosen.

▲ Tomb robbers made their living from breaking into tombs and stealing the contents. It was a family business, passed on from father to son. Robbers took great risks, as they faced death if caught.

Egypt's last pyramids

138 Deir el-Medineh was a village built to house the workers building tombs in the Valley of the Kings. Their kings were buried out of sight in underground tombs, but some workers were buried in tombs with small pyramids above them.

139 The small pyramids at Deir el-Medineh were ordinary people's private tombs. They were built of mud-brick, which was cheap and easy to make. The outside of the pyramid was covered with plaster to give a smooth finish, and pictures were painted on the inside walls.

▼ A cross-section through a small pyramid at Deir el-Medineh on the west bank at Thebes. This pyramid was built for an ordinary Egyptian, not a king.

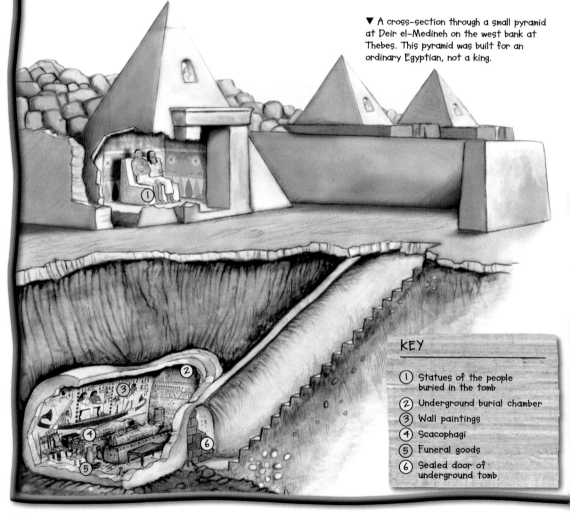

KEY

1. Statues of the people buried in the tomb
2. Underground burial chamber
3. Wall paintings
4. Scacophagi
5. Funeral goods
6. Sealed door of underground tomb

140 Mud-brick was the basic building material in ancient Egypt. Brick-makers collected mud, water and straw, then mixed them by treading them together. This mixture was pressed into brick-shaped wooden frames. The bricks were removed from the frames and left to bake in the sun. They were light and easy to build with.

141 From 770 BC, around 180 small pyramids were built in Nubia, at Meroe. They were built by kings and nobles to be used as tombs. Perhaps Nubian kings wanted to use pyramids to show their royal power.

142 The Nubian pyramids were small and short, had steep sides, and were very pointed. Most were built from sandstone. The last pyramids were built at Meroe, around AD 350 when Nubia was conquered by the Axumites. This was the end of 3000 years of pyramid building in ancient Egypt.

▼ The pyramids at Meroe are in varying states of disrepair due to people breaking into them looking for treasure, as well as stealing the stone blocks.

Ziggurats

143 The people of Mesopotamia built pyramid-shaped buildings called ziggurats. Mesopotamia was the ancient name for the land between the rivers Euphrates and Tigris, in what is now Iraq. The name ziggurat comes from the ancient word 'ziqquratu', meaning 'mountain top'.

144 The first ziggurats were built around 2100 BC at the city of Ur, Mesopotamia. This was roughly the same time that the Egyptian pyramids were built, but the buildings were very different. A pyramid was a pointed tomb with smooth sides, a ziggurat was a tower with a temple, built on a series of platforms.

▶ A ziggurat, or temple tower, in a town in ancient Mesopotamia (Iraq). A priest, wearing a fish costume, leads a procession of worshippers to the temple at the top of the ziggurat.

Tower

Temple

Priest

Procession of worshippers

QUIZ

1. What was at the top of a ziggurat?
2. In which city was the Tower of Babel?
3. True or false: a ziggurat had smooth sides.
4. What were ziggurats made from?

Answers:
1. A temple 2. Babylon
3. False – a ziggurat had stepped sides
4. Mud-brick

145 Ziggurats were the centre of religious life in Mesopotamian cities. There was a constant bustle of priests, officials and worshippers. The faithful believed ziggurats were links between heaven and earth. As they climbed up to the temple they felt that they were getting closer to the gods.

146 A ziggurat was made from several flat platforms, built on top of each other. These were reached by ramps and outer staircases. The building was made from mud-bricks, held together by wooden beams and reed matting. Some outer bricks were coated in bright colours.

147 The largest ziggurat was in the city of Babylon. It was built around 600 BC by King Nebuchadnezzar II. At this time it was called 'Etemenanki', which means 'house of the foundation of heaven on earth'. It had seven platforms, and was 100 metres tall. The Book of Genesis, in the Bible, calls Babylon 'Babel', and refers to a tall brick tower 'that reaches to the heavens'. This probably refers to the ziggurat, which became known as the Tower of Babel.

Pyramids of the Maya

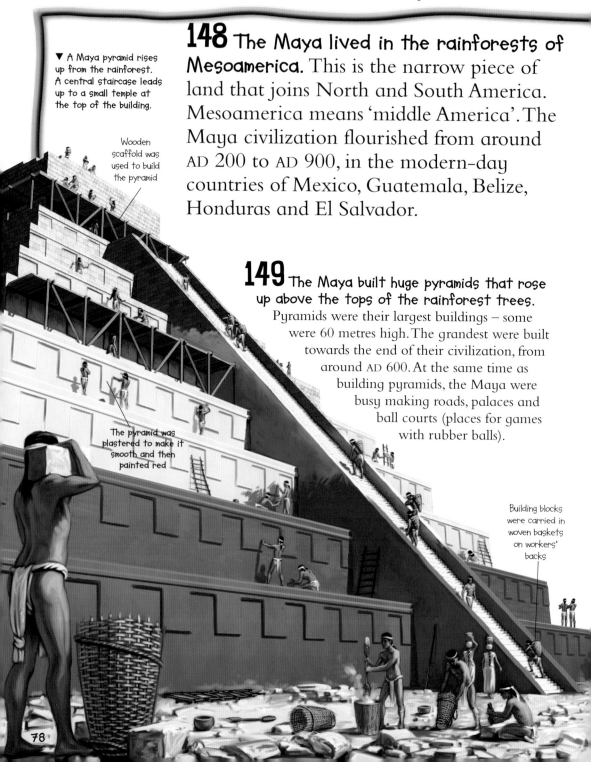

▼ A Maya pyramid rises up from the rainforest. A central staircase leads up to a small temple at the top of the building.

Wooden scaffold was used to build the pyramid

The pyramid was plastered to make it smooth and then painted red

148 The Maya lived in the rainforests of Mesoamerica. This is the narrow piece of land that joins North and South America. Mesoamerica means 'middle America'. The Maya civilization flourished from around AD 200 to AD 900, in the modern-day countries of Mexico, Guatemala, Belize, Honduras and El Salvador.

149 The Maya built huge pyramids that rose up above the tops of the rainforest trees. Pyramids were their largest buildings – some were 60 metres high. The grandest were built towards the end of their civilization, from around AD 600. At the same time as building pyramids, the Maya were busy making roads, palaces and ball courts (places for games with rubber balls).

Building blocks were carried in woven baskets on workers' backs

150 Maya pyramids were not made of solid stone. They were pyramid-shaped mounds of compacted earth and rubble, with stone walls on the outside. The walls were built to form a series of steps. Then they were layered with plaster to make them smooth, and painted red. A temple was built on the top, reached by one or more staircases at the front of the building.

▲ The Temple of the Inscriptions is the tomb of Pacal the Great. It is 23 metres high.

▲ Some Maya pyramids had images of human skulls carved all around them. They represented the skulls of enemies defeated in battle.

152 The Temple of the Inscriptions at Palenque, Mexico, is the most famous of all Maya pyramids. It was built around AD 680, as a tomb for the Maya king Pacal. His tomb was found after archaeologists lifted a stone slab at the top of the pyramid and climbed down a passage. Pacal was buried inside a huge stone sarcophagus. Its carved lid shows the king on his way to the afterlife.

151 Maya pyramids were temples to the gods and tombs for dead kings. During religious ceremonies, priests climbed the steep staircases. They believed the higher they climbed, the nearer they came to their gods. In the temple at the top, prisoners were sacrificed as offerings to the gods. Crowds gathered in courtyards around the pyramid to watch the blood flow.

I DON'T BELIEVE IT!

Pacal was buried with a mask of jade (a hard green stone) covering his face. The mask was stolen from a museum by two students in 1985. Police tracked it down in 1989, and returned it to the museum.

Pyramids of Mexico

153 Many pyramids were built by the ancient peoples of Mexico, such as the Olmecs, the Toltecs and the Aztecs. Some of the oldest and largest are at Teotihuacan. One of the best known is the Pyramid of the Magician, at Uxmal.

154 Long ago, a city called Teotihuacan existed in Mexico. Around AD 500, it was one of the world's largest cities. In the city centre were two huge pyramids – the Pyramid of the Moon and the Pyramid of the Sun.

◀ The Pyramid of the Magician was built by the Maya. They began building it in the AD 500s, and it was in use for about 400 years. It is unusual because it has curved sides, and is an oval shape.

I DON'T BELIEVE IT!

Around AD 500, so many people lived in Teotihuacan, that it was one of the biggest cities in the world!

▲ The Pyramid of the Sun is made from around 2.5 million tonnes of earth and stone.

157 The city of Tula also became important after the fall of Teotihuacan. It was the capital of the Toltecs, who built several temple-pyramids there. At the top of Pyramid B are columns carved decoratively to look like warriors, which supported the temple roof. When the Toltecs lost power, a new group became important in Mexico – the Aztecs.

155 The Pyramid of the Sun, at Teotihuacan, was built around 2000 years ago. According to Mexican legend, it was built at the place where time began. Archaeologists discovered a small shrine built over a sacred cave at the site. Over time the shrine was made bigger, and became a series of platforms rising to 75 metres in height. At the top was a temple. The whole pyramid was covered with painted plaster.

▶ The warrior columns at the top of the Toltec pyramid at Tula are 4.6 metres high.

156 The city of Teotihuacan was abandoned around AD 750. No one really knows why, but its pyramids were burned, statues were broken, and the people left. After the fall of Teotihuacan, other cities rose to power. In the city of Cholula, a huge pyramid-shaped temple was built. The Great Pyramid of Cholula is the largest pyramid in the Americas. Its sides are 450 metres in length, and it is about 66 metres in height.

Pyramids of the Aztecs

158 The Aztecs lived in Mexico from around AD 1325 to AD 1521. Their capital city, Tenochtitlan, was built on an island in the middle of Lake Texcoco. Today, the lake has been drained, and Mexico City has been built over the Aztec capital's ruins. Beneath the modern streets are the remains of a giant Aztec pyramid.

159 Aztec pyramids were built as temples, where sacrifices were made to the gods. They were the main town buildings, and were surrounded by public squares. The squares were viewing places, where the public gathered to watch priests at work at the top of the pyramid.

160 Aztecs sacrificed animals and humans to their gods to ensure that the universe would continue to exist. Every town had sacrificial ceremonies. Many prisoners who were captured in battle slowly walked towards the place of execution. The victims' hearts, limbs and even heads were removed during ceremonies.

▲ An Aztec knife with a stone blade and decorated mosaic handle. It may have been used to sacrifice victims.

161 The Aztec pyramid at Tenochtitlan was built over roughly 200 years. It reached its final shape around AD 1519. At 30 metres high, it was made from gravel and mud. The outside was faced with stone and brightly painted plaster. Twin staircases led to the top, where there were a pair of shrines to the city's gods of rain and war. When the Aztec empire was conquered by Spain in 1521, the pyramid became known as the 'Templo Mayor' (Great Temple).

▼ A reconstruction of the Aztec temples and squares at Tenochtitlan, present-day Mexico City.

Shrine to the god of war

Shrine to the god of rain

Templo Mayor

Public square

◀ The Aztecs sacrificed human victims at shrines built at the top of their pyramids.

MAKE A MOSAIC

You will need:
coloured paper cut into small squares
plain paper   pencil   glue

1. Draw a design onto the plain paper using the pencil.
2. Fill in your design with different coloured squares of paper and stick them down with glue.

Now you have your very own mosaic!

162 The Spanish killed many Aztecs, and destroyed the Great Temple. They believed that human sacrifice was wrong, and that the Aztec religion was false. Some of the stone was used for new buildings, such as the Metropolitan Cathedral, in Mexico City. The pyramid was reduced to a low mound, and became known as the 'Hill of the Dogs' because stray dogs lived there. By chance, in 1978, workmen discovered the pyramid's ruins and archaeologists began excavating them.

A world of pyramids

163 The Romans were experts at copying other people's ideas. For example, in their capital at Rome, Italy, is the Pyramid of Cestius. The Romans ruled Egypt between 30 BC and AD 395, and the Egyptian pyramids had impressed them. The Roman pyramid was built about 12 BC, as a tomb for Gaius Cestius, a Roman politician.

164 There are ancient pyramids in China, but little is known about them. Near the city of Xian are about 100 pyramid-shaped mounds made from soil. Some are quite low, but a few rise up to 60 metres. These are the burial mounds of China's early emperors and empresses, built between 200 BC and AD 800.

▼ The Pyramid of Cestius, Rome, is made from concrete covered with slabs of white marble. It is about 36 metres high.

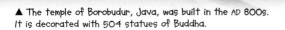

▲ The temple of Borobudur, Java, was built in the AD 800s. It is decorated with 504 statues of Buddha.

QUIZ

1. How tall is the Pyramid of Cestius?
2. In what country are the pyramids near Xian located?
3. Statues of whom can be found at the temple of Borobudur?

Answers:
1. 36 meters tall
2. They are located in China
3. Buddha

165 The ancient Buddhist temple of Borobudur, on the island of Java, looks like a step pyramid. The different levels reflect the ideas of Buddhist faith, and the temple is used as a centre of religious practice. There are several temples at Bagan, Myanmar (Burma), which have tall spires that look like narrow, pointed pyramids.

166 During the 19th century there were even plans to have a pyramid built in London! At this time cemeteries were filling up and people were worried there was not enough space. So they came up with a plan to build a giant pyramid on Primrose Hill, to hold the bodies of five million Londoners. It was never actually built.

RIP

85

Mummies

Journey through the ages and unearth
the mysteries of the mummies.

Afterlife • Tutankhamun • Bog bodies • Amulets
Masks • Tombs • Sacrifices • Pharaohs
Iceman • Ancient Egypt • Spells • Lindow Man
Animals • Myths • Coffins • Jewellery

What is a mummy?

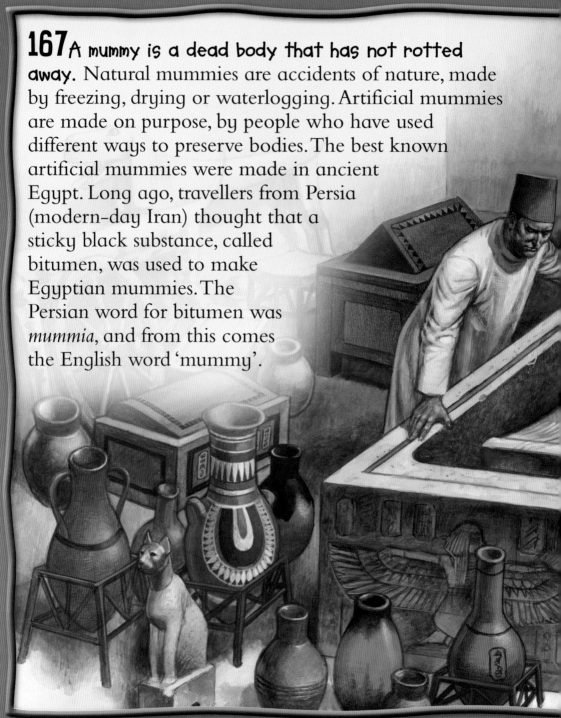

167 **A mummy is a dead body that has not rotted away.** Natural mummies are accidents of nature, made by freezing, drying or waterlogging. Artificial mummies are made on purpose, by people who have used different ways to preserve bodies. The best known artificial mummies were made in ancient Egypt. Long ago, travellers from Persia (modern-day Iran) thought that a sticky black substance, called bitumen, was used to make Egyptian mummies. The Persian word for bitumen was *mummia*, and from this comes the English word 'mummy'.

▲ The 3300-year-old mummy of Egyptian pharaoh Tutankhamun was discovered in 1922 by Howard Carter. This is a good example of an artificial mummy.

The first mummies

168 The first artificial mummies were made 7000 years ago by the Chinchorro people of South America. These people are named after a place in Chile. Here, scientists discovered traces of the way the Chinchorro lived. They were a fishing people who lived in small groups along the coast of the Pacific Ocean.

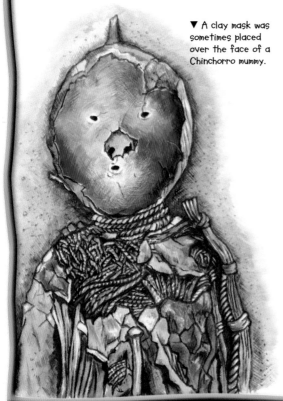

▼ A clay mask was sometimes placed over the face of a Chinchorro mummy.

169 It is thought that the Chinchorro made mummies because they believed in life after death. They tried to make a mummy look as lifelike as possible, which shows they did not want the person's body to rot away. Perhaps they thought the dead could live again if their bodies were preserved.

170 To make a mummy, the Chinchorro first removed all of a dead person's insides. The skin and flesh were then taken off the bones, which were left to dry. Then sticks were tied to the arm, leg and spine bones to hold them together. White mud was spread over the skeleton to build a body shape. The face skin was put back in place, and patches of skin were added to the body. When the mud was dry, it was painted black or red.

◄ Once the Chinchorro had removed all the skin and soft tissue, the body was rebuilt with sticks, mud and paint.

171 The Chinchorro made mummies for about 3000 years. Early mummies were painted black, but by the time of the last mummies, 4000 years ago, the Chinchorro were painting them red.

172 The first Chinchorro mummies were discovered in 1917, when 12 were found buried in northern Chile. In 1983, builders uncovered more of this ancient burial ground. About 100 ancient Chinchorro mummies were dug up at this site, and more have been found elsewhere in Chile.

Iceman of Europe

173 Europe's oldest human mummy is known as the Iceman. He died about 5300 years ago, at the end of the Stone Age. His mummy was discovered by hikers in northern Italy in 1991. They found it lying face down in an icy glacier.

175 When the Iceman was alive, arrows had sharp points made from flint (a type of stone). It was a flint arrowhead that injured the Iceman, piercing his clothes and entering his left shoulder. This arrow caused a deep wound. The Iceman pulled the long arrow shaft out, but the arrowhead remained inside his body. This injury would have made the Iceman weak, eventually causing him to die.

◀ The Iceman is the oldest complete human mummy ever to be found. He is so well preserved, even his eyes are still visible.

176 The mummy's clothes were also preserved by the ice. For the first time, scientists saw how a Stone Age person actually dressed. The Iceman wore leggings and shoes made from leather, a goatskin coat, a bearskin hat and a cape made from woven grass. These would have kept the Iceman warm in the cold climate.

174 The Iceman mummy was found high up in the mountains, where it is very cold. At first, people thought that he was a shepherd, or a hunter on the search for food – or even a traveller on a journey. Then in 2001, an arrowhead was found in the Iceman's left shoulder. He might have fled into the mountains to escape danger.

177 Equipment used by the Iceman was also found with him. He carried a copper axe, a flint dagger, and a bow and quiver with 14 arrows. He also had a leather pouch filled with dried grass, which he would have used for starting fires. If the Iceman had been a hunter, he would have killed animals, such as the mountain ibex (a type of goat), with his arrows.

178 Today, the Iceman mummy and his clothes and equipment are kept at a museum in northern Italy. Visitors are able to peep through a tiny window to see the Iceman, who is kept frozen inside a special room. The mummy must never be allowed to thaw, as this would cause it to rot.

▶ This reconstruction of the Iceman shows how he would have looked on the day he died.

Quiver to hold arrows

Leather pouch

Flint dagger

Copper axe

Shoes stuffed with grass for warmth

I DON'T BELIEVE IT!

At first, the Iceman was thought to be a modern person who had died in a recent accident on the mountain.

Bog bodies

179 Lots of mummies have been found in the peat bogs of northern Europe. Peat is a soily substance that is formed from plants that have fallen into pools of water. The plants sink to the bottom and are slowly turned into peat. If a dead body is placed in a bog, it may be preserved as a mummy. This is because there is little oxygen or bacteria to rot the body.

180 Bog bodies, or mummies, are usually found when peat is dug up. One of the best known bodies was dug up at Tollund, Denmark, in 1950. Tollund Man, as he is known, died 2300 years ago. Around his neck was a leather noose. He was hanged, perhaps as a sacrifice to his gods, and then thrown in the bog. Over the years his face was perfectly preserved, right down to the whiskers on his chin.

▶ The face of Tollund Man is so well preserved, he looks as if he is sleeping.

182 Grauballe Man was also found in a peat bog in Denmark. He was discovered by peat workers near the village of Grauballe in 1852. About 2300 years ago, the man's throat was cut and he bled to death. His body was thrown into a bog, where it was preserved until its discovery.

▲ The head of Grauballe Man. Like all bog bodies, his skin has turned brown due to the acids in the bog.

181 Bog bodies have also been discovered in Germany. At Windeby, the body of a teenage girl was found. The girl, who died 1900 years ago, was wearing a blindfold. It seems she was taken to the bog, her eyes were covered, and then she was drowned. A heavy rock and branches were put on top of her body, so it sank to the bottom of the bog.

▶ The mummy of Windeby Girl revealed that some of her hair had been cut off, or shaved, at the time of her death.

183 From the Netherlands comes the bog body of another teenage girl. Known as Yde (*ay-de*) Girl, she was stabbed, strangled and then dumped in a bog around 1900 years ago. A medical artist made a copy of her skull, then covered it with wax to rebuild her face. The model shows scientists how Yde Girl may have looked when she was alive.

Lindow Man

184 A bog body of a man was found in north-west England in 1984. It was discovered by peat cutters at Lindow Moss, Cheshire. The mummy was named 'Lindow Man', but a local newspaper nicknamed it 'Pete Marsh' because a peat bog is a wet, marshy place. Lindow Man is now on display at the British Museum, London.

185 Lindow Man was about 20 years old when he died. His short life came to an end around 1900 years ago. After his death, his body was put in a bog, where it sank without trace until its discovery by the peat cutters.

▼ The body of Lindow Man was squashed flat by the weight of the peat on top of it.

186 Lindow Man did not die peacefully. Before he died, he ate food with poisonous mistletoe in it. It's impossible to say if the poison was put there on purpose, or by accident. The marks on his body tell the story of his last moments alive. Someone hit him hard on the head, a cord was tightened around his neck and he was strangled. Then, to make sure he was dead, his throat was cut.

187 It took four years to find most of Lindow Man's body. The machine used to cut the peat had sliced it into pieces, which were found at different times. His top half, from the waist up, was found in 1984, and four years later his left leg turned up. His right leg is missing, possibly still buried in the peat bog.

▲ In this reconstruction, Lindow Man eats a meal containing burnt bread. This may have been part of a ceremony in which he was sacrificed to the gods.

I DON'T BELIEVE IT!

Visitors to the British Museum have come up with names for Lindow Man, including Sludge Man and Man in the Toilet!

188 In Lindow Man's time, gifts were given to the gods. The greatest gift was a human sacrifice, which is what may have happened to Lindow Man. After eating a meal mixed with mistletoe, he was killed and put in a bog. People may have thought he was leaving this world and entering the world of the gods.

Mummies of ancient Egypt

189 **The most famous mummies were made in ancient Egypt.** The Egyptians were skilled embalmers (mummy-makers). Pharaohs (rulers of Egypt) and ordinary people were made into mummies, along with many kinds of animal.

▲ Even pet dogs were mummified in ancient Egypt.

▲ Two people walk through the Field of Reeds, which was the ancient Egyptian name for paradise.

190 Mummies were made because the Egyptians thought that the dead needed their bodies in a new life after death. They believed a person would live forever in paradise, but only if their body was saved. Every Egyptian wanted to travel to paradise after death. This is why they went to such trouble to preserve the bodies of the dead.

191 Ancient Egypt's first mummies were made by nature. When a person died, their body was buried in a pit in the desert sand. The person was buried with objects to use in the next life. Because the sand was hot and dry, the flesh did not rot. Instead, the flesh and skin dried and shrivelled until they were stretched over the bones. The body had been mummified. Egypt's natural mummies date from around 3500 BC.

◀ This man died 5200 years ago in Egypt. His body slowly dried out in the hot, desert conditions, and became a natural mummy.

193 The ancient Egyptians made their first artificial mummies around 3400 BC. The last mummies were made around AD 400. This means the Egyptians were making mummies for 4000 years! They stopped making them because as the Christian religion spread to Egypt, mummy-making came to be seen as a pagan (non-Christian) practice.

192 When an old grave was found, perhaps by robbers who wanted to steal the grave goods, they got a surprise. Instead of digging up a skeleton, they uncovered a dried-up body that still looked like a person! This might have started the ancient Egyptians thinking – could they find a way to preserve bodies themselves?

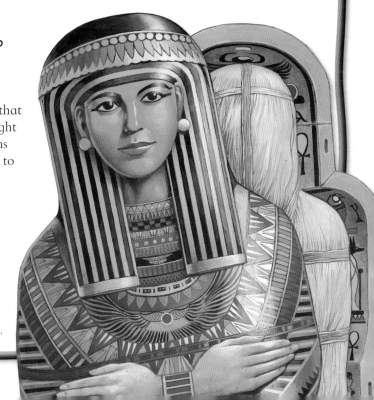

▶ Many Egyptian coffins were shaped like a person and beautifully painted and decorated.

Egypt's first mummy

194 The ancient Egyptians told a myth about how the very first mummy was made. The story was about Osiris, who was ruler of Egypt. It explained how Osiris became the first mummy, and because it had happened to him, people wanted to follow his example and be mummified when they died.

195 The story begins with the murder of Osiris. He had a wicked brother called Seth, and one day Seth tricked Osiris into lying inside a box. The box was really a coffin. Seth shut the lid and threw the coffin into the river Nile, and Osiris drowned. Seth killed his brother because he was jealous of him – he felt the people of Egypt did not love him as much as they loved Osiris.

196 Isis was married to Osiris, and she could not bear to be parted from him. She searched throughout Egypt for his body, and when she found it, she brought it home. Isis knew that Seth would be angry if he found out what she had done, and so she hid the dead body of Osiris.

QUIZ

1. Who killed Osiris?
2. Who was the wife of Osiris?
3. How many pieces did Seth cut Osiris into?
4. Which three gods helped Isis?
5. What did Osiris become in the afterlife?

Answers:
1. Seth 2. Isis 3. 14
4. Ra, Anubis, Thoth
5. King of the dead

▶ Isis, Anubis and Thoth rebuild the body of Osiris to make the first mummy.

197 However, Seth found out, and he took the body of Osiris from its hiding place. Seth cut Osiris into 14 pieces, which he scattered far and wide across Egypt. At last, he thought, he had finally got rid of Osiris.

198 Seth might have destroyed Osiris, but he could not destroy the love that Isis had for him. Once again, Isis searched for Osiris. She turned herself into a kite (a bird of prey), and flew high above Egypt so she could look down upon the land to see where Seth had hidden the body parts of Osiris. One by one, Isis found the pieces of her husband's body, except for one, which was eaten by a fish.

199 Isis brought the pieces together. She wept at the sight of her husband's body. When Ra, the sun god, saw her tears, he sent the gods Anubis and Thoth to help her. Anubis wrapped the pieces of Osiris' body in cloth. Then Isis, Anubis and Thoth laid them out in the shape of Osiris and wrapped the whole body. The first mummy had been made. Isis kissed the mummy and Osiris was reborn, not to live in this world, but to live forever in the afterlife as the king of the dead.

A very messy job

200 Mummies were made in Egypt for almost 4000 years. Mummy-makers experimented with different methods of preserving the dead, some of which worked better than others. The best mummies were made during a time of Egyptian history called the New Kingdom, between 3550 and 3069 years ago.

201 An ancient Greek called Herodotus wrote down one way the Egyptians made mummies. Herodotus visited Egypt in the 400s BC. He was told that it took 70 days to make a mummy – 15 days to cleanse the body, 40 days to dry it out and 15 days to wrap it.

202 Mummy-makers worked in open-air tents. Their simple workshops, which were far from villages and towns, were along the west bank of the river Nile. The tents were left open so that bad smells were carried away on the breeze. They were near the river as water was needed in the mummy-making process.

I DON'T BELIEVE IT!

In the 1800s, Egyptian cat mummies were shipped to England where they were crushed up to make fertilizer!

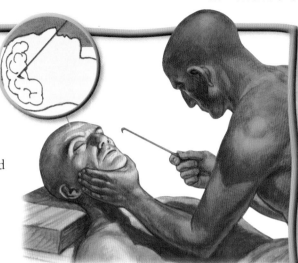

▶ To remove the brain, a metal hook was pushed up through the left nostril. It was then used to pull the brain out through the nose.

203 Mummy-making skills were handed down from one generation to the next. It was a job for men only, and it was a father's duty to train his son. A boy learned by watching his father at work. If his father worked as a slitter – the man who made the first cut in the body – his son also became a slitter.

204 The first 15 days of making a mummy involved cleaning the body. In the Place of Purification tent, the body was washed with salty water. It was then taken to the House of Beauty tent. Here, the brain was removed and thrown away. Then a slit was made in the left side of the body and the liver, lungs, intestines and stomach were taken out and kept.

205 The heart was left inside the body. The Egyptians thought the heart was the centre of intelligence. They believed it was needed to guide the person in the next life. If the heart was removed by mistake, it was put back inside. The kidneys were also left inside the body.

◀ A dead body was carefully washed with salty water before its organs were removed.

Drying the body

206 After the insides had been taken out, the body was dried. Mummy-makers used a special salt called natron to do the drying. The salt was a powdery-white mixture and was found along the edges of lakes in the north of Egypt. The natron was put into baskets, then taken to the mummy-makers.

209 The liver, lungs, intestines and stomach were also dried. Each of these organs was placed in a separate pottery bowl, and natron was piled on top. Just like the body, these organs were also left for 40 days, during which time the natron dried them out.

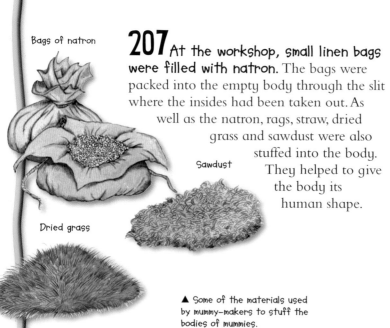

Bags of natron

Sawdust

Dried grass

207 At the workshop, small linen bags were filled with natron. The bags were packed into the empty body through the slit where the insides had been taken out. As well as the natron, rags, straw, dried grass and sawdust were also stuffed into the body. They helped to give the body its human shape.

▲ Some of the materials used by mummy-makers to stuff the bodies of mummies.

208 Next, the body was placed on its back on a table and covered in a thick layer of natron. No flesh was left exposed. The body was left to dry out under the natron for 40 days.

210 Fisherman first used natron to dry the fish they caught. They realized that natron's salty crystals sucked juices out of dead flesh, leaving it dry. Dried, or salted, fish did not rot. This was why the mummy-makers began to use natron to preserve the dead.

211 During the 40 days of drying, the natron absorbed the body's juices. At the end of this time, the mummy-makers scraped away the natron and removed the materials used to stuff the body. The dried body had lost about three-quarters of its original weight and was shrivelled, hard and blue-black in colour. It hardly looked like a body at all.

▲ The body was covered in natron, a kind of salt, to dry it out. Up to 225 kilograms were needed.

Wrapped from head to toe

212 The next job was to make the body appear lifelike. The body cavity was filled and the skin was rubbed with oil and spices to make it soft and sweet-smelling. Then it was given false eyes and a wig, and make-up was applied. Lastly, tree resin was poured over it. This set into a hard layer to stop mould growing.

213 The dried-out organs were wrapped in linen, then put into containers called canopic jars. The container with the baboon head (the god Hapi) held the lungs, and the stomach was put into the jackal-headed jar (the god Duamutef). The human-headed jar (the god Imseti) protected the liver, and the intestines were placed in the falcon-headed jar (the god Qebehsenuef).

214 The cut on the left side of the body was rarely stitched up. Instead, it was covered with a wax plaque. On the plaque was a design known as the Eye of Horus. The Egyptians believed it had the power to see evil and stop it from entering the body through the cut.

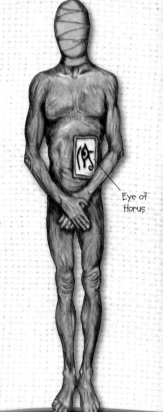

① Head wrapped

Eye of Horus

Hapi

Imseti

◀ The four canopic jars represented the sons of the god Horus.

Duamutef

Qebehsenuef

106

215 **In the final part of the process, the body was wrapped.** It took 11 days to do this. The body was wrapped in strips of linen, 6 to 20 centimetres wide. There was a set way of wrapping the body, which always started with the head. Lastly, the body was covered with a sheet of linen, tied with linen bands.

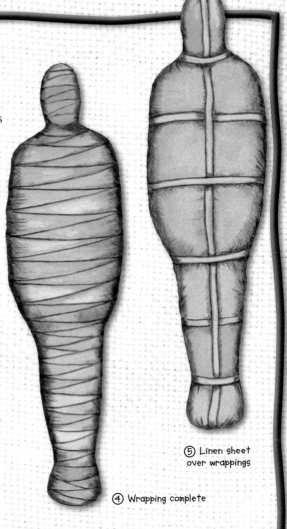

⑤ Linen sheet over wrappings

④ Wrapping complete

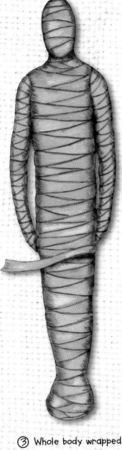

③ Whole body wrapped

▲ There was a five-stage sequence for wrapping the body, which always started with the head.

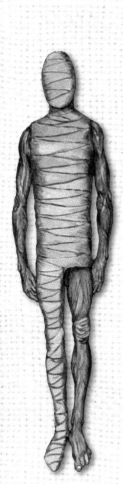

② Limbs and torso wrapped

216 **During the wrapping, amulets (lucky charms) were placed between the layers of linen.** These protected the person from harm on their journey to the afterlife. Magic spells written on the wrappings were another form of protection. After it was wrapped, resin was poured over the mummy to make it waterproof. Last of all, it was given a face mask.

Tombs and tomb robbers

217 **The body was placed in a wooden coffin.** Simple coffins were made from planks of wood, and expensive ones were shaped like a person. They were decorated with spells. A picture on the inside of the coffin showed the route to the afterlife.

218 The earliest pharaohs (kings) were buried in pyramid tombs. The first pyramid was built about 2650 BC, for Pharaoh Djoser. For the next 800 years, all pharaohs were buried in pyramids. However, robbers found their way into all of them. Later pharaohs were buried in tombs cut into a rocky valley, known as the Valley of the Kings. Robbers found many of these tombs too, but not all.

219 On the day of burial, the mummy was lifted out of its coffin and stood upright. A priest used a Y-shaped stone tool to touch the mummy's mouth, eyes, nose and ears. This was the Opening of the Mouth ceremony. It was done so that the person's speech, sight, hearing and smell came back to them for use in the next life.

▲ A priest (right) about to touch a mummy (left) in the Opening of the Mouth ceremony.

220 Mummies were buried with grave goods. These were items for the person to use in the next life. Ordinary people were buried with basic items, such as food and drink. Pharaohs and wealthy people were buried with everything they would need in their next life, such as furniture, clothes, weapons, jewellery and musical instruments.

221 Tombs were tempting places to robbers. They knew what was inside them, and took great risks to break in and steal the goods. Not even a mummy was safe – the tomb robbers smashed coffins open, and cut their way through the layers of linen wrappings to get at the masks, amulets and jewellery. Tomb robbery was a major crime, and if a robber was caught he was put to death.

◀ A funeral procession on its way to the Valley of the Kings. Oxen pulled the coffin on a wooden sledge shaped like a boat. This represented the deceased's journey to the next life.

Tutankhamun, the boy-king

222 **Tutankhamun is one of Egypt's most famous pharaohs.** He became king in 1334 BC when he was eight years old. Because he was too young to carry out the important work of ruling Egypt, two of his ministers took charge. They were Ay, chief minister, and Horemheb, head of the army. They made decisions on Tutankhamun's behalf.

▲ This model of Tutankhamun was buried with him in his tomb.

223 **Tutankhamun was pharaoh for about nine years.** He died when he was 17 years old. His body was mummified and buried in a tomb cut into the side of a valley. Many pharaohs were laid to rest in this valley, known as the Valley of the Kings. Tutankhamun was buried with valuables for use in the next life.

224 **The tombs in the Valley of the Kings were meant to be secret.** However, robbers found them, and stole the precious items buried there. They found Tutankhamun's tomb, but were caught before they could do much damage. Years later, when the tomb of Rameses VI was being dug, rubble rolled down the valley and blocked the entrance to Tutankhamun's tomb. After that, it was forgotten about.

225 In 1922, British archaeologist Howard Carter discovered the tomb of Tutankhamun. He had spent years searching for it. Other archaeologists thought he was wasting his time. They said all the tombs in the valley had already been found. Carter refused to give up, and in November 1922 he found a stairway that led to the door of a tomb.

◀ Found covering the head and shoulders of Tutankhamun's mummy, this beautiful mask features a royal cobra and a vulture's head, representing the unification of Upper and Lower Egypt.

▲ Tutankhamun's throne. The back is decorated with a picture of the pharaoh, who is seated, and a princess.

226 Behind the door was a corridor. At the end of it was a second door, which Carter made a hole in. He peered through the hole, and said he could see 'wonderful things'. It took ten years to remove all the objects from the tomb – jewellery and a gold throne were among the treasures. A gold mask covered the king's head and shoulders. It was made of 10 kilograms of pure gold.

Magnificent mummies!

227 The mummy of pharaoh Ramses II was found in 1871. It had been buried in a tomb, but had been moved to prevent robbers finding it. Ramses II had bad teeth, probably caused by eating gritty bread. He was in his eighties when he died and had arthritis, which would have given him painful joints. In 1976 his mummy was sent to France for treatment to stop mould from damaging it.

228 Mummy 1770 is in the Manchester Museum, in the UK. This is a mummy of a teenage girl, whose real name is not known. Her lower legs and feet are missing, and the mummy-makers had given her false ones to make her appear whole. It's a mystery what happened to her, but she might have been bitten by a crocodile, or even a hippo, as she paddled in the river Nile 3000 years ago.

▼ The mummy of Ramses II. Scientific studies have shown that particularly fine linen was used to stuff and bandage the body.

229 A trapped donkey led to the discovery of thousands of mummies! It happened in 1996, when a donkey slipped into a hole at Egypt's Bahariya Oasis. The owner freed it, then climbed down into an underground system of chambers lined with thousands of mummies of ordinary people. The site is called the Valley of the Golden Mummies, as many of the mummies have golden masks over their faces. They are about 2000 years old.

230 Djedmaatesankh – Djed for short – is an Egyptian mummy in the Royal Ontario Museum, Toronto, Canada. She lived around 850 BC, and in 1977 she entered the history books as the first Egyptian mummy to have a whole-body CAT scan (computerized axial tomography). The CAT images revealed that Djed had a serious infection in her jaw, which may have caused her death.

QUIZ

1. What was damaging Rameses II?
2. What is false about Mummy 1770?
3. What did a donkey help to find?
4. Which mummy had the first CAT scan?

Answers:
1. Mould 2. Her legs and feet 3. The Valley of the Golden Mummies 4. Djed

Mummies of Peru

231 Mummies were made in Peru, South America, for hundreds of years. The first were made in the 400s BC, and the last probably in the early 1500s. A body was put into a sitting position, with its knees tucked under its chin. Layers of cloth were wrapped around it to make a 'mummy bundle'. The body was preserved by the dry, cold environment.

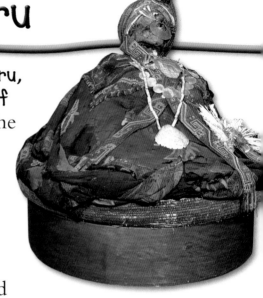

▲ This mummy from Peru is more than 500 years old. It was covered in cloth to make a 'mummy bundle'.

▲ Mummies of emperors were carried through the streets and put on display to the public.

232 In the 1500s, the mummies of Inca emperors were paraded through the streets of Cuzco, Peru. People thought that by doing this the souls of the dead were well-cared for, and this helped them on their journey into the afterlife. People also believed that this practice pleased the gods, who then ensured that living people were healthy and happy.

I DON'T BELIEVE IT!

When Spaniards came to Peru in the 1500s, they destroyed thousands of Inca mummies – they got rid of 1365 in just four years!

233 The Incas sacrificed children to their gods. They hoped that in return the gods would provide rain for crops, good health and prosperity. The children's bodies were left at the tops of freezing mountains, where they slowly turned into natural mummies.

234 In 1995, the mummy of a teenage Inca girl was found. She was led to her death 500 years ago, as a sacrifice to the gods. Her body was left 6300 metres up Mount Ampato, Peru, with offerings of cloth, food, gold and silver. The icy conditions preserved her body.

▶ Inca children stand in front of a priest as they prepare to be sacrificed to the gods in a religious ceremony.

Mummies from Asia

235 More than 2500 years ago, the Pazyryk people of Siberia, Russia, buried their leaders in the region's frozen ground. In 1993, a Pazyryk burial mound was dug up, and inside was the frozen mummy of the 'Ice Princess'. She was dressed in clothes made from silk and wool, and she wore a pair of riding boots. When her body thawed from the ice, pictures of deer were found tattooed on her skin.

▲ The Pazyryk people tattooed images of snow leopards, eagles and reindeer onto their bodies. Those found on the 'Ice Princess' may have been a mark of her importance, or rank.

236 Lady Ch'eng is one of the world's best-preserved mummies. She was found in China, and is 2100 years old. Her body had been placed inside a coffin filled with a strange liquid that contained mercury (a silvery liquid metal, also known as quicksilver). The coffin was sealed and placed inside another, and then another. The coffins were buried under a mound of charcoal and clay, and in this watertight, airtight tomb, her body was preserved.

◀ This artist's impression shows how Lady Ch'eng may have looked when she was alive more than 2000 years ago.

237 Mummies have been found in China's Taklamakan Desert. It hardly rains here, and the salty sand means that human bodies do not rot. It was a surprise when mummies were found in this remote place. They are about 3000 years old, and look Indo-European, not Chinese. It seems that long ago, a group of tall, light-skinned people settled in the east, where they died and were buried.

238 Vu Khac Minh was a Buddhist monk from Vietnam. In 1639, when he was near the end of his life, he locked himself in his room. He told his fellow monks to leave him alone for 100 days while he meditated (prayed). When this time was up, the monks found that he had died. His body was perfectly preserved and was put on view for all to see.

◄ Cherchen Man was just one of the many mummies found in the Taklamakan Desert.

117

North American mummies

239 **At 9000 years old, Spirit Cave Man is one of the oldest mummies.** The mummy was found in Spirit Cave, Nevada, USA, in 1940. It was wearing a cloak of animal skins, leather moccasins on its feet, and was wrapped inside mats made of tough grass. The cool, dry air in the cave had dried the body, turning it into a natural mummy.

▲ The mummy of Spirit Cave Man. Although it was discovered in 1940, the mummy's actual age was not determined until 1994.

240 **The mummy of the North American Iceman no longer exists.** It was found in 1999, in Canada. The Iceman had died in the 1400s, and was preserved in a glacier. Native North Americans claimed that the man was their ancestor, so the mummy was handed to them. It was cremated, and the ashes buried near where the mummy had been found.

241 **A mummy family was found on Greenland in 1972.** The bodies of six Inuit women and two children had been placed on a rocky ledge, in about 1475. The cold conditions had preserved them, slowly freeze-drying their bodies.

▶ An Inuit mummy of a baby boy. He was killed so that he could stay with his mother in the afterlife.

I DON'T BELIEVE IT!

Hazel Farris, like Elmer McCurdy, was an American outlaw whose mummified body was put on show at funfairs.

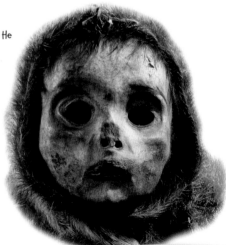

243 **Elmer McCurdy was an American outlaw who became a mummy.** He was shot dead in 1911 after robbing a train. His body was taken to an undertakers where it was preserved, but no one claimed the body. Eventually, McCurdy's mummy was sold to a fairground. In 1976, a TV programme was being filmed at a ghost ride, and a 'dummy' turned out to be the mummy of Elmer McCurdy! He was finally buried in 1977.

242 **The mummies of three British sailors lie in the frozen ground of the Arctic.** They are John Torrington, John Hartnell and William Braine, who died in 1845 during a voyage from England to find a sea route across the Arctic Ocean. Their bodies were examined in 1984, and it was discovered that they had suffered from lead poisoning, caused by eating contaminated food. The sailors were reburied, and the Arctic began to freeze their bodies again.

▼ The crew of HMS *Terror* try to dig their ship out of the Arctic ice. The men eventually died, and some of their remains were mummified in the freezing conditions.

Studying mummies

244 Until recently, mummies were studied by opening them up. Unwrapping Egyptian mummies was popular in the 1800s, and was often done in front of an audience. Thomas Pettigrew (1791–1865) was an English surgeon who unwrapped many mummies at this time. He wrote some of the finest books about Egyptian mummies.

▲ An audience looks on as a mummy is unwrapped in the 1800s. This process destroyed lots of historical evidence.

245 There is no need to open up mummies today. Instead, mummies are studied by taking X-rays of bones, while scans reveal soft tissue in great detail. Mummies can even be tested to work out which families they came from.

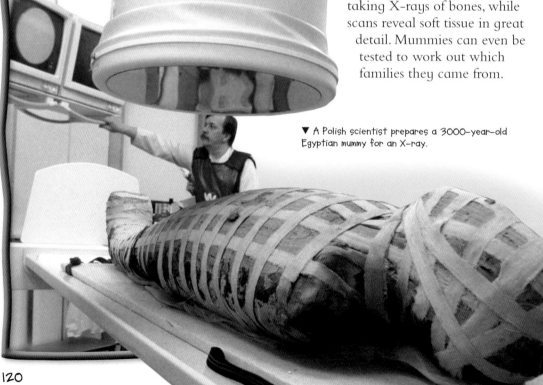

▼ A Polish scientist prepares a 3000-year-old Egyptian mummy for an X-ray.

▶ This X-ray of a mummy's skull reveals that a fractured skull was the cause of death.

247 We can learn about the diseases and injuries people suffered by studying mummies. Egyptian mummies have been studied the most. We can tell they had problems with their health. Gritty bread damaged their teeth, parasites (worms) entered their bodies when they drank polluted water, insect bites caused fevers, and hard manual work led to problems with their joints and bones.

246 French emperor Napoleon Bonaparte was fascinated by mummies. After defeating the British in 1798, Napoleon and his troops became stranded in Egypt. With Napoleon were 150 scientists, who began to study Egypt and its mummies.

▼ When Napoleon left Egypt in 1799, he left behind a team of historians and scientists to study Egypt for him.

Animal mummies

248 **Animals were mummified in ancient Egypt, too!** Birds and fish were mummified as food for a dead person in the next life. Pet cats, dogs and monkeys became mummies so they could keep their dead owners company. Some bulls were believed to be holy as it was thought the spirits of the gods lived inside them. When they died, the bulls were mummified and buried in an underground tomb.

▲ Crocodiles were sacred to the Egyptian god Sobek. They were probably mummified in the same way as humans, then wrapped up.

▼ Fur is still visible around the feet of Dima, the baby mammoth.

249 **A baby mammoth was found in the frozen ground of Siberia in 1977.** Many of these ancient elephant-like animals have been found in this part of Russia. What made this one special was the near-perfect state of its body. The animal was about a year old when it died, and was named Dima, after a stream close to where it was discovered.

250 The world's oldest mummy is a dinosaur. It is the fossil of *Edmontosaurus*, which was found in Wyoming, USA, in 1908. This dinosaur died 65 million years ago, but instead of becoming a skeleton, its body was baked dry by the sun. When US fossil hunter Charles Sternberg discovered it, the skin and insides had been fossilized, as well as the bones.

▲ This frog was naturally mummified in 2006 when it died in a plant pot. The sun baked it dry.

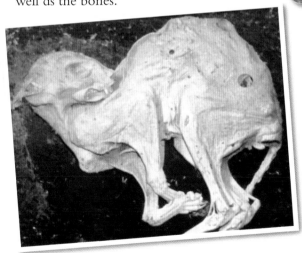

▲ This mummified cat was found in 1971 in Sudbury, Suffolk, UK. It had been walled up in an old mill to protect the building from harm.

251 Cats have been made into mummies for thousands of years. In ancient Egypt, cats were linked to the goddess, Bastet. They were bred to be killed as religious offerings at temples. Cat mummies are sometimes found behind the walls of old houses in Europe. It was believed a cat could bring good fortune, so a cat's body was sometimes walled up, after which it dried out until it was a natural mummy.

Ancient Greece

Take a step back in time and explore one of the world's greatest civilizations.

Kings • City-states • Temples • Gods and goddesses
Slaves • War • Farming • Fishing • Education • Family
Fashion • Food and drink • Olympic Games
Theatres • Festivals

Greece was great

252 **Ancient Greece was a small country, but its people had great ideas.** From around 2000 BC, they created a splendid civilization that reached its peak between 500–400 BC. All citizens contributed to a society that respected people's rights, encouraged the best in human nature and lived in harmony with the natural world. Today, we still admire Greek sport, medicine, drama, politics, poetry and art.

▲ The agora (town square) of Athens was a meeting place for citizens and an open-air market. Traders sold fresh fruit and vegetables and craftworkers sold cloth and pottery.

Greek homelands

253 The Greeks thought that they were better than other people. They saw all foreigners as uncivilized 'barbarians' who did not share the same values and beliefs, or follow the Greeks' lifestyle. Even worse, they did not speak or understand the elegant Greek language.

254 Lifestyle was shaped by the seasons. Winters were cold with icy winds, pouring rain and storms. Summers were very hot and dry with droughts, dust and forest fires. Spring was green and fresh – a time to plant crops and fight wars. Autumn with its harvest of ripe olives, grapes and grain was the busiest time for farmers.

▼ Neat rows of olive trees growing on a Greek farm. Olives were mixed with salt then stored in jars to eat, or crushed to make oil.

▼ The Greeks' homeland included mainland Greece and over 2000 islands in the Aegean Sea and the Ionian Sea, together with the coast of Asia Minor.

Th

MACEDONIA

Mount Olympus

GREECE

IONIAN SEA

Olympia

Athens

Sparta

▲ The land of Greece was rugged and mountainous. Today, the stony soil is bare. In ancient Greek times there would have been more trees.

Troy

ASIA MINOR

Ephesus

255 Ancient Greece was bigger than Greece is today. The power and influence of Greek civilization travelled far beyond mainland Greece and the nearby islands. Greek people, ideas, designs and language could be found along the Mediterranean and the Black Sea coasts.

256 Sited in an active earthquake zone, Greece was regularly hit by tremors. Some quakes were minor, but others were more serious. They knocked down houses, started fires and landslides, wrecked water supplies and blocked important harbours. Earthquakes killed and injured many citizens.

I DON'T BELIEVE IT!
Around 1450 BC, a Greek island disappeared! Most of Thera vanished when a volcano erupted there. The explosion triggered earthquakes, tsunamis and dust clouds that damaged many other Greek islands.

Steeped in history

257 The ancient Greeks were proud of their beautiful country. There were high snowy mountains, swift rushing streams, thick forests, flowery meadows and narrow, fertile plains beside the sea. Around the coast there were thousands of rocky islands, some small and poor, others large and prosperous.

◀ A carved stone figure of a woman found in the Cyclades Islands. The design is very simple but strong and graceful.

258 Greek civilization began on the islands. Some of the first evidence of farming in Greece comes from the Cyclades Islands. Around 6000 BC, people living there began to plant grain and build villages.

259 They buried their dead in graves filled with treasures. These included carved marble figures, pottery painted with magic sun symbols and gold and silver jewellery.

▼ This timeline shows some of the important events in the history of ancient Greece.

TIMELINE OF GREECE

c. 40,000 BC
First people in Greece. They are hunters and gatherers

c. 2000–1450 BC
Minoan civilization on the island of Crete

c. 1250 BC
Traditional date of the Trojan War

c. 900–700 BC
Greek civilization grows strong again

c. 6000 BC
First farmers in Greece

c. 1600–1100 BC
Mycenean civilization on mainland Greece

c. 1100–900 BC
A time of decline – kingdoms weaken, writing stops

c. 776 BC
Traditional date of first Olympic Games

◄ This jar, made around 900 BC, is rather dull and plain. It suggests that times were troubled and Greek people had no money to spare for art.

260 **Between 1100–900 BC, the history of Greece is a mystery.** From 2000–1100 BC, powerful kings ruled Greece. They left splendid buildings and objects behind them, and used writing. But between around 1100–900 BC, there were no strong kingdoms, little art, few new buildings – and writing disappeared.

▲ Alexander the Great conquered an empire stretching from Greece to India.

261 **Migrants settled in distant lands.** By around 700 BC, Greece was overcrowded. There were too many people, not enough farmland to grow food and some islands were short of water. Greek families left to set up colonies far away, from southern France to North Africa, Turkey and Bulgaria.

262 **When the neighbours invaded, Greek power collapsed.** After 431 BC, Greek cities were at war and the fighting weakened them. In 338 BC, Philip II of Macedonia (a kingdom north of Greece) invaded with a large army. After Philip died, his son, Alexander the Great, made Greece part of his mighty empire.

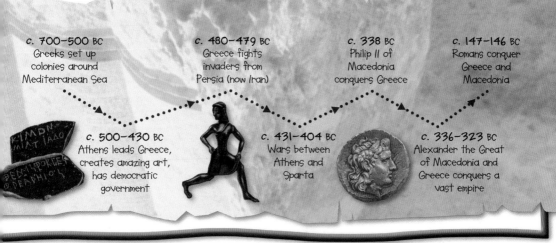

c. 700–500 BC
Greeks set up colonies around Mediterranean Sea

c. 480–479 BC
Greece fights invaders from Persia (now Iran)

c. 338 BC
Philip II of Macedonia conquers Greece

c. 147–146 BC
Romans conquer Greece and Macedonia

c. 500–430 BC
Athens leads Greece, creates amazing art, has democratic government

c. 431–404 BC
Wars between Athens and Sparta

c. 336–323 BC
Alexander the Great of Macedonia and Greece conquers a vast empire

Kings and warriors

263 King Minos ruled an amazing palace city. The first great Greek civilization grew up at Knossos on the island of Crete. Historians call it 'Minoan' after its legendary king, Minos. Around 2000 BC, Minoan kings built an amazing palace-city, with rooms for 10,000 people. It was decorated with wonderful frescoes (wall paintings), statues and pottery.

▲ A section of the palace at Knossos on the island of Crete. A succession of powerful kings ruled a rich kingdom here.

264 Minoan Greeks honoured a monster. Greek myths describe how a fearsome monster was kept in a labyrinth (underground maze) below the palace. It was called the Minotaur, and it was half-man, half-bull.

▲ Greek legends told how the young hero Theseus bravely entered the labyrinth and killed the Minotaur.

QUIZ

1. What was the Minotaur?
2. What was the labyrinth?
3. Where was Knossos?

Answers:
1. A monster – half-man, half-bull 2. A maze underneath the Minoan royal palace 3. On the Greek island of Crete

▶ This golden mask was found in one of the royal tombs at Mycenae. It covered the face of a king who died around 1500 BC.

Oule = Hello

Khaire = Goodbye

265 Invaders brought the Greek language. Between around 2100–1700 BC, warriors from the north arrived in mainland Greece. They brought new words with them and their language was copied by everyone else living in Greece.

▼ Works of art found at Knossos include many images of huge, fierce bulls with athletes leaping between their horns in a deadly religious ritual.

266 Mycenae was ruled by warrior kings. Around 1600 BC new kings took control of Minoan lands from forts on the Greek mainland. The greatest fort was at Mycenae, in the far south of Greece. Mycenaean kings sent traders to Egypt and the Near East to exchange Greek pottery and olive oil for gold, tin and amber. They used their wealth to pay for huge tombs in which they were buried.

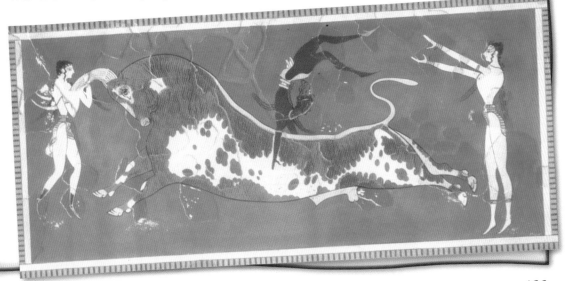

War with Troy

267 A famous Greek poem, the Iliad, describes a terrible war between the Greeks and the Trojans. The Trojans lived in a rich city on the west coast of Asia Minor (now Turkey). The Iliad was first written down around 750 BC. Ancient Greeks said the writer was a blind poet called Homer.

▼ A scene from the 2004 film *Troy*, starring Brad Pitt. The war between the Trojans and the Greeks still thrills people today. Some of the story is legend, but it may be based on real, half-remembered, facts.

MAKE HELEN'S CROWN

You will need:
gold-coloured card   ruler   scissors
sticky tape   glue   gold plastic
'jewels' or sequins   strings of beads

1. Cut a strip of gold-coloured card about 15 cm wide and 65 cm long.
2. Stick the ends of the strip together, using tape to make a circular 'crown'.
3. Decorate your crown with 'jewels' or sequins.
4. Add strings of beads hanging down at the back and the sides.

268 Queen Helen loved a Trojan prince. According to legend, the Trojan War started because Helen, the wife of Greek King Menelaus, ran away with (or was captured by) Paris, a Trojan prince. However, historians believe the main reason for the war was because the Greeks and the Trojans were rival traders.

269
The Greeks could not break through Troy's walls until they thought of a clever plan. They made a huge, hollow, wooden horse, hid warriors inside and persuaded the Trojans to accept it as an offering to the gods. The Trojans hauled the horse into their city, then the Greeks leapt out and defeated them.

270
Odysseus survived to have amazing adventures. Another famous Greek poem tells how the warrior Odysseus fought at Troy, then on the way home survived extraordinary encounters with gods, giants, witches, one-eyed monsters, sea-serpents and a man-eating whirlpool.

▶ The Cyclops was a one-eyed giant. He trapped Odysseus and his soldiers in a cave and planned to eat them. But Odysseus blinded the Cyclops, escaped from the cave and sailed away.

▶ The Iliad describes how, for ten years, the Greeks besieged the city of Troy. They eventually won the war by offering a wooden horse to the Trojans. Once inside the city walls, warriors leapt out of the horse and destroyed the city.

City-states

271 The power of Mycenaean kings collapsed around 1200 BC. By 700 BC, Greece had been divided into 300 city-states, which were cities and the land around them. Some city-states were ruled by kings, some by tyrants (men who governed by force) and some by oligarchs (small groups of rich, powerful men).

▶ Merchant ships carried goods from all around the Mediterranean Sea to sell in Greek markets. They could only travel in the summer, as winter seas were too stormy.

272 Most city-states grew rich by buying and selling. The agora (market-place) was the centre of many cities. Goods on sale included farm produce such as grain, wine and olive oil, salt from the sea, pottery, woollen blankets, sheepskin cloaks, leather sandals and slaves.

273 Top craftsmen made fine goods for sale. Cities were home to many expert craftsmen. They ran small workshops next to their homes, or worked as slaves in factories owned by rich businessmen. Greek craftworkers were famous for producing fine pottery, stone-carvings, weapons, armour and jewellery.

274 Coins displayed city wealth and pride. They were invented in the Near East around 600 BC. Their use soon spread to Greece, and each city-state issued its own designs, stamped out of real silver. Coins were often decorated with images of gods and goddesses, heroes, monsters and favourite local animals.

▶ The design on the top coin shows the head of Alexander the Great. The other is decorated with an owl, the symbol of Athens' guardian goddess, Athena.

◀▲ The walls and gates guarding the city of Mycenae were made of huge stone slabs. The gate had a huge sculpture of two lions above it.

275 Cities were defended by strong stone walls. City-states were proud, independent and quarrelsome. They were often at war with their rivals, and were also in constant danger of attack from neighbouring nations, especially Persia (now Iran). To protect their homes, temples, workshops, market-places and harbours, citizens built strong wooden gates and high stone walls.

▶ Many Greek ships were wrecked together with their cargoes. Some have survived on the seabed for over 2000 years and are studied by divers today.

QUIZ

1. What was a city-state?
2. What was the centre of many cities?
3. What were coins made of?
4. How did the Greeks defend their cities?

Answers:
1. A city and the land around it 2. The agora (market-place) 3. Real silver 4. With strong wooden gates and high stone walls

Citizens, foreigners, slaves

▶ Slaves for sale. Men, women and children captured in war or snatched by pirates were put on display for rich families to buy.

276 Within most city-states, there were different classes of people. Citizens were men who had been born in the city-state, together with their wives and children. Foreigners were traders, sailors or travelling artists and scholars. Slaves belonged to their owners.

277 In wealthy city-states almost half the population were slaves. Household slaves did the shopping, cooking, housework and childcare. Gangs of slave-labourers worked for rich citizens or city governments as builders, road-menders, miners and security guards. Slaves could be very badly treated. The conditions for slaves working in mines and on building sites were grim and many died.

QUIZ

1. What is democracy?
2. Where was it established?
3. What is an ostrakon?
4. What was it used for?

Answers:
1. Rule by the people 2. Athens 3. A piece of broken pottery 4. Voting to ban an unpopular person from Athens. Citizens scratched the person's name on the ostrakon

278 In 508 BC, Athenian leader Cleisthenes established a new system of government called 'democracy' (rule by the people). All male citizens over 18 years old could speak and vote at city Assemblies, elect the officials that ran their city-state and be elected as city councillors. Women, foreigners, children and slaves had no democratic rights.

279 In Athens, citizens could make speeches at the Assembly to propose new laws for their community. They served as jurors in the city-state law courts, hearing the evidence against accused criminals and deciding whether they were innocent or guilty. Citizens could also take part in debates on important government decisions, such as whether to declare war.

▼ Speeches at the Athenian Assembly were carefully timed (and kept short) so that all citizens would have a chance to share in the debate.

▼ You can see the names of two unpopular Athenian citizens scratched on these pieces of pottery. Left, top line: Themistokles. Right, top line: Kimon.

280 Once a year, Athenian citizens voted to ban unpopular people from their city for ten years. They scratched the name of the person they wanted to remove on an ostrakon (piece of broken pottery). If 6000 citizens (about a quarter of the whole Assembly) voted to ban the same man, he had to leave the city within ten days.

Mighty Athens

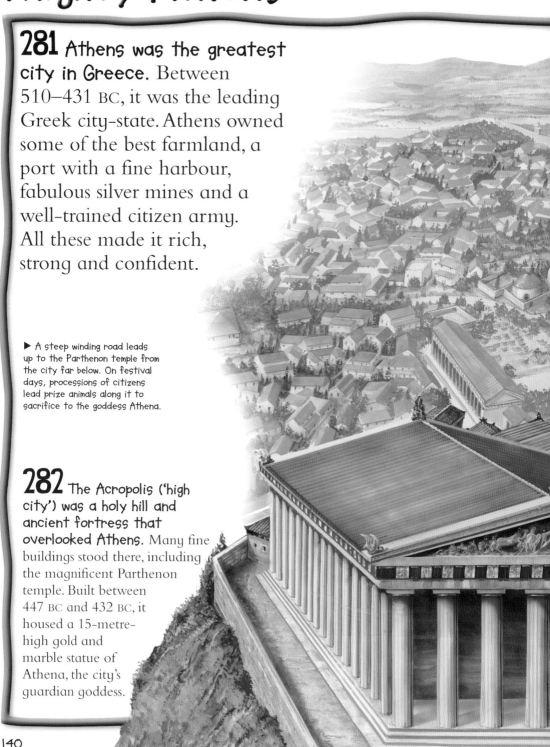

281 **Athens was the greatest city in Greece.** Between 510–431 BC, it was the leading Greek city-state. Athens owned some of the best farmland, a port with a fine harbour, fabulous silver mines and a well-trained citizen army. All these made it rich, strong and confident.

▶ A steep winding road leads up to the Parthenon temple from the city far below. On festival days, processions of citizens lead prize animals along it to sacrifice to the goddess Athena.

282 **The Acropolis ('high city') was a holy hill and ancient fortress that overlooked Athens.** Many fine buildings stood there, including the magnificent Parthenon temple. Built between 447 BC and 432 BC, it housed a 15-metre-high gold and marble statue of Athena, the city's guardian goddess.

283 In 490 and 480 BC, armies from Persia (now Iran) invaded Greece. They were defeated, but Greek city-states felt threatened. They joined together in a League against the Persians. Athens took charge of the League, built a splendid navy and sent soldiers and government officials to 'advise' other city-states. By around 454 BC, Athens had taken control of most of Greece.

284 Athenian city leaders paid for fine works of art. They invited the best artists, architects, sculptors, scientists and scholars to live and work in their city, and gave money to build temples, monuments and public buildings. They vowed to make their city 'an education to Greece'.

285 Athenians are famous today – after more than 2000 years. Pericles was a great general and political leader. Socrates and Plato were philosophers and teachers who taught how to think and question. Aristotle was a scientist who pioneered a new way of studying by carefully observing and recording evidence.

Sparta

286 Sparta was Athens' great rival. It was a city-state set in wild mountain country in the far south of Greece. Sparta had kings who ruled together with a small elite group of citizens. Other Spartans were either free craftsmen who were not allowed to vote, or helots who had few rights but made up 80 percent of the population.

287 Sparta was always ready for war. Kings and citizens lived in fear that the helots might rebel. So all male Spartans had to train as warriors. After this, they were sent to live in barracks with other soldiers, ready to fight at any time.

288 All Spartan citizens were warriors. Soldiers were famous for their bravery and loyalty – and for their bright red cloaks and long curling hair. Their main duty was to fight. They had no time to grow food, keep farm animals, build houses, make clothes or buy and sell. All these tasks, and more, were done by helot families.

I DON'T BELIEVE IT!

When their sons were marching off to war Spartan women said "Come back carrying your shield (victorious) or carried on it (dead!)".

▶ This bronze (metal) statue shows a Spartan girl running a race. Unlike other Greek women, she wears a short tunic and her hair is loose and free.

290 Women in Sparta were strong, like men. Young girls were made to do tough physical training. The Spartans believed this would make them grow up to produce strong, warlike sons. The girls were educated in reading and writing to the same level as the boys. Spartan women had to be emotionally tough as they spent most of their lives apart from their husbands and had to give up their children to serve the city-state.

289

Spartan children were trained to be tough. Citizen children were sent to state training camps. There, boys were treated very harshly so that they would learn to be tough and not complain. From seven years old they were taught to fight, kept cold and hungry and beaten so that they would learn to endure pain.

▼ The legendary toughness of Spartan warriors has inspired artists and film-makers. This scene, from the film *300*, shows the Spartans' metal helmets, sharp spears and round shields.

War on land and sea

291 As teenagers, all Greek male citizens were trained to fight. They had to be ready to defend their city whenever danger threatened. City-states also employed men as bodyguards and mercenary troops with special skills.

▼▶ Soldiers had different duties. Cavalrymen were messengers and spies. Peltasts had to move fast and were armed with javelins. Mercenaries fought for anyone who would pay them.

Peltast

Cavalry

Hoplite

Mercenary

292 Each soldier paid for his own weapons and armour. Most soldiers were hoplites (soldiers who fought on foot). Their most important weapons were swords and spears. Poor men could not afford swords or armour. Their only weapons were slings for shooting stones and simple wooden spears.

293 Soldiers rarely fought on horseback. At the start of a battle, hoplites lined up side by side with their shields overlapping, like a wall. Then they marched towards the enemy while the peltasts threw their javelins. When they were close enough, the hoplites used their spears to fight the enemy.

◀ A Corinthian-style helmet. Soldiers tried to protect themselves from injury with bronze helmets, breastplates, greaves (shin guards) and round wooden shields.

▼ Greek ships were made of wood. If they were holed below the waterline they sank very quickly.

294 City-states paid for fleets of fast, fearsome wooden warships, called triremes. Each ship had a crew of about 170 oarsmen who sat in three sets of seats, one above the other. They rowed the ship as fast as they could towards enemy vessels, hoping that the sharp, pointed ram at its prow would smash or sink them. The most famous naval battle in Greece was fought at Salamis, near Athens, in 480 BC, when the Greeks defeated the Persians.

Farming and fishing

295 **Cities were surrounded by fields and farms.** Everyone living inside the walls relied on country people to grow crops, raise animals and bring food to sell at city markets. Some rich families owned country farms as well as city houses and workshops. They paid for servants or slaves to work the land for them.

▲ Satyrs (legendary monsters) picking and crushing ripe grapes to extract the juice to make wine.

296 **Farmers worked hard to make a living.** The climate was harsh and they had no big machines to help them. Men ploughed the soil, cut down trees, sheared sheep and harvested grain. Women milked sheep and goats, made cheese, grew vegetables, kept chickens and bees and gathered wild herbs and berries. Children scared birds from crops and watched over sheep and goats.

▼ Sheep's wool was cleaned, combed, spun into thread then woven to make warm clothes, rugs and blankets.

297 **Grain, grapes and olives were the most valuable crops.** Barley was the chief grain crop. It was used to make porridge or flour. Grapes were dried in the sun, or trampled by bare feet to extract the juice. This was turned into wine. Olives were crushed to produce oil. This was used in cooking, for burning in lamps or for cleaning and smoothing the skin.

▶ A wild boar hunt (top) pictured on a Greek pot made around 600 BC.

298 The Greeks hunted in wild countryside. Mountains and steep valleys were covered in thick forests. Wild creatures lived there, such as wolves, bears, boar and deer. Huntsmen tracked and killed them for their skins or meat. They also trapped wild birds and stole eggs from their nests, and caught small creatures to eat such as hares and rabbits.

299 Seaside communities made a living from fishing. Every day fishermen sailed out to catch tuna, mullet, squid, octopus and many other sea creatures. Villagers worked as boat-builders and sail-makers, or made ropes and fishing nets. Women prepared bait and preserved fish by drying or smoking to eat in winter.

300 Divers searched for sea produce to sell. They plunged deep underwater, holding their breath for as long as they could. They searched for shellfish (to eat and use as dye for cloth) and sponges, which the Greeks used when bathing. Sponges were also useful for doctors – they soaked up blood.

▼ A modern display of Greek seafood. Fish and shellfish might have been even better in ancient Greek times because the Mediterranean Sea was less polluted.

▶ This wall painting from Minoan Crete shows a fisherman carrying home his catch of gleaming fresh fish.

Food and drink

301 Greek food was plain, hearty and healthy. It included whole grains, cheese, beans and lentils, fruits, vegetables, olives and for special occasions, a little meat or fish.

► Preparing a meal in an open-air kitchen in the courtyard of a house. Food was cooked over a wood fire in a stone hearth.

Mixing barley and honey to make cakes

Oil and wine stored in jars

Slabs of stone or pottery tiles for floor

All the cooking was done by hand

Stone hearth with metal racks for cooking

302 Main meals were breakfast and dinner. Breakfast was bread dipped in olive oil or stale wine. Dinner was olives, then eggs, dried bean stew or hot barley porridge. This was followed by vegetables, fruit and honeycomb. Some people ate a light lunch of bread with fruit or cheese.

▼ A pottery bowl decorated with tasty-looking fish.

303 Greek cooking was very simple. Boiling, stewing or grilling were the only methods of cooking. Many foods were eaten raw, such as fruit, herbs and some shellfish. The Greeks disapproved of cooked dishes with lots of different ingredients, saying that they were too indulgent.

I DON'T BELIEVE IT!

A Greek dinner party might go on for hours and hours. Guests discussed sport and politics, listened to music, played silly games – and sometimes fell asleep between courses!

king pots
ored on
den shelf

Walls of rough plaster

Table of scrubbed wood

304 The Greeks enjoyed wine – but always mixed it with water. Wine could be rough, strong and unsuitable for drinking. People also thought that drunkenness was shameful, except at parties for men only. They did not want to see their guests disgracing themselves.

305 There might be hungry months in winter. Meals were based on preserved foods and grain from the summer harvest. If these ran out or decayed, families went hungry. The only food preservation techniques were smoking, pickling, steeping in olive oil or drying in the sun.

306 Dinner parties were for men only. When husbands invited their male friends to a symposion (dinner party), their wives and daughters stayed away. At a party, male diners reclined on couches while slaves served food and wine.

▶ Male guests at a symposion relax while listening to a girl – probably a slave – playing the double flute.

Family life

307 **Families were very important.**
A person's wealth, rank and
occupation all depended on their
family circumstances, as did the
part they played in community life.
Some families were very active in
politics and had powerful friends –
and enemies.

308 **Fathers were the heads of families.** They had
power over everyone in their
households – wives, children
and slaves. However, families
also worked as a team to find
food, make a safe, comfortable
home and train their children
in all the skills they would
need in adult life.

Bedrooms were
upstairs

Pottery tiles

Mud-brick walls
covered with
plaster

Slaves cooked in
the kitchen

Prayers were said
around the altar
each morning

309 **All Greek parents longed
for a son.** Boys passed on the family
name to the next generation and they
could protect family property and run
businesses or farms. However, girls had to
be fed and housed at the family's expense,
before they left to get married.

▲ Greek houses were designed to provide security
and privacy. They had high, windowless outer walls
and a hidden inner courtyard, which only the
inhabitants and trusted visitors could see.

310 Most girls married very young, aged around 13 years. Their husbands, who were several years older, were chosen by their fathers for political or business reasons. A marriage linked two familes together. Romantic love was not important in marriage – the Greeks thought it was dangerous!

▼ Weddings took place at dusk. The bride was driven to the bridegroom's family home, accompanied by guests carrying flaming wooden torches.

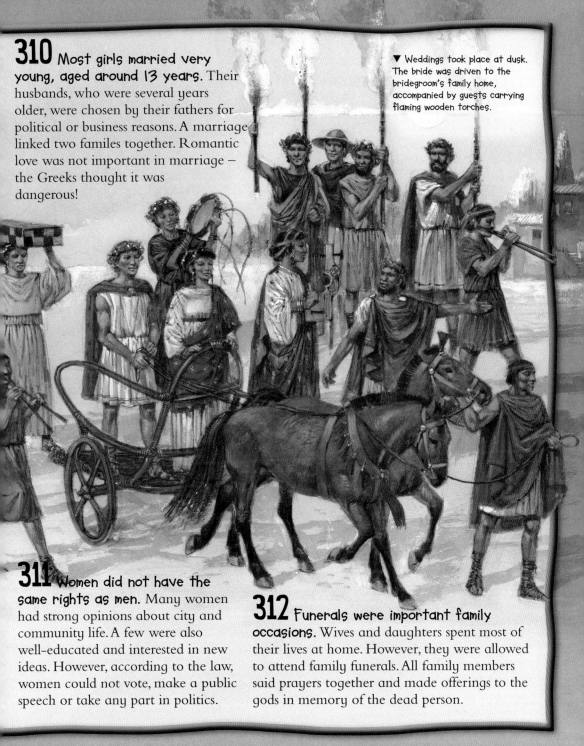

311 Women did not have the same rights as men. Many women had strong opinions about city and community life. A few were also well-educated and interested in new ideas. However, according to the law, women could not vote, make a public speech or take any part in politics.

312 Funerals were important family occasions. Wives and daughters spent most of their lives at home. However, they were allowed to attend family funerals. All family members said prayers together and made offerings to the gods in memory of the dead person.

Education

313 From their earliest days, children were expected to play their part in the family. This meant being well-behaved, obedient, sharing family worship of the gods and showing respect to their parents.

▲ A schoolroom scene, pictured on a Greek pot, showing a music lesson, a writing lesson and a slave. The slave is there to make sure that his master's son behaves and works hard.

314 From around seven years old, boys from wealthy families went to school. They learnt reading, writing, simple arithmetic, how to sing or play a musical instrument and how to debate and recite poetry. They also practised favourite Greek sports such as running, jumping, wrestling and throwing the javelin.

315 School was not for girls. They stayed at home and learnt skills such as spinning, weaving and cookery. Wealthy women taught their daughters how to read and write, keep accounts, manage a big houshold and give orders. Older women also passed on traditional songs and dances so that girls could take part in religious festivals.

▲ This statue shows a slave girl mixing flour, yeast and water to make bread.

317 Socrates was a scholar and teacher who lived in Athens. He encouraged his students to try to discover the truth by asking careful, thoughtful questions. However, his constant questioning alarmed political leaders who accused him of misleading young people. Socrates was condemned to death by the Athens law courts and given poison. He died in 399 BC.

316 Most boys left school when they were 14 years old. Older boys might study with local scholars or sophists (travelling teachers). Around 380 BC, a man called Plato opened a study centre in Athens called the Academy. He planned to train young men to work for the city-state, but attracted the best students in Greece who became famous for their brilliant ideas.

▶ Plato believed that thinking and learning were essential for a good life.

Clothes and fashion

318 Greek clothes were just draped around the body. They were loose and flowing, for comfort in the hot summer months. For extra warmth in winter, both men and women draped a thick woolly himation (cloak) over their shoulders.

319 Each piece of cloth used to make a garment was specially made. It had to be the right length and width to fit the wearer. All cloth was handwoven, usually by women in their homes. Cool, smooth linen was the favourite cloth for summer. In winter, Greeks preferred cosy wool. Very rich people wore fine clothes of silk imported from India.

▶ Men's clothing was designed for action. Young men wore short tunics so they could work — and fight — easily. Older men's robes were longer.

◀ Women's clothing was modest and draped the body from top to toe. Respectable women covered their heads and faces with a veil when they went outside the house.

MAKE A GREEK CHITON

You will need:
length of cloth twice as wide as your outstretched arms and half your height
safety pins   belt or length of cord

1. Fold the cloth in half.

2. Fasten two edges of the cloth together with safety pins, leaving a gap of about 30 cm in the middle.

3. Pull the cloth over your head so that the safety pins sit on your shoulders.

4. Fasten the belt or cord around your waist. Pull some of the cloth over the belt so that the cloth is level with your knees.

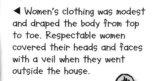

320 Women – and men – took care of their skin. To keep their skin smooth and supple, men and women rubbed themselves all over with olive oil. Rich women also used sunshades or face powder to achieve a fashionably pale complexion. They did not want to look sun-tanned – that was for farm workers, slaves – and men!

Before 500 BC

500–300 BC

After 300 BC

321 Curls were very fashionable. Women grew their hair long and tied it up with ribbons or headbands, leaving long curls trailing over their shoulders. Men, except for Spartan warriors, had short curly hair. Male and female slaves had their hair cropped very short – this was a shameful sign.

▲ Before 500 BC, long, natural hairstyles were popular. Between 500–300 BC, women tied their hair up and held it in place with ribbons or scarves. After 300 BC, curled styles and jewelled hair ornaments were popular and men shaved off their beards.

322 The Greeks liked to look good and admired fit, slim, healthy bodies. Women were praised for their grace and beauty. Young men were admired for their strong figures, and often went without clothes when training for war or taking part in sports competitions. Top athletes became celebrities, and were asked by artists to pose for them as models.

323 Sponges, showers and swimming helped the Greeks keep clean. Most houses did not have piped water. So people washed themselves by standing under waterfalls, swimming in streams or squeezing a big sponge full of water over their heads, like a shower.

◄ Athletes and their trainer (left) pictured on a Greek vase.

Gods and goddesses

324 To the Greeks, the world was full of dangers and disasters that they could not understand or control. There were also many good things, such as love, joy, music and beauty, that were wonderful but mysterious. The Greeks thought of all these unknown forces as gods and goddesses who shaped human life and ruled the world.

▶ This statue of the goddess Aphrodite was carved from white marble – a very smooth, delicate stone. It was designed to portray the goddess' perfect beauty. Sadly, it has been badly damaged over the centuries.

▶ Poseidon was god of the sea and storms. He also sent terrifying earthquakes to punish people – or cities – that offended him.

325 Gods and goddesses were pictured as superhuman creatures. They were strong and very beautiful. However, like humans, gods and goddesses also had weaknesses. Aphrodite was thoughtless, Hera was jealous, Apollo and his sister Artemis were cruel, and Ares was bad-tempered.

▲ Odysseus and his shipmates were surrounded by the Sirens — beautiful half-women, half-bird monsters. They sang sweet songs, calling sailors towards dangerous rocks where their ships were wrecked.

326 The Greeks believed in magic spirits and monsters. These included Gorgons who turned men to stone, and Sirens – bird-women whose song lured sailors to their doom. They also believed in witchcraft and curses and tried to fight against them. People painted magic eyes on the prows of their ships to keep a look-out for evil.

▶ Herakles was a hero – a man who became a god. He performed amazing feats of strength and fought against many monsters. This statue shows him killing a centaur, half-man, half-horse.

327 Individuals were often anxious to see what the future would bring. They believed that oracles (holy messengers) could see the future. The most famous oracles were at Delphi, where a drugged priestess answered questions, and at Dodona, where the leaves of sacred trees whispered words from the gods.

328 Poets and dramatists retold myths and legends about the gods. Some stories were explanations of natural events – thunder was the god Zeus shaking his fist in anger. Others explored bad thoughts and feelings shared by gods and humans, such as greed and disloyalty.

Temples and festivals

329 In Greece and the lands where the Greeks settled, we can still see the remains of huge, beautiful temples. They were built as holy homes for gods and goddesses. Each city-state had its own guardian god and many temples housed a huge, lifelike statue of him or her. People hoped that the god's spirit might visit them and live in the statue for a while.

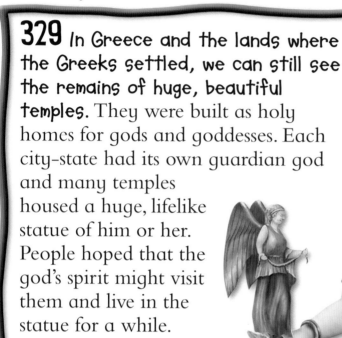

▶ This gigantic statue of the goddess Athena was 15 metres high and was made of gold and ivory. It stood inside her finest temple, the Parthenon in Athens. In her right hand, Athena holds Nike, the goddess of victory.

330 As well as visiting a temple, people hoped — or feared — that they might meet a god or goddess in a forest or on a mountain top. It was thought that all the gods met at Mount Olympus to feast, love, quarrel and make plans. Another high peak, Mount Parnassus, was sacred to the Muses — nine graceful goddesses who guided the arts, such as music and drama.

▲ The summit of the tallest mountain in Greece, Mount Olympus (1951 metres), was often hidden in clouds. It was remote, dangerous and mysterious — a suitable home for the mighty gods.

▼ The first temples were made of wood and shaped like ordinary houses. By around AD 600, temples were built of stone.

c. 800 BC tree trunks hold up the roof. Small inner room.

331 People offered prayers and sacrifices (gifts) to their gods and goddesses. Gifts might be just a few drops of wine or a valuable live animal. The meat of the sacrifice was cooked and shared among the worshippers and the bones and skin were burned on the altar. People thought that smoke carried their prayers up to the gods.

c. 600 BC tree trunks replaced by stone columns. More rooms inside.

332 City-states held festivals to honour their guardian gods. There would be a procession towards the city's main temple or to a shrine (holy place). At temples, crowds watched priests and priestesses making special sacrifices. At shrines, citizens might take part in secret rituals. Afterwards there could be music and drama or sports contests.

c. 440 BC temples are huge, with rows of columns and carved decorations.

159

Olympic Games

333 **The Olympic Games began as a festival to honour Zeus.** Over the centuries, it grew into the greatest sports event in the Greek world. A huge festival complex was built at Olympia with a temple, sports tracks, seats for 40,000 spectators, a campsite and rooms for visitors and a field full of stalls selling food and drink.

▶ Victory! The Greeks believed that winners were chosen by the gods. The first known Olympic Games was held in 776 BC, though the festival may have begun years earlier.

334 Every four years athletes travelled from all over Greece to take part in the Olympic Games. They had to obey strict rules – respect for Zeus, no fights among competitors and no weapons anywhere near the sports tracks. In return they claimed protection – the holy Olympic Peace. Anyone who attacked them on their journeys was severely punished.

160

335 The most popular events were running, long jump, wrestling and boxing. Spectators might also watch chariot races, athletes throwing the discus and javelin or weightlifting contests. The most prestigious event was the 200-metre sprint. There was also a dangerous fighting contest called *pankration* (total power).

▲ Boxers did not wear gloves. Instead they wrapped their hands in bandages.

336 Many events featured weapons or skills that were needed in war. One of the most gruelling competitions was a race wearing heavy battle armour. The main Olympic Games were for men only – women could not take part. There was a separate women's games held at Olympia on different years from the men's competitions.

▲ Throwing the discus was a test of strength and balance. It was also useful training for war.

337 Athletes who won Olympic contests were honoured as heroes. They were crowned with wreaths of holy laurel leaves and given valuable prizes of olive oil, fine clothes and pottery. Poets composed songs in their praise and their home city-states often rewarded them with free food and lodgings for life!

▲ Swimmer Michael Phelps sets a new world record at the Beijing Olympics, 2008. The modern Olympics is modelled on the ancient games and since 1896 has remained the world's greatest sports festival.

▶ A crown of laurel leaves was given to winning athletes as a sign of their god-like strength and speed.

Plays and poems

338 Greek drama originated at religious festivals. In the earliest rituals, priests and priestesses sometimes played the part of gods or goddesses. They acted out stories told about them or famous local heroes. Over the years, these ancient rituals changed into a new art form – drama.

339 Drama became so popular that many city-states built splendid new open-air theatres. Greek theatres were built in a half-circle shape with tiers (raised rows) of seats looking down over an open space for performers. Most seats were filled by men – women were banned from many plays.

▶ The theatre at Epidaurus, in southern Greece, is one of the largest built by the ancient Greeks. It had seats for over 10,000 spectators.

ANCIENT GREECE

340 All the parts in a play were performed by men. They wore masks, wigs and elaborate costumes to look like women or magic spirits and monsters. Some theatres had ladders and cranes so that actors playing gods could appear to fly or sit among the clouds.

341 In some city-states, especially Athens, drama remained an important part of several religious festivals. Writers competed for prizes for the best new plays. They wrote serious plays called tragedies and lively comedies. Some plays lasted all day long. Others had extra 'satyr plays' added on. These were short, funny pieces.

342 Plays were written like poetry. The main actors were always accompanied by singers and dancers. Poems were also recited to music. Tunes were sad for tragic poems or rousing for those about war. Poets performed at men's dinner parties and in rich families' homes. Public storytellers entertained crowds by singing poems in the streets.

Barbarian – or monster – with wild, shaggy hair

Angry young man

▶ Actors wore masks to show which character they were playing. Bright-coloured masks were for cheerful characters and dark-coloured masks were more gloomy. Some masks were double-sided so that the actors could change parts quickly.

Huge, funnel-shaped mouths helped the actors' words reach the audience

Masks with beards and bald heads were for actors playing old men

163

Scientists and thinkers

343 The Greeks liked to ask questions and discuss. Although they believed in gods and magic, they also wanted to investigate the world in a practical way. They learnt some mathematics and astronomy from the Egyptians and Babylonians then used this knowledge to find out more for themselves.

▶ Hipparchus (170–126 BC) observed and recorded the position of over 800 stars and worked out a way of measuring their brightness.

344 Mathematicians and astronomers made important discoveries. Aristarchus was the first to understand that the Earth travels around the Sun. Hipparchus mapped the stars. Thales discovered mathematical laws about circles and triangles. Pythagoras worked out the mathematics behind music and measured the movements of the Sun and the Moon.

345 Many people believed that illness was a punishment sent by the gods. However doctors, led by Hippocrates (460–370 BC), tried to cure people with good food, fresh air, exercise and herbal medicines. They carefully observed patients for signs of illness and recorded the results of their prescriptions. That way they could prove scientifically which treatments worked best for each disease.

▲ This stone carving shows a doctor treating an injured arm. Greek doctors were some of the first in the world to treat patients scientifically.

▼ Archimedes was the most famous Greek engineer. He invented (or improved) a spiral pump to make water flow uphill, for example, from rivers into fields.

Handle turns wooden screw

Water is lifted round and round and then pushed out

Water is pulled in as the screw turns

346 Engineers designed many clever machines. Speakers at the Athenian Assembly were timed by a water-powered clock and there were machines that used hot air to open temple doors. Archimedes (287–211 BC) discovered how objects float and how they balance. He also designed a 'sun gun' (huge glass lens) to focus the Sun's rays on enemy ships to set them on fire.

347 Greek thinkers thought about thinking! As well as investigating the world and creating new inventions they also wanted to understand people and society. They asked questions such as 'How do we think?', 'How do we see and feel?', 'What is good?' and 'How can we live the best lives?'.

Ancient Rome

Take your seat in the arena
and let the games begin!

Gladiators • Army • Food • Slaves • Shopping
Chariots • School • Empire • Medicine
Emperors • Baths • Roads • Laws • Clothes
Farming • Entertainment • Family

The centre of an empire

348 **Rome was a city in central Italy, and it ruled one of the world's greatest empires.**
An empire is made up of many different countries governed by a single ruler. Rome began around 1000 BC as a village of wooden huts, but soon grew rich and powerful. It was busy, crowded, noisy and exciting, with many beautiful buildings. By 200 BC the Romans ruled most of Italy, and started to invade neighbouring lands. They conquered a vast empire that stretched between what we now call Scotland and Turkey.

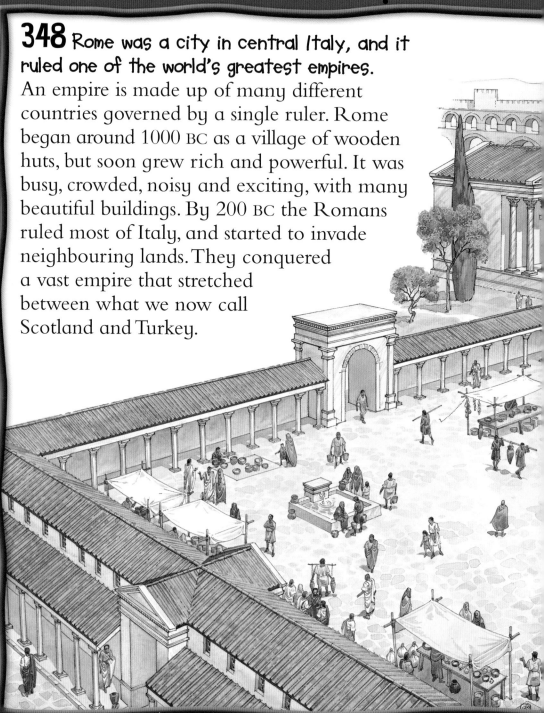

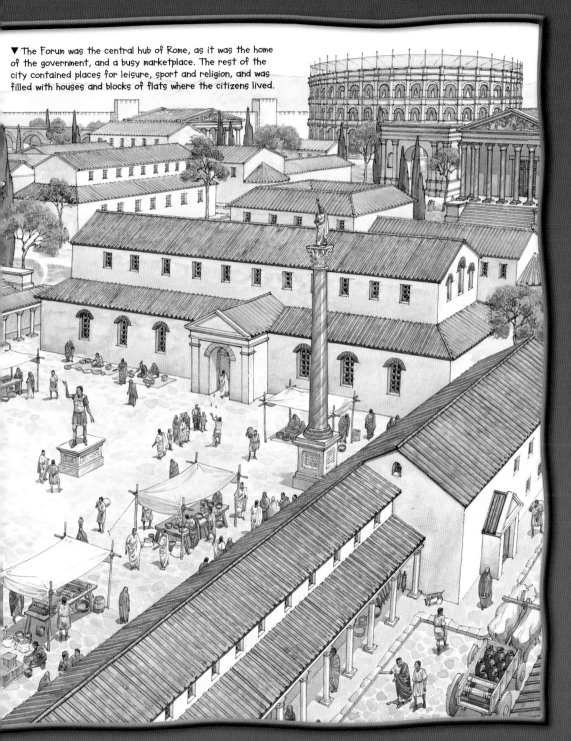

▼ The Forum was the central hub of Rome, as it was the home of the government, and a busy marketplace. The rest of the city contained places for leisure, sport and religion, and was filled with houses and blocks of flats where the citizens lived.

Capital city

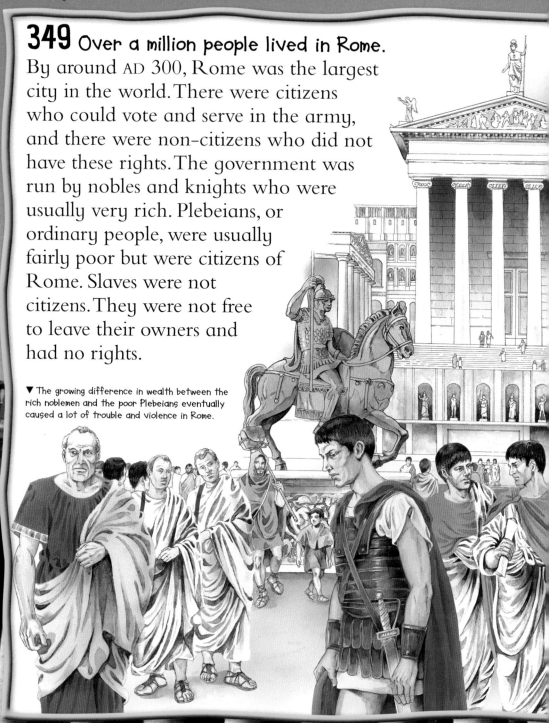

349 **Over a million people lived in Rome.**
By around AD 300, Rome was the largest
city in the world. There were citizens
who could vote and serve in the army,
and there were non-citizens who did not
have these rights. The government was
run by nobles and knights who were
usually very rich. Plebeians, or
ordinary people, were usually
fairly poor but were citizens of
Rome. Slaves were not
citizens. They were not free
to leave their owners and
had no rights.

▼ The growing difference in wealth between the
rich noblemen and the poor Plebeians eventually
caused a lot of trouble and violence in Rome.

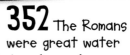

350 The Forum was the government district in the centre of Rome.
People went there to meet their friends and business colleagues, discuss politics, and to listen to famous orators who made speeches in the open air.
The Forum was mainly a market-place, surrounded by government buildings such as offices and law-courts.

352 The Romans were great water engineers. They designed aqueducts, raised channels to carry water from streams in faraway hills and mountains to the city. The richest Roman homes were supplied with constant running water carried in lead pipes. Ordinary people had to drink from public fountains.

Aqueduct

353 Rome relied on its drains. The city was so crowded that good drains were essential. Otherwise, the citizens could have caught diseases from sewage and died. The largest sewer, called the 'cloaca maxima', was so high and so wide that a horse and cart could drive through it.

Roman soldier

351 Rome was a well-protected city.
It was surrounded by 50 kilometres of strong stone walls to keep out attackers. All visitors had to enter the city through one of its 37 gates, which were guarded by soldiers and watchmen.

I DON'T BELIEVE IT!
Roman engineers also designed public lavatories. These lavatories were convenient, but not private. Users sat on rows of seats, side by side!

City life

354 **The Romans built the world's first high-rise apartments.** Most of the people who lived in Ostia, a busy port close to Rome, had jobs connected with trade, such as shipbuilders and money-changers. They lived in blocks of flats known as 'insulae'. A typical block was three or four storeys high, with up to a hundred small, dirty, crowded rooms.

355 Rich Romans had more than one home. Rome was stuffy, dirty and smelly, especially in summer. Wealthy Roman families liked to get away from the city to cleaner, more peaceful surroundings. They purchased a house (a 'villa urbana') just outside the city, or a big house surrounded by farmland (a 'villa rustica') in the countryside far away from Rome.

▲ On the ground floor of an *insula* were shops, and on the first floor were flats and apartments for families. The poorest families lived in single rooms on the top floor.

▼ Pools were also used to collect and store rainwater for cooking or washing.

356 Many Roman homes had a pool, but it was not used for swimming! Pools were built for decoration, in the central courtyards of large Roman homes. They were surrounded by plants and statues. Some pools had a fountain; others had mosaics – pictures made of tiny coloured stones or squares of glass – covering the floor.

You will need:

large sheet of paper   scissors   pencil   glue
scraps of coloured and textured paper

Draw the outlines of your design on a large
sheet of paper. Plan which colours to use
for different parts of the mosaic.

Cut the paper scraps into small squares, all
roughly the same size. The simplest way
to do this is to cut strips, then snip the
strips into squares.

Stick the paper squares onto the large
sheet of paper following the outlines
of your design.

357 **Fortunate families had hot
feet.** Homes belonging to wealthy
families had underfloor central heating.
Blasts of hot air, warmed by a wood-
burning furnace, circulated in channels
built beneath the floor. The furnace
was kept burning by slaves
who chopped wood
and stoked the fire.

▼ For the rich, a heating system made
cold winters much more bearable.

Space in walls
for hot air to
circulate

Fire for
heating

Space under the
floor for hot air

358 **Rome had its own
fire brigade.** The 7000
firemen were freed slaves,
who had all been specially
trained. Ordinary families
could not afford central
heating, so they warmed
their rooms with fires in big
clay pots which often set the
house alight.

Going shopping

359 Rome housed the world's first shopping mall. It was called Trajan's Market, and was built on five different levels on the slopes of the Quirinal Hill in the centre of Rome. It contained over 150 different shops together with a large main hall.

360 The Romans liked a bargain. Most prices were not fixed. People haggled until they had agreed on a deal.

◄ Most shops occupied the ground floors of the *insulae*. Only the most expensive shops were located in the Forum. Markets sold cheaper goods at wooden stalls, while the poorest traders sold by the roadside.

CAN YOU MEASURE IN ROMAN?

The Romans had different measurements to us. Find out below what they were!

A 'pes' equals 29 centimetres. If you are 1 metre 16 centimetres tall, how tall would you be in Roman measurements?

A Roman 'libra' is 326 grams. How many does your favourite toy weigh?

A 'sextarius' is 450 millilitres. How many of these can you fit in a saucepan?

361 Roman shoppers had to get up early. Many shops and market-stalls closed at noon. Shoppers also had to walk a long way to make purchases as different goods were sold in different parts of the city.

Eating and drinking

362 Most Romans ate very little during the day. They had bread and water for breakfast and a light snack of bread, cheese or fruit around midday. They ate their main meal at about 4 o'clock. In rich people's homes, a meal would have three separate courses, and could last for up to three hours. Poor people ate much simpler foods, such as soups made with lentils and onions, barley porridge, peas, cabbage and tough, cheap cuts of meat stewed in vinegar.

▲ The Romans were famous for eating huge meals of luxurious food and drink. This was only for the rich, of course.

363 Only rich Roman people had their own kitchen. They could afford to employ a chef with slaves to help him in the kitchen. Ordinary people went to 'popinae' (cheap eating houses) for their main meal, or bought ready-cooked snacks from roadside fast food stalls.

▲ Meat and bread were large parts of a Roman's diet, as well as wine.

364 At parties, the Romans ate lying down. Men and women lay on long couches arranged round a table. They also often wore crowns of flowers, and took off their sandals before entering the dining room.

REAL ROMAN FOOD!

PATINA DE PIRIS (Pear Soufflé)
Ingredients:

1 kg pears (peeled and cored)	oil
	pinch of salt
	½ tsp cumin
6 eggs (beaten)	ground pepper
4 tbsp honey	

Ask an adult to help you with this recipe.
Mash the pears together with the pepper, cumin, honey, and a bit of oil. Add the beaten eggs and put into a casserole dish. Cook for approximately 30 minutes in a moderate oven. Serve with a little pepper sprinkled on top.

◄ Dishes served at a Roman banquet might include shellfish, roast meat, eggs, vegetables, fresh fruits, pastries and honeyed wine. The Romans enjoyed strong-flavoured, spicy food, and also sweet-sour flavours.

School days

365 **Roman boys learned how to speak well.** Roman schools taught three main subjects, reading, maths and public speaking. Boys needed all three skills for their future careers. There were no newspapers or television, so politicians, army leaders and government officials all had to make speeches in public, explaining their plans and policies to Roman crowds. Boys went to school from around seven years old and left aged 16.

▼ Roman schoolboys practise reading with their slave schoolmaster.

366 **Roman girls did not go to school.** They mostly stayed at home, where their mothers, or slave women, taught them how to cook, clean, weave cloth and look after children. Girls from rich families, or families who ran a business, also learned to read, write and keep accounts.

▼ A girl is taught to play the lyre.

367 **Many of the best teachers were slaves.** Schoolmasters and private tutors often came from Greece. They were purchased by wealthy people who wanted to give their sons a good education. The Greeks had a long tradition of learning, which the Romans admired.

368 The Romans wrote a lot – but not on paper. They used thin slices of wood for letters and day-to-day business. For notes Romans used flat, wooden boards covered with wax, as the wax could be smoothed over and used again. For important documents that they wanted to keep, the Romans used cleaned, polished calfskin or papyrus.

370 Rome had many libraries. Some were public, and open to everyone, others belonged to rich families and were kept shut away in their houses. It was fashionable to sponsor writers and collect their works.

371 Many Romans read standing up – it was easier that way. It took time and patience to learn how to read from a papyrus scroll. Most were at least 10 metres long. Readers held the scroll in their right hand, and a stick in their left hand. They unrolled a small section of the scroll at a time.

Papyrus scroll

Ink pot

Pens

Stylus, to use with a wax tablet

Wax tablet

369 Romans made ink from soot. To make black ink, the Romans mixed soot from wood fires with vinegar and a sticky gum that oozed from tree bark. Some Roman writing has survived for almost 2000 years.

LEARN SOME WORDS!

The Romans spoke a language called Latin. It forms the basis of many languages today, and below you can learn some Latin for yourself!.

liber = book   epistola = letter
bibliotheca = library
vellum = calfskin
stylus = writing stick
librarii = slaves who work in a library
grammaticus = schoolmaster
paedagogus = private tutor

Father knows best!

372 A Roman father had the power of life and death over his family. According to Roman law, each family had to be headed by a man. He was known as the 'paterfamilias' (father of a family), and was usually the oldest surviving male. The buildings of the house and its contents belonged to him, and he had the right to punish any family members who misbehaved. Even his mother and other older female relatives were expected to obey him.

▲ The Romans gave a good luck charm, called a bulla, to their babies.

373 Roman families included more than blood relations. To the Romans, a 'family' meant all the people living and working together in the same household. So families included many different slaves and servants, as well as a husband, wife and their children.

▲ Most Roman laws and customs were related to family, as it was the basis of people's lives.

▲ This carving shows a Roman wedding. The bride and groom are in the centre, with a priestess behind them.

I DON'T BELIEVE IT!

The Romans invented Valentine's Day, but called it Lupercalia. Boys picked a girl's name from a hat, and she was meant to be their girlfriend for the year!

374 Sons were valued more than daughters. Boys would grow up to carry on the family name. They might also bring fame and honour to a family by achievements in government, politics and war. They might marry a rich wife, which helped to make the whole family richer, or win friends among powerful people.

375 Childhood was short for a Roman girl. Roman law allowed girls to get married at 12 years old, and many had become mothers by the time they were 15. They could not choose their husband, especially if they came from rich or powerful families. Instead, marriages were arranged by families, to gain political power or encourage business deals. Love was not important.

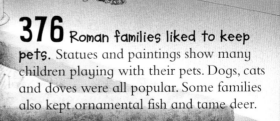

376 Roman families liked to keep pets. Statues and paintings show many children playing with their pets. Dogs, cats and doves were all popular. Some families also kept ornamental fish and tame deer.

Roman style

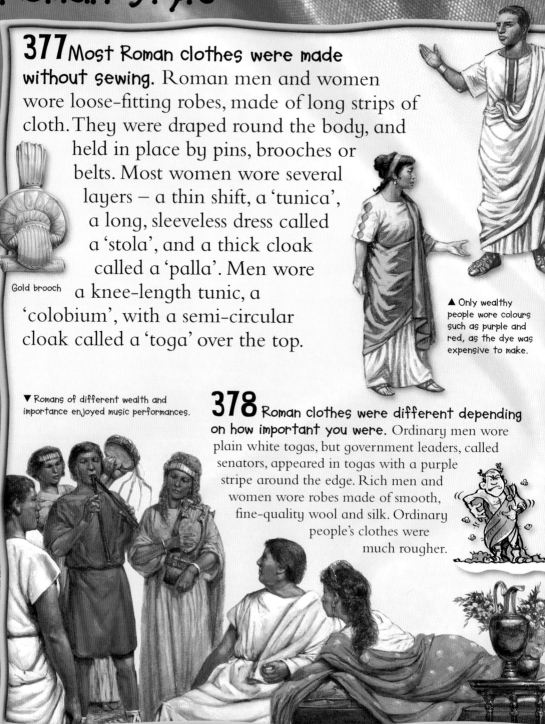

377 **Most Roman clothes were made without sewing.** Roman men and women wore loose-fitting robes, made of long strips of cloth. They were draped round the body, and held in place by pins, brooches or belts. Most women wore several layers – a thin shift, a 'tunica', a long, sleeveless dress called a 'stola', and a thick cloak called a 'palla'. Men wore a knee-length tunic, a 'colobium', with a semi-circular cloak called a 'toga' over the top.

Gold brooch

▲ Only wealthy people wore colours such as purple and red, as the dye was expensive to make.

▼ Romans of different wealth and importance enjoyed music performances.

378 **Roman clothes were different depending on how important you were.** Ordinary men wore plain white togas, but government leaders, called senators, appeared in togas with a purple stripe around the edge. Rich men and women wore robes made of smooth, fine-quality wool and silk. Ordinary people's clothes were much rougher.

379 **Clothes told the world who you were.** People from many different cultures and races lived in lands ruled by the Romans. They wore many different styles of clothes. For example, men from Egypt wore wigs and short linen kilts. Celtic women from northern Europe wore long, woollen shawls, woven in brightly coloured checks. Celtic men wore trousers.

▼ Sandals known as 'crepidae' were worn by men and women all year round.

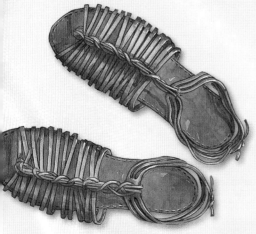

▼ These Roman sandals have metal studs in the soles to make sure that they don't wear down too quickly.

TOGA TIME!

Ask an adult for a blanket or sheet. White is best, like the Romans.

Drape the sheet over your left shoulder. Now pass the rest behind your back.

Pull the sheet across your front, so that you're wrapped up in it.

Finally, drape the last end over your right hand and there you have it, a Roman toga!

380 **Roman boots were made for walking!** Roman soldiers and travellers wore lace-up boots with thick leather soles studded with iron nails. Other Roman footwear included 'socci', loose-fitting slippers to wear indoors. Farmers wore shoes made of a single piece of ox-hide wrapped round the foot, called 'carbatinae'. There were also 'crepidae', comfortable lace-up sandals with open toes.

Looking good

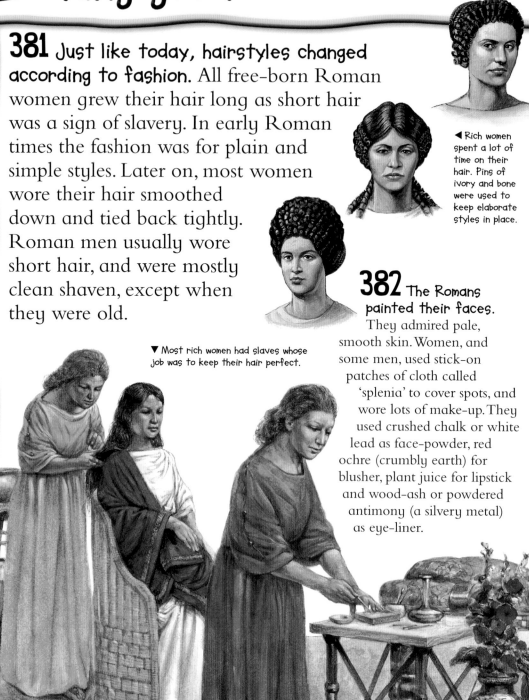

381 Just like today, hairstyles changed according to fashion. All free-born Roman women grew their hair long as short hair was a sign of slavery. In early Roman times the fashion was for plain and simple styles. Later on, most women wore their hair smoothed down and tied back tightly. Roman men usually wore short hair, and were mostly clean shaven, except when they were old.

◄ Rich women spent a lot of time on their hair. Pins of ivory and bone were used to keep elaborate styles in place.

▼ Most rich women had slaves whose job was to keep their hair perfect.

382 The Romans painted their faces. They admired pale, smooth skin. Women, and some men, used stick-on patches of cloth called 'splenia' to cover spots, and wore lots of make-up. They used crushed chalk or white lead as face-powder, red ochre (crumbly earth) for blusher, plant juice for lipstick and wood-ash or powdered antimony (a silvery metal) as eye-liner.

383 Blonde hair was highly prized. Most Romans were born with wiry, dark-brown hair. Some fashionable people admired delicate, blonde hair because it was unusual. Roman women used vinegar and lye (an early form of soap, made from urine and wood-ash) to bleach their own hair.

384 Going to the barbers could be very painful. In Roman times, sharp scissors and razors had not been invented. Barbers used shears to trim men's hair and beards. When a smooth, close-shaven look was in fashion barbers would pull men's beards out by the roots, one hair at a time!

QUIZ
If you had to dress up as a Roman, how would you look? Use the information on this and the previous page to help you draw a picture of the clothes you would need and how to arrange your hair. Will you be a rich governor, a Celtic warrior or a soldier?

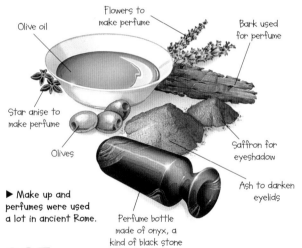

Olive oil

Flowers to make perfume

Bark used for perfume

Star anise to make perfume

Olives

Saffron for eyeshadow

Ash to darken eyelids

▶ Make up and perfumes were used a lot in ancient Rome.

Perfume bottle made of onyx, a kind of black stone

386 Roman combs were made from bone, ivory or wood. Like combs today, they were designed to smooth and untangle hair, and were sometimes worn as hair ornaments. But they had another, less pleasant, purpose – they were used for combing out all the little nits and lice!

385 Romans liked to smell sweet. They used olive oil (made from the crushed fruit of the olive tree) to cleanse and soften their skin, and perfumes to scent their bodies. Ingredients for perfume came from many different lands – flowers came from southern Europe, spices came from India and Africa, and sweet-smelling bark and resin came from Arabia.

Comb

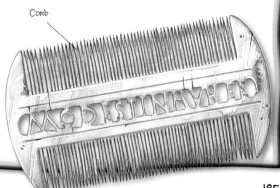

Bath time

387 **The Romans went to the public baths in order to relax.** These huge buildings were more than a place to get clean. They were also fitness centres and places to meet friends. Visitors could take part in sports, such as wrestling, do exercises, have a massage or a haircut. They could buy scented oils and perfumes, read a book, eat a snack or admire works of art in the baths' own sculpture gallery.

◀ There were public baths in most districts of Rome. They were built by Roman emperors or rich families as a gift to the citizens. The finest were the baths of Caracalla (opened around AD 215), which had room for 1600 bathers at a time.

▶ Roman bathing involved five different stages that took place in separate areas of the baths.

388 Men and women could not bathe together. Women usually went to the baths in the mornings, while most men were at work. Men went to the baths in the afternoons.

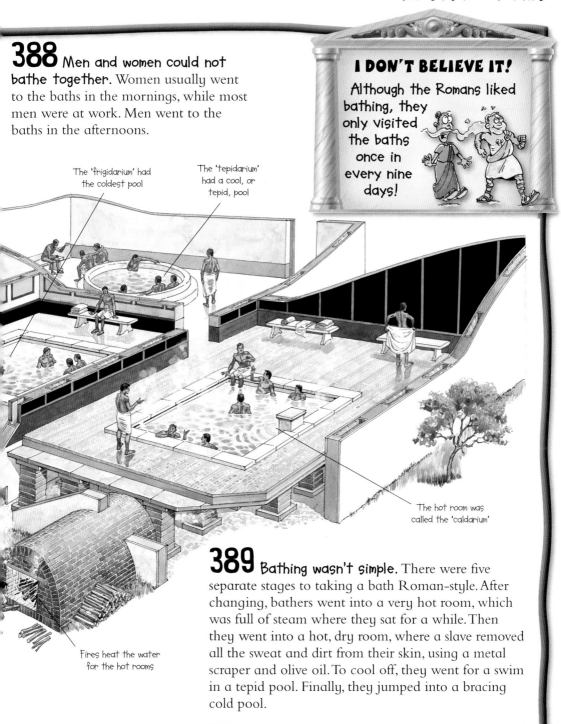

The 'frigidarium' had the coldest pool

The 'tepidarium' had a cool, or tepid, pool

The hot room was called the 'caldarium'

Fires heat the water for the hot rooms

389 Bathing wasn't simple. There were five separate stages to taking a bath Roman-style. After changing, bathers went into a very hot room, which was full of steam where they sat for a while. Then they went into a hot, dry room, where a slave removed all the sweat and dirt from their skin, using a metal scraper and olive oil. To cool off, they went for a swim in a tepid pool. Finally, they jumped into a bracing cold pool.

Having fun

390 The Romans liked music and dancing. Groups of buskers played in the streets, or could be hired for parties. Among ordinary families, favourite instruments included pipes, flutes, cymbals, castanets and horns. However, rich, well-educated people thought the noise they made was vulgar. They preferred the gentler sound of the lyre, which was played to accompany poets and singers.

▲ Roman buskers played music in the street.

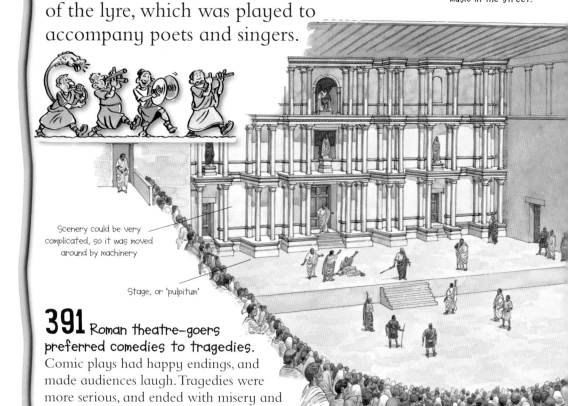

Scenery could be very complicated, so it was moved around by machinery

Stage, or 'pulpitum'

391 Roman theatre-goers preferred comedies to tragedies. Comic plays had happy endings, and made audiences laugh. Tragedies were more serious, and ended with misery and suffering. The Romans also liked clowns, and invented mime, a story told without words, through gestures, acrobatic movements and dance.

392 Plays were originally part of religious festivals. Many famous dramas showed scenes from ancient myths and legends, and were designed to make people think about morals and politics. Later, plays were written on all sorts of topics – including politics and current affairs. Some were paid for by rich politicians, to spread their political message. They handed out free tickets to Roman citizens, hoping to win votes.

394 Roman actors wore masks to help the audience in big theatres see what each character was feeling. They were carved and painted in bright colours, with larger than life features and exaggerated expressions. Some masks were frightened, some were happy, some were sad.

◀ ▲ Most plays only had a small number of characters, so the masks were easily recognised by the audience.

395 Other favourite pastimes included games of skill and chance. Adults and children enjoyed dice and knucklebones, which needed nimble fingers. Draughts relied on luck and quick thinking. They played these for fun, but adults also made bets on who would win.

Draughts, kuncklebones and dice

◀ All the parts in Roman plays were performed by men. For women's roles, men wore masks and dressed in female costume. Women could not be actors, except in mime.

393 Theatres were huge, well-built structures. One of the best preserved Roman theatres is at Orange, in southern France. It has seats for almost 10,000 people. It is so cleverly designed that the audience can hear the actors even from the back row.

I DON'T BELIEVE IT!
Roman actors were almost all men. Some were as popular as TV stars today. Women weren't allowed to sit near the stage, in case they tried to arrange a date with one of the stars!

189

Let the games begin!

396 Romans admired gladiators for their strength, bravery and skill. However, gladiators' lives were short and their deaths were horrible. They were sent to the arena to fight – and suffer – until they died.

Large fork, called a trident

Net to trap opponent

Gladius, a gladiator's sword

Greaves to protect the legs

397 Most gladiators did not choose to fight. They were either prisoners-of-war or criminals who were sold to fight-trainers who organized gladiator shows. Some were specially trained, so that they would survive for longer and provide better entertainment for the watching crowds.

398 Gladiators fought wild beasts, as well as each other. Fierce wild animals were brought from distant parts of the Roman empire to be killed by gladiators in the arenas in Rome. So many lions were taken from North Africa that they became extinct there.

399 The Colosseum was an amazing building for its time. Also known as the Flavian Amphitheatre, the Colosseum was a huge oval arena in the centre of Rome, used for gladiator fights and mock sea-battles. It opened in AD 80, and could seat 50,000 people. It was built of stone, concrete and marble and had 80 separate entrances. Outside, it was decorated with statues of famous Roman heroes.

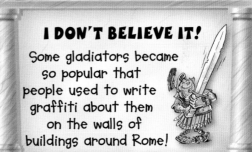

401 **Chariots often collided and overturned.** Each charioteer carried a sharp knife, called a 'falx', to cut himself free from the wreckage. Even so, many horses and charioteers were killed.

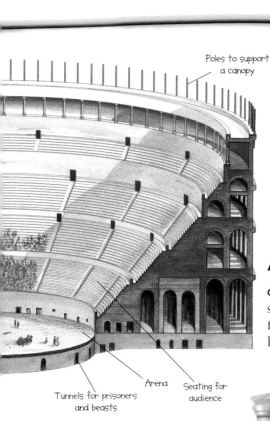

Poles to support a canopy

Arena

Seating for audience

Tunnels for prisoners and beasts

▲ The Colosseum was the largest amphitheatre in the Roman empire.

400 **Some Romans preferred a day at the races.** Horses pulled fast chariots round race-tracks, called 'circuses'. The most famous was the Circus Maximus in Rome, which had room for 250,000 spectators. There could be up to 24 races each day. Twelve chariots took part in each race, running seven times round the oval track – a total distance of about 8 kilometres.

I DON'T BELIEVE IT!

Some gladiators became so popular that people used to write graffiti about them on the walls of buildings around Rome!

402 **Racing rivalries sometimes led to riots.** Races were organized by four separate teams – the Reds, Blues, Greens and Whites. Charioteers wore tunics in their teams' colours. Each team had a keen – and violent – group of fans.

191

Ruling Rome

403 Rome used to be ruled by kings.

According to legend, the first king was Romulus, who came to power in 753 BC. Six more kings ruled after him, but they were unjust and cruel. The last king, Tarquin the Proud, was overthrown in 509 BC. After that, Rome became a republic, a state without a king. Every year the people chose two senior lawyers called consuls to head the government. Many other officials were elected, or chosen by the people, too. The republic lasted for over 400 years.

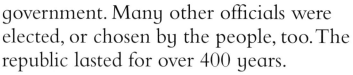

▲ Roman coin showing Emperor Constantine.

▼ Senators were men from leading citizen families who had served the Roman republic as Judges or state officials. They made new laws and discussed government plans.

404 In 47 BC a successful general called Julius Caesar declared himself dictator.

This meant that he wanted to rule on his own for life. Many people feared that he was trying to end the republic, and rule like the old kings. Caesar was murdered in 44 BC by a group of his political enemies. After this, there were many years of civil war.

Julius Caesar

405 In 27 BC an army general called Octavian seized power in Rome.

He declared himself 'First Citizen', and said he would bring back peace and good government to Rome. He ended the civil war, and introduced many strong new laws. But he also changed the Roman government forever. He took a new name, 'Augustus', and became the first emperor of Rome.

Octavian

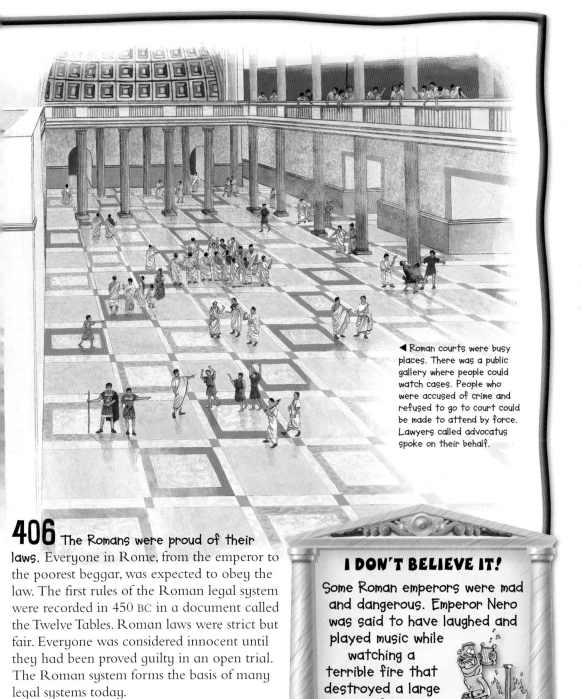

◄ Roman courts were busy places. There was a public gallery where people could watch cases. People who were accused of crime and refused to go to court could be made to attend by force. Lawyers called advocatus spoke on their behalf.

406 The Romans were proud of their laws. Everyone in Rome, from the emperor to the poorest beggar, was expected to obey the law. The first rules of the Roman legal system were recorded in 450 BC in a document called the Twelve Tables. Roman laws were strict but fair. Everyone was considered innocent until they had been proved guilty in an open trial. The Roman system forms the basis of many legal systems today.

I DON'T BELIEVE IT!

Some Roman emperors were mad and dangerous. Emperor Nero was said to have laughed and played music while watching a terrible fire that destroyed a large part of Rome.

In the army

407 **Being a soldier was a good career, if you did not get killed!** Roman soldiers were well paid and well cared for. The empire needed troops to defend its land against enemy attack. A man who fought in the Roman army received a thorough training in battle skills. If he showed promise, he might be promoted and receive extra pay. When he retired after 20 or 25 years of service, he was given money or land to help him start a business.

408 **The Roman army contained citizens and 'helpers'.** Roman citizens joined the regular army, which was organized into legions of around 5000 men. Men who were not citizens could also fight for Rome. They were known as auxiliaries, or helpers, and were organized in special legions of their own.

409 **Roman troops carried three main weapons.** They fought with javelins, swords and daggers. Each man had to buy his own set. He looked after them carefully – one day, his life might depend on them.

▶ Soldiers used their shields to make a protective shell called a 'testudo', or tortoise.

▼ Roman troops defended the empire from attack. They were well paid but it was a dangerous job.

411 The army advanced 30 kilometres every day. When they were hurrying to put down a rebellion, or moving from fort to fort, Roman soldiers travelled quickly, on foot. Troops marched along straight, well made army roads. On the march, each soldier had to carry a heavy pack. It contained weapons, armour, tools for building a camp, cooking pots, dried food and spare clothes.

Shield, or *scutum*

410 Soldiers needed many skills. In enemy territory, soldiers had to find or make everything they needed to survive. When they first arrived they built camps of tents, but soon afterwards they built permanent forts defended by strong walls. Each legion contained men with a wide range of skills, such as cooks, builders, doctors, carpenters, blacksmiths and engineers – but they all had to fight!

▼ Forts were built by the troops themselves, using carpentry and engineering skills.

Protective wall

Barracks, where soldiers slept

Exercise yard

Gate

412 Soldiers worshipped their own special god. At forts and army camps, Roman soldiers built temples where they honoured Mithras. They believed he protected them, and gave them life after death.

Ruled by Rome

413 **More than 50 million people were ruled by Rome.** Celts, Germans, Iberians, Dacians and many other peoples lived in a territory conquered by Roman armies. They spoke many different languages, and had different customs and beliefs. Roman rulers sent armies to occupy their lands, and governors to rule them. They forced conquered peoples to pay Roman taxes and obey Roman laws.

▲ A Roman tax collector assesses a farmer for taxes.

▼ Boudicca, queen of the Iceni tribe, led a revolt against the Romans.

415 Cleopatra used beauty and charm to stop the Romans invading. Cleopatra was queen of Egypt, in North Africa. Cleopatra knew that the Egyptian army would not be able to defeat Roman soldiers. Two Roman army generals, Julius Caesar and Mark Antony, fell in love with her. She stopped the Romans invading for many years, but Egypt was eventually conquered.

414 A few conquered kings and queens refused to accept Roman rule. For example, in AD 60 Boudicca, queen of the Iceni tribe who lived in eastern England, led a rebellion against the Romans in Britain. Her army marched on the city of London and set fire to it, before being defeated by Roman soldiers. Boudicca survived the battle, but killed herself by taking poison so that she would not be captured by Roman troops.

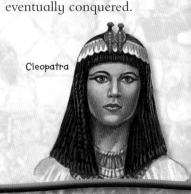
Cleopatra

▼ A carving from Trajan's column of Roman legionaries boarding ships.

Roman writers reported how Celtic warriors decorated their faces and bodies with patterns before going into battle. They believed that the paint was magic, and would protect them. The Celts used a deep-blue dye made from a plant called woad. If you have some special face-painting make-up (make sure you ask an adult), then try making up some scary war-paint designs of your own.

416 Roman conquerors built monuments to celebrate their victories. Trajan, who ruled from AD 98–117, was a famous soldier who became emperor of Rome. He led Roman armies on one of their most successful conquests, in Dacia (Romania) in AD 106. To record this achievement, he gave orders for a tall stone pillar (now known as Trajan's Column) to be built in the Forum in Rome. It was almost 30 metres high, and was decorated with carvings of 2500 Roman soldiers winning wars.

Trajan's column

▲ A carving from Trajan's column of Roman soldiers building the walls of a new fort.

The farming life

417 **Rome relied on farmers.** Most people in Roman times lived in the countryside and worked on farms. Farmers produced food for city-dwellers. Without them, the citizens would not have survived. Food was grown on big estates by teams of slaves, and on small peasant farms where single families worked together.

418 **Farm produce was imported from all over the empire.** Wool and honey came from Britain, wine came from Greece, and 400,000 tonnes of wheat were shipped across the Mediterranean Sea from Egypt every year. It was ground into flour, which was used to make bread, the Romans' basic food.

Pots containing produce

419 **Farmers didn't have big machines to help them.** Heavy work was done by animals, or by human hands. Ploughs were pulled by oxen. Ripe crops were harvested by men and women with curved knives called sickles, and loaded by hand onto farm carts. Donkeys turned mill wheels to crush olives and grind grain, and to raise drinking water from wells.

▼ A large Roman farm estate with slaves working the land.

Beehives for honey

Treading grapes for wine

Owner of the farm

Sheep kept in the fields

Olive tree

Threshing wheat

Pressing olives

Vegetable patch

Vineyard and orchard

Farmworkers harvesting grain

421 **The most valuable fruit was small, hard, green and bitter!** It came from olive trees. Olives could be pickled in salty water to eat with bread and cheese, or crushed to provide oil. The Romans used olive oil as a medicine, for cooking and preserving food, for cleaning and softening the skin, and even for burning in lamps.

420 Roman grapes grew on trees. Vines, climbing plants that produce grapes, were planted among fruit trees in orchards. They provided support for the vine stems, and welcomed shade to stop the grapes getting scorched by the sun. Grapes were one of the most important crops on Roman farms. The ripe fruits were picked and dried to become raisins, or pulped and made into wine.

QUIZ

Imagine that you are a Roman farmer talking to a visitor from the city. How would you answer these questions?

What crops do you grow?

Why do you keep oxen?

Who will harvest the grain?

How do you grind grain into flour?

Why are you growing olives?

Work like a slave!

422 **Roman people were not all equal.** There were different classes within Roman society. Throughout the Roman Empire, the biggest difference between people was whether they were slaves or free. Free-born men and women had rights that were guaranteed by law; for example, to find their own work, or travel from one place to another. In Rome, citizens also had the right to vote for government officials, and to receive free hand-outs of food. But slaves had hardly any rights at all. They belonged to their owners just like dogs or horses.

423 **Slaves were trained to do all sorts of tasks.** Slaves did everything their owners demanded, from babycare to hard labour on farms. Many slaves were trusted by their owners, who valued their skills. A few slaves became respected chefs or doctors.

▶ Slaves were bought and sold at slave-markets. They were paraded before the citizens to be chosen or rejected. The slaves could not leave, or choose what work to do. They could be cruelly punished, neglected or given away.

424 There were many different ways of becoming a slave. Slaves might be captured in war, purchased from a slave-trader or born to slave parents. They could also be people condemned to slavery as punishment for a serious crime.

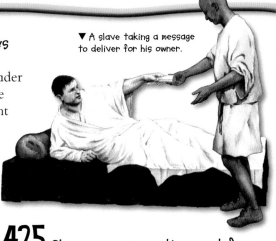
▼ A slave taking a message to deliver for his owner.

425 Slaves were sometimes set free by their owners. Freedom could be a reward for loyalty or long service. Some sick or dying slave-owners gave orders that their slaves should be freed. They did not want their slaves to pass to a new owner who might treat them badly.

I DON'T BELIEVE IT!

From 73 BC to 71 BC a slave called Spartacus led a revolt in southern Italy. He ran away to a hideout in the hills where 90,000 other slaves joined him.

426 Some slaves did very well after they were freed. Former slaves used the skills they had learned to set up businesses of their own. Many were successful, and a few became very rich.

Roman know-how

427 **The Romans pioneered many new building materials and designs.** They discovered concrete, which was much cheaper and easier to use than solid building stone. They made bricks of clay baked at high temperatures, which lasted much longer than unbaked ones. They found out how to use arches to create tall, strong walls and doorways. They designed massive domes for buildings that were too big to be roofed with wooden beams.

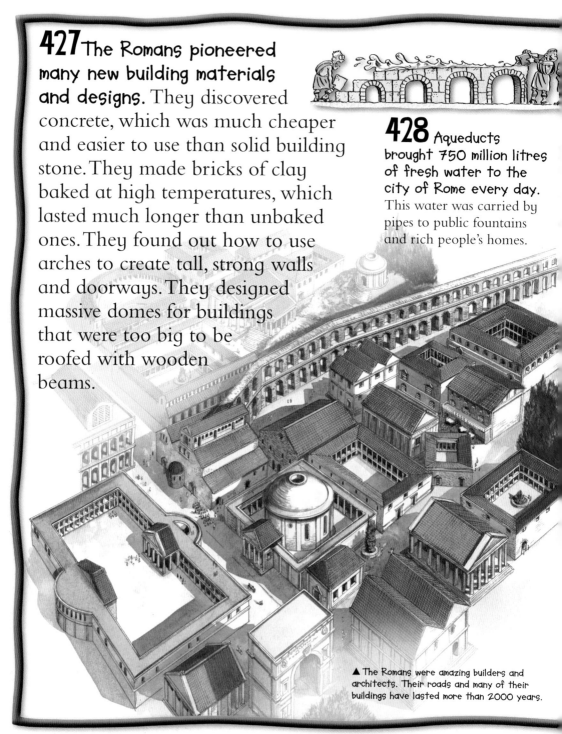

428 Aqueducts brought 750 million litres of fresh water to the city of Rome every day. This water was carried by pipes to public fountains and rich people's homes.

▲ The Romans were amazing builders and architects. Their roads and many of their buildings have lasted more than 2000 years.

◀ ▲ Romans used valves to pump water uphill. Water would then come out of fountains.

429 The Roman's water supplies were so advanced that no one had anything better until the 1800s! They invented pumps with valves to pump water uphill. This went into high tanks above fountains. Gravity pulled the water out of the fountain's spout.

431 Even the best doctors often failed to cure their patients. But Roman doctors were skilled at sewing up cuts and joining broken bones. They also used herbs for medicines and painkillers.

▼ Romans believed in the ability of doctors to cure illnesses.

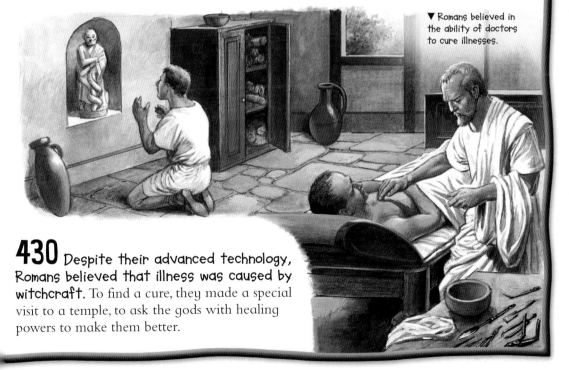

430 Despite their advanced technology, Romans believed that illness was caused by witchcraft. To find a cure, they made a special visit to a temple, to ask the gods with healing powers to make them better.

Prayers and sacrifices

432 **The Romans worshipped many different gods.** Some were worshipped just in Rome, others through the whole of the ancient world. There were also gods of the city, the country, and of the underworld, and some were worshipped by people of certain professions. However, the empire was so large that it came to include countries with very different beliefs. These were often adopted by the Romans. Ideas and gods from Greece had a very big impact.

Jupiter, king of the gods   Juno, queen of the gods

Mercury, messenger the go

Neptune, god of the sea

Mars, god of war

Minerva, goddess of war

Diana, goddess of the moon and hunting

Pan, god of the mountainside, pastures, sheep and goats

Venus, goddess of love

Dis (Pluto), god of the underworld

433 **The Roman emperor was also chief priest.** As part of his government duties he said prayers and offered sacrifices to the gods who protected Rome. He was given a special name 'pontifex maximus', which meant chief bridge-builder, because people believed he acted as a bridge between the gods and ordinary people.

A curse written on a piece of stone

434 Families made offerings to the gods every day.
They left food, wine and incense in front of a shrine in their house. A shrine is like a mini temple. It contained statues of ancient gods called the 'lares' and 'penates'. The lares were ancestor spirits who looked after living family members. The penates guarded the family's food.

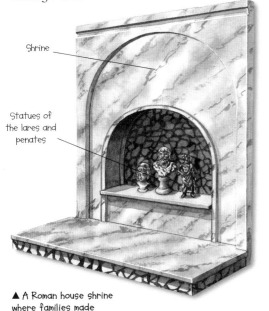

Shrine

Statues of the lares and penates

▲ A Roman house shrine where families made offerings to the gods.

436 Roman men and women could ask the gods to curse their enemies.
They wrote their enemies' names, plus curse words, on metal or pottery scraps and left them at temples. They hoped that the gods would see them and harm the people named.

▲ A Christian in Roman times praying in a catacomb.

437 Some of the world's first Christians lived in Rome.
But until AD 313 Christianity was banned in the Roman Empire. Christians met secretly, in underground passages called catacombs, to say prayers and hold services. They also used the catacombs as a burial place.

435 Roman people were very superstitious.
They decorated their homes with magic symbols, and hung good luck charms around children's necks. They believed that they could foretell the future by observing animals, birds, insects and even the weather! For example, bees were a sign of riches and happiness but a hooting owl foretold danger.

I DON'T BELIEVE IT!
After an animal had been sacrificed to the gods, a priest, called a 'haruspex', examined its liver. If it was diseased, bad luck was on the way!

On the move

KEY
▨ Roman Empire
⌒ Roads

438 All roads led to Rome. The city was at the hub of a network of roads that stretched for more than 85,000 kilometres. They had been built to link outlying parts of the empire to the capital, so that Roman armies or government officials could travel quickly. To make travel as quick as possible, roads were built in straight lines, taking the shortest route.

▲ Thousands of kilometres of road ran across the whole empire.

440 Some Roman roads have survived for over 2000 years. Each road was made of layers of earth and stones on top of a firm, flat foundation. It was surfaced with stone slabs or gravel. The centre had a camber, a curved surface, so that rainwater drained away into ditches on either side.

439 Rome's first main road was built in 312 BC. Its name was the Via Appia ('via' is the Latin word for road), and it ran from the city of Rome to the port of Brundisium on the south-east coast of Italy. Many travellers from Greece arrived there, and the new road made their journey to Rome quicker and easier.

▼ The building of a Roman road. Trained men worked out the route, and slaves did the heavy labour. Army roads were built by soldiers.

Large surface slabs

Drainage ditch

Route accurately marked out

Solid foundations

441 Roman engineers used tools to help them to make accurate surveys. They made careful plans and took measurements before starting any building project, such as a new road or city walls.

▶ These road builders are using a 'groma' to measure straight lines.

442 Poor people had to walk everywhere. They could not afford to hire a horse or a donkey, or a cushioned carriage, pulled by oxen. If they were lucky, they might manage to hitch a lift in a farm wagon – but this would not give them a comfortable ride!

◀ A rich man travelling through the streets in a litter.

443 Town streets were crowded and very dirty. Rich people travelled in curtained beds called litters, carried shoulder-high by slaves. Ordinary people used stepping-stones to avoid the mud and rubbish underfoot.

444 Heavy loads often travelled by water. There were no lorries in Roman times. Ships powered by sails and by slaves rowing carried people and cargo across the sea and along rivers. But water-transport was slow, and could be dangerous. Roman ships were often attacked by pirates, and shipwrecks were common.

▲ The Romans' knowledge of ship-building came from the Greeks. The Romans, though, were not really sailors, and they did not improve the designs.

Gladiators

Prepare to do battle with the
finest warriors of ancient Rome!

Colosseum • Training • Politics • Julius Caesar
Schools • Armour • Prisoners • Shields • Helmets
Games • Animals • Arenas • Slaves • Weapons
Water fights • Parades

The great games

445 Gladiators were made to fight to the death to please the crowd. They fought in an arena (open space surrounded by tiered seats) and used lots of different swords, spears, knives and other weapons. Not every gladiatorial fight ended in death. Some gladiators were allowed to live if they fought bravely and with skill. Most fights took place in Rome, but cities throughout the Roman Empire had arenas for these events. The arenas were also used for wild animal hunts and for the execution of criminals. For the ancient Romans, violence and bloodshed were used as entertainment.

▼ A defeated gladiator appeals for mercy from the crowd by raising his left hand. The victorious fighter awaits the instruction to kill or spare his rival.

The first gladiators

446 **The first gladiators were not from Rome.** The Romans did not invent the idea of gladiators. They believed the idea of men fighting in an arena probably came to Rome from the region of Etruria. But the first proper gladiators probably came from Campania, an area of Italy south of Rome.

▲ The first gladiators probably came from Campania, in the south, and more fought in this area than in Rome.

447 **The first Roman gladiators fought in 264 BC.** Six slaves were set to fight each other with swords, but they were not allowed to wear any armour. The fights did not last for long before one of the slaves in each pair was killed.

▶ The gladius was the standard weapon used by early gladiators. It was kept in a sheath called a scabbard.

448 **The first gladiatorial fights were always part of a funeral.** The name for a gladiatorial show, a munus, means a duty owed to the dead. The first fights were held at the funerals of politicians and noblemen, who ordered the games in their wills.

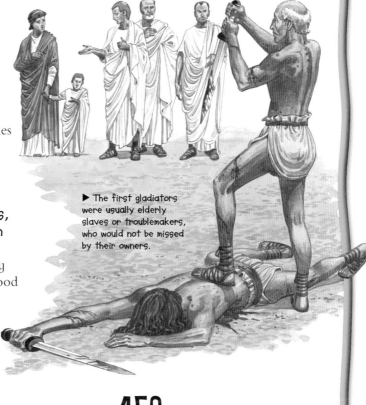

▶ The first gladiators were usually elderly slaves or troublemakers, who would not be missed by their owners.

449 **In early funeral games, food was more important than gladiators.** The Romans used funerals to show off how wealthy and important they were. Free food and drink were laid out at the funeral for any Roman citizen who wanted to come along. Gifts of money, jewellery and clothing were also handed out. The family of the person being buried would wear their finest clothes. The first gladiator fights were just one part of the whole funeral.

450 **Gladiators were named after their weapons.** The word gladiator means 'a man who uses a gladius'. The gladius was a type of short, stabbing sword that was used by Roman soldiers. It was about 40 centimetres long and had a very sharp point. It was generally used for slashing, not for cutting. Not all gladiators used the gladius, but the name was used for all fighters in the arena.

Scabbard

Gladius

Prisoners of war

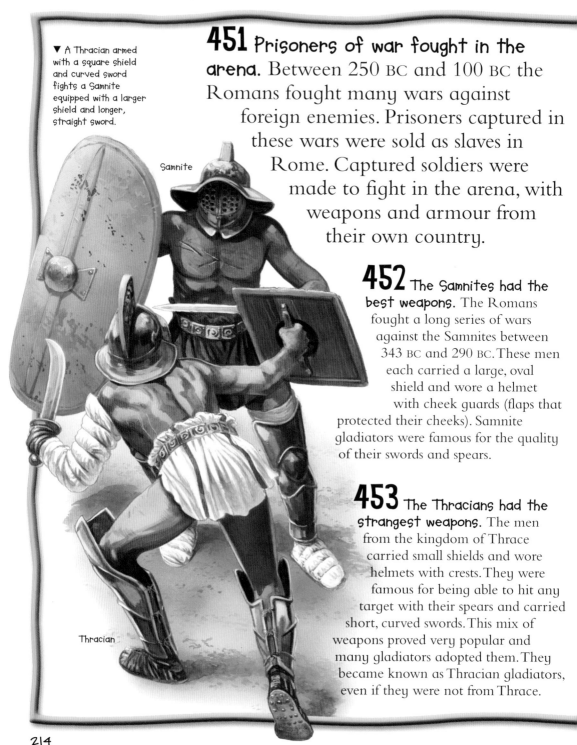

▼ A Thracian armed with a square shield and curved sword fights a Samnite equipped with a larger shield and longer, straight sword.

Samnite

Thracian

451 **Prisoners of war fought in the arena.** Between 250 BC and 100 BC the Romans fought many wars against foreign enemies. Prisoners captured in these wars were sold as slaves in Rome. Captured soldiers were made to fight in the arena, with weapons and armour from their own country.

452 **The Samnites had the best weapons.** The Romans fought a long series of wars against the Samnites between 343 BC and 290 BC. These men each carried a large, oval shield and wore a helmet with cheek guards (flaps that protected their cheeks). Samnite gladiators were famous for the quality of their swords and spears.

453 **The Thracians had the strangest weapons.** The men from the kingdom of Thrace carried small shields and wore helmets with crests. They were famous for being able to hit any target with their spears and carried short, curved swords. This mix of weapons proved very popular and many gladiators adopted them. They became known as Thracian gladiators, even if they were not from Thrace.

I DON'T BELIEVE IT!

At the end of a war the prisoners were auctioned as slaves in the Forum (market square). Sometimes so many prisoners had been taken that the auction lasted for many days.

▶ The tall, fair-skinned Celts decorated their bodies and shields with bright colours.

454 Celts painted their bodies before going into battle. The Celts were the only people to have captured Rome, in 390 BC. They lived in northern Italy and across Europe. The Romans forced many Celtic prisoners to fight in their native clothes and with native weapons.

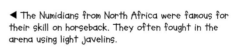

◀ The Numidians from North Africa were famous for their skill on horseback. They often fought in the arena using light javelins.

455 The Numidians fought on horseback. Numidia was an area of northern Africa in what is now Algeria. The area was famous for breeding quality horses and its army included large numbers of cavalry (soldiers on horseback). Prisoners of war from Numidia rode horses when they appeared in the arena.

215

Gladiators and politics

▲ A person's ashes were stored in a pot or urn until the funeral.

456 Funerals were delayed for years. Gladiatorial shows were organized as part of the funerals of rich and powerful noblemen. However, the heir of the man who had died would want to hold the show when he was standing for election so that he could impress the voters.

457 A good gladiator show could win an election. In ancient Rome, votes were not cast in secret. Each voter had to give his name to an official called a censor and then declare how he was voting. The men standing for election stood near the censor to see how people voted. Putting on an impressive gladiator show could gain votes.

▼ A citizen waiting to vote at an election. The censor kept a list of everyone entitled to vote and people had to prove who they were before voting.

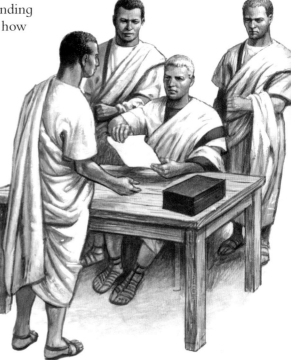

I DON'T BELIEVE IT!

In 165 BC, a play was interrupted when the entire audience left the theatre to watch a gladiatorial show. The actors were left alone in the theatre!

458 Some politicians hired gangs of gladiators to beat up their opponents. If a citizen could not be persuaded, by gladiator shows or the payment of money, to vote for a certain candidate, the candidate might use gladiators to bully him. Gladiators were armed with clubs and given the names of citizens who should be threatened. Every election was accompanied by this sort of violence.

▲ Men were posted at the entrance to the arena to ensure that only voters entered.

459 The best seats went to men who donated money to the election campaign. Standing for an election cost a lot of money in ancient Rome. Rich men would give or lend money to the candidate they preferred. In return they would get the best seats in a gladiatorial show and would expect to receive titles or government money if their candidate won.

460 Only voters could watch the games. The purpose of holding spectacular gladiatorial shows was to influence voters. Only citizens of Rome could vote, so only they were allowed to attend the shows. Citizens who were known to be voting for an opponent were turned away, as were slaves and foreigners who could not vote.

◀ Roman coins were made of gold, silver or bronze and carried a portrait of the emperor on one side.

Caesar's games

461 **Julius Caesar borrowed money to buy his gladiators.** Caesar rose to become the ruler of the Roman Empire. Early in his career he staged spectacular games to win votes in elections. But Caesar was too poor to afford to pay the bills, so he borrowed money from richer men. When he won the elections, Caesar repaid the men with favours and titles.

▲ Julius Caesar (102–44 BC) was a politician who won several elections after staging magnificent games to entertain the voters.

▲ War elephants were popular attractions, and gladiators were specially trained in how to fight against them.

462 **Caesar's gladiators fought in silver armour.** In 65 BC, Julius Caesar staged the funeral games for his father, who had died 20 years earlier. Caesar was standing for election to be chief priest of Rome. To make his games even more special, Caesar dressed his 640 gladiators in armour made of solid silver.

463 **Caesar brought war elephants to Rome.** In 46 BC Julius Caesar celebrated a victory in North Africa by staging gladiatorial games in Rome. Among the prisoners of war forced to fight in the arena were 40 war elephants, together with the men trained to fight them.

464 **Caesar turned senators (governors of Rome) into gladiators.** On one occasion Caesar forced two rich noblemen to fight in the arena. They had been sentenced to death by a court, but Caesar ordered that the man who killed the other in the arena could go free.

465 **Caesar's final show was too big for the arena.** The games staged by Julius Caesar when he wanted to become dictator of Rome were the grandest ever held. After weeks of shows and feasts, the final day saw a fight between two armies of 500 infantry (foot soldiers) and 30 cavalry. The battle was so large it had to be held in the enormous chariot race course, Circus Maximus.

▲ Chariot racing was a hugely popular sport that thrilled the crowds in ancient Rome.

QUIZ

1. Did Caesar's gladiators wear armour made of silver, gold or bronze?
2. Was Caesar's final show a big or small show?
3. Where did Caesar get the money to buy gladiators?

Answers:
1. Silver. 2. It was a big show. 3. He borrowed money from richer men.

The mob

466 **The Roman mob could overpower emperors.** Over a million people lived in ancient Rome. Many were voting citizens who did not have regular jobs. Even the most powerful emperors had to keep this vast mob of Romans happy. If an emperor did not put on impressive gladiatorial shows he could be booed, attacked or even killed.

▲ Emperor Vitellius (AD 69) was murdered by a mob of Romans after failing to put on any impressive games.

◄ The seats in the arena were numbered and cushions were sometimes provided for extra comfort.

467 **Each seat was saved for a particular person.** People attending the gladiator games had their own seats. The row and seat number were written on small clay tablets that were handed out by the organizer of the games. Some seats were given to whoever queued up outside the arena.

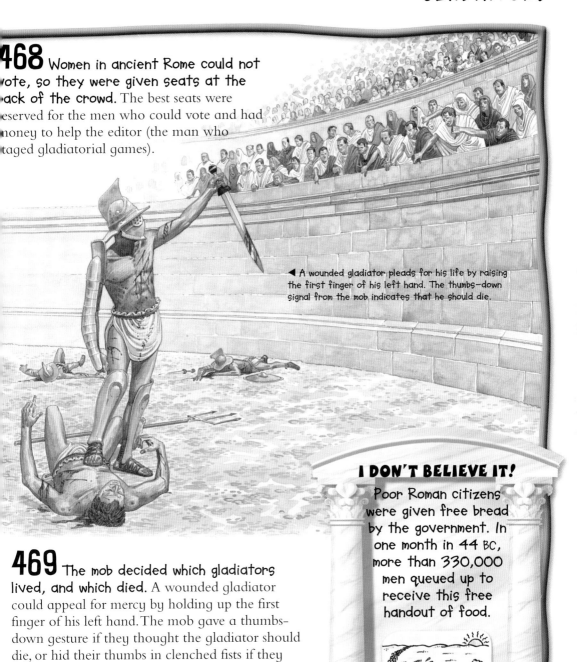

468 Women in ancient Rome could not vote, so they were given seats at the back of the crowd. The best seats were reserved for the men who could vote and had money to help the editor (the man who staged gladiatorial games).

◄ A wounded gladiator pleads for his life by raising the first finger of his left hand. The thumbs-down signal from the mob indicates that he should die.

469 The mob decided which gladiators lived, and which died. A wounded gladiator could appeal for mercy by holding up the first finger of his left hand. The mob gave a thumbs-down gesture if they thought the gladiator should die, or hid their thumbs in clenched fists if they thought he should live. The editor usually did what the mob wanted because he wanted them to vote for him.

I DON'T BELIEVE IT!

Poor Roman citizens were given free bread by the government. In one month in 44 BC, more than 330,000 men queued up to receive this free handout of food.

221

Amazing arenas

470 The first gladiator fights took place in the cattle market. The cattle market, or Forum Boarium, was a large open space by the river Tiber. Cattle pens were cleared away to make space for fighting, while the audience watched from shops and temples.

◀ The crowd watched early gladiatorial fights in the cattle market from shops and pavements.

471 Most fights took place in the Forum. This was the largest open square in the centre of Rome. The most important temples and government buildings stood around the Forum. After about 150 BC, gladiatorial games were held in the Forum and temporary wooden stands were erected in which spectators could sit.

472 One fight took place in a swivelling arena. In 53 BC, the politician Gaius Scribonius Curio put on a gladiator show and impressed the crowd by staging two plays in back-to-back theatres. The theatres swivelled around to form an arena for a small gladiator show. The crowd loved the new idea and Curio went on to win several elections.

473
The first purpose-built arena had the emperor's name carved on it. In 29 BC an amphitheatre (an open-air building with rows of seats, one above the other) was built to the north of Rome by the politician Titus Statilius Taurus. The amphitheatre was built of stone and timber to replace temporary wooden stands in the Forum. Taurus wanted to impress Emperor Augustus so he carved the name 'Augustus' over the entrance.

▼ The name Augustus dominated the entrance to the arena built by Taurus.

AUGUSTUS

474
Every arena had the same layout. Arenas were oval with an entrance at each end. The gladiators came into the arena through one entrance, and the other was reserved for servants and for carrying out any dead gladiators. The editor sat in a special section of the seating called the tribunal editoris, which was on the north side in the shade.

▼ All gladiatorial stadiums were oval in shape, with blocks of seating rising from the central arena.

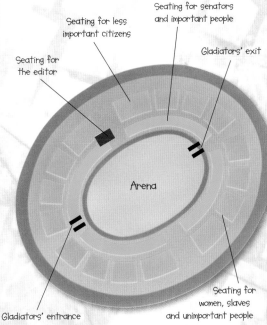

Seating for less important citizens

Seating for senators and important people

Gladiators' exit

Seating for the editor

Arena

Gladiators' entrance

Seating for women, slaves and unimportant people

The mighty Colosseum

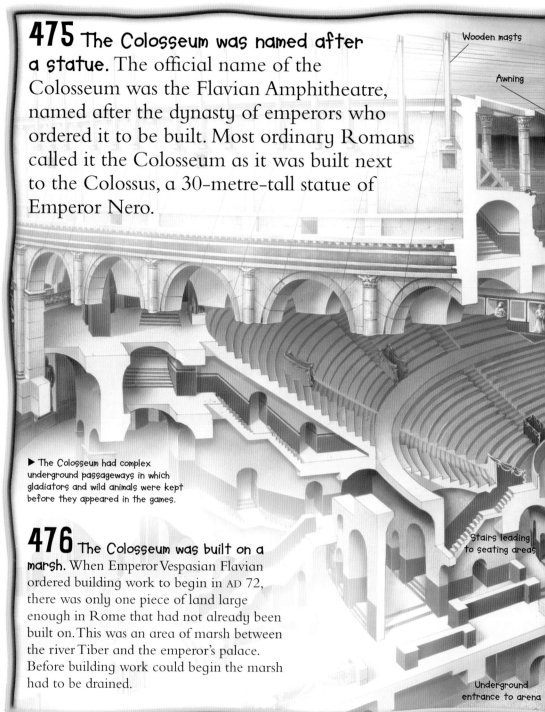

475 **The Colosseum was named after a statue.** The official name of the Colosseum was the Flavian Amphitheatre, named after the dynasty of emperors who ordered it to be built. Most ordinary Romans called it the Colosseum as it was built next to the Colossus, a 30-metre-tall statue of Emperor Nero.

Wooden masts

Awning

▶ The Colosseum had complex underground passageways in which gladiators and wild animals were kept before they appeared in the games.

476 **The Colosseum was built on a marsh.** When Emperor Vespasian Flavian ordered building work to begin in AD 72, there was only one piece of land large enough in Rome that had not already been built on. This was an area of marsh between the river Tiber and the emperor's palace. Before building work could begin the marsh had to be drained.

Stairs leading to seating areas

Underground entrance to arena

477 The Colosseum could seat 50,000 spectators. The huge seating area was divided into over 80 sections. Each section had a door and flight of steps that led to the outside of the Colosseum. The standing room at the top was reserved for slaves and may have held another 4000 people.

478 The Colosseum was probably the largest building in the world. The outer walls stood 46 metres tall and covered an area 194 metres long by 160 metres wide. The walls were covered in stone, but the structure was made of brick or concrete.

479 The first games in the Colosseum lasted 100 days. The Colosseum was finished in AD 80, during the reign of Emperor Titus. He wanted to show that he was the most generous man ever to live in Rome, so he organized gladiatorial games to last for 100 days. Thousands of gladiators and animals fought in these games.

Tiered seating

Trapdoors

Arena floor

Network of corridors and machinery beneath arena floor

Who were the gladiators?

480 Gladiators were divided into types based on their weapons. Not all gladiators used the same weapons or fought in the same way. Some gladiators fought with weapons that had been popular in other countries or were used by different types of soldiers. Others used weapons and armour that were made especially for the arena.

Murmillo

481 Murmillo gladiators used army weapons and military armour. Their shields and swords were similar to those used by infantry in the Roman army. The shield was one metre long and 65 centimetres wide. The sword was used for stabbing, not cutting.

482 Thracian gladiators used lightweight armour. The weapons of the Thracians were based on those used by soldiers from the kingdom of Thrace. The shield was small and square and the leg armour had long metal guards. The sword had a curved blade and the helmets were decorated with a griffin's head (a griffin was an imaginary bird).

Thracian

◄ ▲ ► Thracian, Murmillo and Provocator gladiators were all equipped with armour and heavy weapons. They usually fought each other, sometimes in teams. The lightly equipped Retiarius only had a net and trident.

483 **Provocator gladiators wore the heaviest armour of all gladiators.** They had a breastplate that protected the chest, a round helmet and leg armour that reached above the knees. The shield was about 80 centimetres long and 60 centimetres wide. They used a short, stabbing sword with a straight blade.

MAKE A SHIELD

You will need:
cardboard scissors
string coloured paints

1. Take the sheet of cardboard and cut out a rectangular shape with rounded corners.
2. Ask an adult to make a pair of holes close to each long side and tie string through them to make handles.
3. Paint the front of the shield with a bright, colourful design.

Retiarius

Provocator

484 **Retiarius gladiators had a fishing net and trident.** These gladiators wore very little armour. They relied on speed and skill to escape attacks from heavily equipped gladiators, such as the Provocator gladiators. The fishing net was used to try to trip or entangle an opponent. The trident, a spear with three points, was usually used by fishermen.

Special fighters

◀ The equite gladiators began their combat on horseback, but if one fell off his horse, the other had to fight on foot as well.

485 **Equite gladiators were equipped in the same way as the Roman army's cavalry.** They used a small, leather shield, a medium-length sword and a lance about 2.5 metres long. Only the helmet was different from that of the army. The army helmet had an open face and no brim. Whenever these gladiators appeared in a show, they were the first to fight.

486 Female gladiators were rare. They first appeared around AD 55 in Rome as a novelty act. They fought only against other women or animals. Female gladiators were banned in AD 200.

▲ Female gladiators fought in the same style as the male gladiators.

487 **The andabatae (an-dab-AH-tie) fought blindfolded.** The Romans loved anything new or unusual. Andabatae gladiators wore helmets with no eye-holes. They listened carefully for sounds of their opponent, then attacked with two swords. Sometimes the andabatae would fight on horseback.

488 **British gladiators fought from chariots.** Known as the essedarii (ess-e-DAH-ree-ee), meaning chariot-man, these gladiators first appeared after Julius Caesar invaded Britain in 55 BC. The first chariot gladiators were prisoners of war.

▲ Andabatae helmets had no eye-holes — the gladiators had to rely on their hearing.

ANDABATAE FIGHT

Recreate the combat of the andabatae with this game

You will need:
blindfold   four or more players

1. One player is the andabatae. Tie on the blindfold, making sure the player can see nothing.
2. Other players run around the andabatae calling out their name.
3. The andabatae tries to catch someone. When they catch a person, that person puts on the blindfold and becomes the andabatae. The game continues for as long as you like.

489 Special clowns who fought with wooden weapons were known as paegniarii (payeg-nee-AH-ree-ee). They appeared at shows during gaps between gladiator fights. They were skilled acrobats and would sometimes tell jokes or make fun of important people in the audience.

▶ The paegniarii used wooden weapons and put on comic displays to entertain the crowd between gladiator fights.

Recruiting gladiators

490 **The first gladiators were household slaves.** The will of the dead man who was being honoured by the games would name his slaves who were to fight. They were made to fight during the funeral. Those who were killed were then buried with their owner.

AUGUSTUS

JULIUS

SPARTACUS

CLAUDIUS

▲ Before a show, the names of the gladiators who were to fight were written on a scroll.

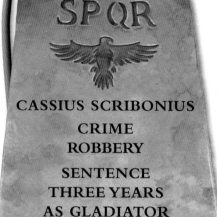

SPQR

CASSIUS SCRIBONIUS

CRIME
ROBBERY

SENTENCE
THREE YEARS
AS GLADIATOR

◀ When convicted, the name, crime and sentence of each criminal was inscribed on a tablet.

491 Criminals could be sent to the arena. The Romans did not have prisons so criminals were usually fined, flogged or executed. Men guilty of some crimes might be ordered to become gladiators for a set period of time – such as three years for robbery. These men would be given a tablet showing the details of their crime and sentence.

I DON'T BELIEVE IT!
When the lanista wanted to buy slaves to become gladiators, he would choose big, strong men. On average a gladiator was about 5 centimetres taller than an ordinary Roman.

492 Some gladiators were volunteers. These volunteers were often former soldiers who wanted to earn money for their retirement. They signed up for a period of time or for a set number of fights and received a large payment of money if they survived.

494 Gladiators were recruited by the lanista. Every gladiator school was run by the lanista, the owner and chief trainer. The lanista decided who to recruit and how to train them. He would choose the strongest men to fight in heavy armour and the quickest men to fight as Retiarius gladiators.

◀ Slaves for sale were paraded in front of potential buyers. They were sold to the highest bidder.

493 Strong slaves were sold to become gladiators. In ancient Rome, slaves were treated as property, and had no human rights. If a man wanted to raise money, he might sell a slave. The lanista would pay a high price for strong male slaves. Many young slaves were also sold to become gladiators.

▶ The price of slaves varied, but a slave might cost about the same as an average workman's wages for a year.

Learning to fight

495 Gladiators lived in a special training school called a ludus. Most early schools were located near Naples, but they later moved to Rome. Some schools specialized in a particular type of gladiator, but others trained all types. The school was run by the lanista, and some were owned by wealthy noblemen.

▲ Wooden training swords were the same size as real weapons.

496 Gladiators trained with wooden weapons. The weapons made sure that gladiators were not seriously injured during training. It also made it more difficult for gladiators to organize a rebellion, as Spartacus had done. Some wooden weapons were bound with heavy lead weights so that when gladiators fought with normal weapons they could fight for longer.

◄ Most arenas and gladiator schools had a small shrine dedicated to the war god Mars.

497 A special oath (promise) was taken by trainee gladiators in front of a shrine to the gods. The oath made the gladiator obey the lanista without question or endure branding, flogging, chains or death. Gladiators were allowed to keep any prize money they won.

498 New trainees fought against a wooden post called a palus. A trainer, known as a doctor, taught the recruits how to use their weapons and shields to strike at the 2-metre-high wooden post. Only when the basic tactics had been learned did the recruits practise against other gladiators.

▼ Gladiators trained for several hours every day, being instructed on fighting techniques by retired gladiators and more experienced men.

499 The buildings of a gladiator school were constructed around a square training ground. This was where the gladiators did most of their training, exercises and other activities. Around the training ground were rooms where the gladiators lived. Recruits slept in dormitories, but fully trained gladiators had their own rooms.

Armour, shields and helmets

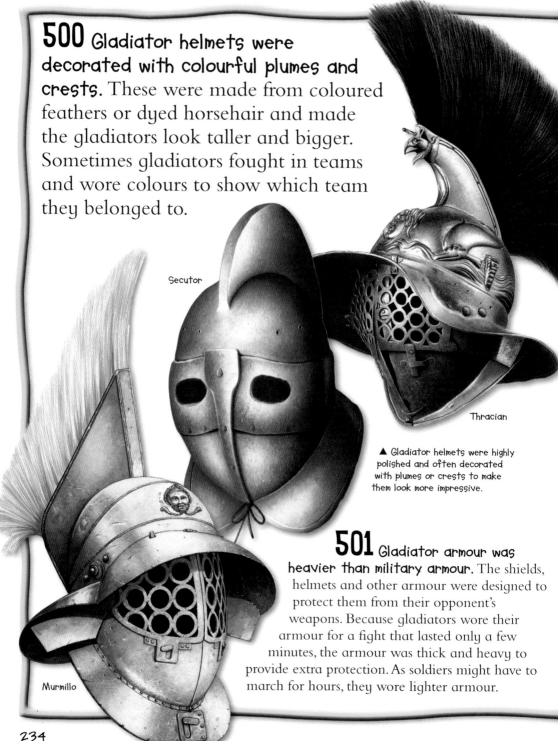

500 Gladiator helmets were decorated with colourful plumes and crests. These were made from coloured feathers or dyed horsehair and made the gladiators look taller and bigger. Sometimes gladiators fought in teams and wore colours to show which team they belonged to.

Secutor

Thracian

▲ Gladiator helmets were highly polished and often decorated with plumes or crests to make them look more impressive.

501 Gladiator armour was heavier than military armour. The shields, helmets and other armour were designed to protect them from their opponent's weapons. Because gladiators wore their armour for a fight that lasted only a few minutes, the armour was thick and heavy to provide extra protection. As soldiers might have to march for hours, they wore lighter armour.

Murmillo

502 Some armour was covered with gold. Most gladiator armour was decorated with carvings and reliefs of gods such as Mars, god of war, or Victory, goddess of success. These decorations were often coated with thin sheets of pure gold.

503 Padded armour was worn on the arms and legs. Thick layers of cloth and padding gave protection from glancing blows from the weapons or from being hit by the shield of the opponent.

Final shape

Leather binding

▲ Gladiator shields were painted and decorated with gold to impress the audience.

Cloth padding

▲ Arms and legs were often covered with layers of woollen cloth tied on with leather bindings.

504 The body was usually left without any armour at all. This meant that a single blow could kill them, or injure them so seriously that they had to ask for mercy. Gladiators needed to be skilful with both weapons and shields to survive.

I DON'T BELIEVE IT!
Gladiator helmets were very heavy – they weighed about 7 kilograms, twice as much as an army helmet!

Get ready for the games

505 **The first decision when staging gladitorial games (munus) was how much money to spend.** The man who hosted the event was known as the editor. A munus was an expensive event but most editors wanted to put on the most impressive show possible. They would spend as much money as they could spare.

506 **The editor would choose different features for his show.** A lanista would be hired to organize the show. Together, they would decide how many gladiators would fight and how many musicians and other performers were needed. The lanista would make sure the event was a success.

▲ Musicians and dancers were popular at gladiator shows. Shows often included a parade of entertainers before the gladiators.

507 **A dead gladiator cost more than a wounded one.** The editor would sign a contract with the lanista. This set down everything that would appear at the munus and the cost. If a gladiator was killed, a special payment was made so that the lanista could buy and train a replacement. Many editors granted mercy to a wounded man to avoid paying extra.

508 Everything was hired — even the clothes worn by the organizer.

The editor would hire expensive clothes and jewellery for himself and his family. He wanted to make sure that they looked their best when they appeared at the games. The editor wanted to impress his fellow citizens and make sure they would vote for him.

509 The star of the show was the editor.

Everything was arranged so that the editor of the games looked as important as possible. As well as wearing special clothes, he was given the most prominent seat in the amphitheatre and all the gladiators and other performers bowed to him. He was paying for the show and wanted to make sure he got all the credit.

▼ Smart clothes were hired for the editor and his family so that they could show off to the audience.

A laurel wreath signified an honour granted by the Roman government

A toga was a special item of clothing that indicated the wearer's rank within society.

Gold jewellery indicated a family's wealth

Brightly coloured silk from China showed wealth and sophistication

Purple was the most expensive dye in ancient Rome

Showtime!

510 Advertising for the show began days beforehand. The lanista sent out slaves to paint signs on walls, while others shouted announcements on the street. The slaves told people when and where the show was and what it included. They also told them the name of the editor of the show.

511 The show began with a parade, which was led into the arena by the editor. He was dressed in beautiful clothes and often rode in a chariot. Behind him came the musicians playing lively tunes. Then came the gladiators, each followed by a slave who carried the gladiator's weapons and armour. Then came statues of gods including the war god Mars. Finally the servants, referees and other officials entered the arena.

512 Gladiators were carefully paired against each other. Before the show began, the editor and lanista would decide which gladiators would fight each other. The show would start with beginners fighting each other, with the expert veterans appearing towards the end of the show. The results would be shouted out by a herald and written on a sign, or tabella, at one end of the arena.

513 The probatio was a crucial ceremony. Before the first fight of the show, the editor and lanista would enter the arena for the probatio. This ceremony involved the men testing the weapons and armour to be used in the show. Swords were tested by slicing up vegetables, and armour by being hit with clubs.

◀ Each gladiator show began with a grand parade of everyone involved in the show, led by the editor in a chariot.

514 Musicians performed first. The band included trumpets, curved horns and the hydraulis. This was a loud instrument like a modern church organ. The musicians entertained the crowd between fights and played music during the show ceremonies.

TRUE OR FALSE?

1. The hydraulis was an instrument like a modern trumpet.
2. Weapons were tested before the show to make sure they were sharp.
3. Gladiators wore their armour during the opening parade.

Answers:
1. FALSE The hydraulis was an instrument like a modern organ. 2. TRUE Weapons were tested during the probatio ceremony. 3. FALSE Slaves carried the armour behind the gladiators.

Water fights

515 Some gladiatorial shows took place on water. The most impressive of all were the naumachiae, or sea fights. For these shows, an artificial lake 557 metres long by 536 metres wide was dug beside the river Tiber. Small warships were brought up the river and launched on the lake when a sea fight was due to take place.

516 Naval fights were recreations of real battles. In 2 BC, Emperor Augustus staged a naumachia that recreated a battle fought 400 years earlier between the Greeks and the Persians. Emperor Titus staged a battle that originally started between the Greeks and Egyptians. These battles did not always end with the same winner as the real battle.

▼ Recreated naval battles were extremely expensive to stage, so didn't take place very often.

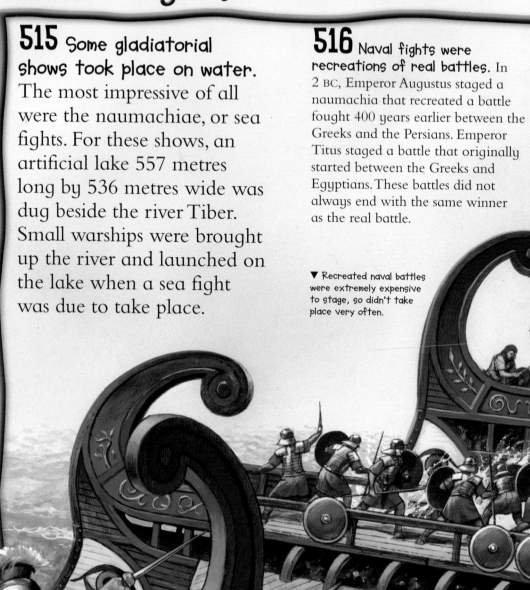

517 **The first naval gladiators did not try to kill each other.** The first of the sea battles were staged by Julius Caesar to celebrate a naval victory. The show was designed to impress the audience with the skills of the sailors and the way Caesar had won his victory.

518 **One naval show involved 19,000 men.** Emperor Claudius staged a sea battle on Lake Fucino. The men fighting were not sailors or gladiators but criminals condemned to death. Most of the men died and any survivors were sent to work as slaves.

519 **The Colosseum in Rome could be flooded for naval fights.** When the Colosseum was first built it had special pipes that could fill the arena with water and then drain it away again. The flooded arena was used for fights between special miniature warships crewed by gladiators. Later, the pipes were replaced by trapdoors and stage scenery.

I DON'T BELIEVE IT!

On one occasion, gladiators took one look at the poor condition of the warships and refused to board them.

Wild animal hunts

520 The first wild animal show was to celebrate a military victory. In 164 BC Rome defeated the powerful North African city of Carthage. The victorious general, Publius Cornelius Scipio, was given the nickname Africanus. He brought back to Rome hundreds of African wild animals, such as elephants, crocodiles and lions. After parading the animals through the streets, he included them in his gladiatorial games.

▲ This ancient mosaic shows the capture of wild animals, such as lions and gazelles. · They were then shipped to Rome to fight in the arenas.

521 One elephant hunt went badly wrong. In 79 BC General Gnaeus Pompey staged a wild elephant hunt with 20 elephants in a temporary arena in Rome. The crowd was protected by a tall iron fence, but two of the elephants charged at the fence, smashing it down. The elephants were quickly killed by hunters, but several people were injured.

522 The design of the arena changed to make it safer for the crowds. As the wild animal shows became more popular, the need to keep the watching crowd safe meant changes to the arena had to be made. The arena was sunk about 3 metres into the ground and surrounded by a vertical wall of smooth stone. No animal could leap up the wall or break it down, so the spectators were safe from attack.

523 Some animal shows were fantastic and strange. The Romans loved to see animals fighting each other. Sometimes a group of lions or wolves would be set to attack zebras or deer. At other times two hunting animals would be made to fight each other. They were often chained together to encourage them to fight. Some pairings were very odd – a snake was set against a lion, a seal set to fight a wolf or a bull against a bear.

524 One of the most popular animal fights was when a lion was set against a tiger. So many lions and tigers were sent to Rome to die in the fights that they became extinct in some areas of North Africa and the Middle East.

I DON'T BELIEVE IT!
The Romans loved watching animals that had been trained to perform tricks. One animal trainer put on shows in which an ape drove a chariot pulled by camels.

▼ A wild tiger attacks a gladiator, as seen in the 2000 movie *Gladiator*. Wild animals were part of most arena shows.

Outside Rome

525 More gladiators fought in southern Italy than in Rome. The idea of gladiatorial fights came from Campania, the area of Italy around Naples. For hundreds of years, the gladiator schools in Campania produced the best-trained gladiators and had more than anywhere else. One school had over 5000 gladiators training at one time.

526 The city of London had a small arena for gladiatorial games and other events. It stood inside the city walls beside the army fortress, near what is now St Paul's Cathedral. The 30-metre-long amphitheatre was built of stone and timber and could seat around 4000 spectators. St Albans, Chester and Caerleon also had amphitheatres.

▼ The arena at Pompeii. The oval shape, banked seating and two exits were the common design for all arenas.

527 All gladiatorial shows had to honour the emperor. By about AD 50, political power was in the hands of the emperor. It was the emperor who decided who could stand for election, and who would win the election. The editor of a gladiator show always began by dedicating the show to the emperor.

528 The best gladiators were sent to Rome. Gladiators who fought in provinces such as Britain or Spain were owned by lanistas who travelled from city to city to put on a show. Agents from Rome would watch these shows and any gladiator who was particularly good would be taken to Rome to fight in the the Colosseum.

▼ A gladiator fight reaches its end, as seen in the 1960 movie *Spartacus*.

▲ A statue of an emperor. Such a statue stood in most arenas and other public buildings.

529 Some towns banned gladiators. Not everyone enjoyed the fights. Many Romans refused to attend the games. Some cities, particularly in Greece and the eastern provinces, did not have an amphitheatre and refused to put on combats. Some people thought the fights were a waste of good slaves.

The last gladiators

▲ A scene from the 2000 movie *Gladiator*. The bloodshed in gladiator fights appalled some Romans.

530 Gladiatorial games became less and less popular. Seneca, a wise man and a great thinker, wrote that attending the games made Romans more cruel and inhuman than they had been before. The writer Artemidorus of Daldis said that the games were dishonourable, cruel and wicked. However most Romans approved of the games and enjoyed watching them.

531 In AD 324, Christian bishops tried to ban gladiatorial fights. After AD 250, Christianity became popular in the Roman Empire. Christians believed that the fights were sinful and they asked Emperor Constantine I to ban the fights. He banned private games, but allowed state games to continue.

QUIZ
1. Which philosopher thought watching gladiator fights made people cruel?
2. Which emperor closed down the gladiator schools in Rome?
3. Which emperor banned private gladiatorial games?

Answers:
1. Seneca. 2. Emperor Honorius. 3. Emperor Constantine I.

532 In AD 366 Pope Damasus used gladiators to murder rival churchmen. When Pope Liberius died the cardinals of Rome could not agree on a successor. Followers who wanted Ursinus to be the next pope were meeting in the church of St Maria Trastevere when Damasus hired a gang of gladiators to attack them. The gladiators broke into the church and killed 137 people. Damasus then became pope.

533 The Christian monk Telemachus was the first to stop a gladiator fight. During a show in the Colosseum in AD 404, Telemachus forced apart two fighting gladiators. He made a speech asking for the shows to stop, but angry spectators killed him. Emperor Honorius then closed down all the gladiator schools in Rome.

▲ Heavily armed gladiators were sometimes hired by ambitious politicians and churchmen to murder their rivals.

534 The last gladiators fought in around AD 445. In AD 410, the city of Rome was captured by a tribe of barbarians. The Roman Empire was falling to pieces. People were too busy trying to escape invasions or to earn a living to organize gladiatorial fights.

◄ The monk Telemachus managed to stop a gladiator fight, but paid for his actions with his life.

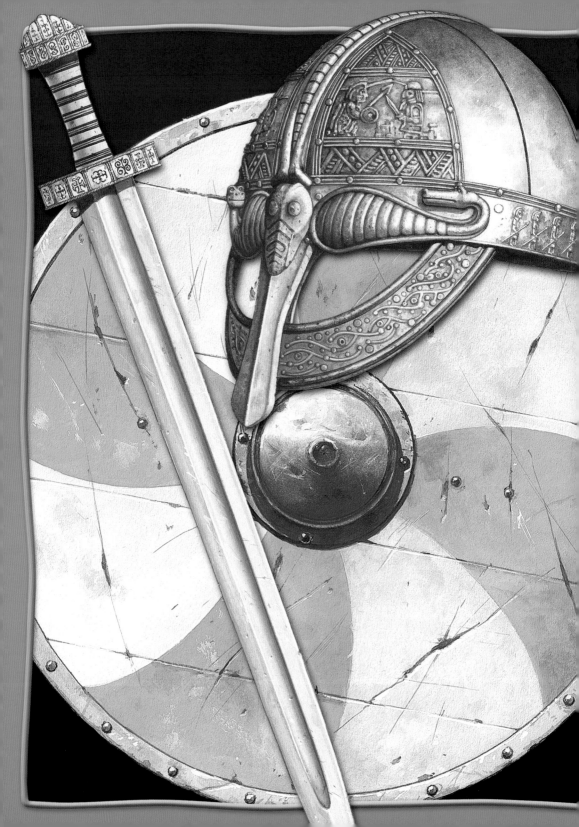

Vikings

Begin your voyage on board a dragon ship
and discover what life was like as a Viking.

Kings • Weapons • Warriors • Clothes
Family • Food • Explorers • Raiders • Legends
Law • Homes • Gods and goddesses • Traders
Farmers • Jewellery • Sailors • Craftworkers

Who were the Vikings?

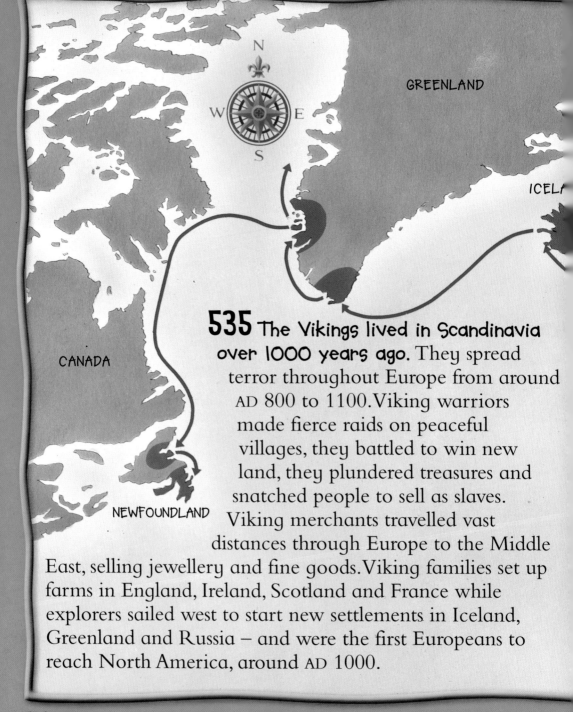

GREENLAND

ICELA

CANADA

NEWFOUNDLAND

535 **The Vikings lived in Scandinavia over 1000 years ago.** They spread terror throughout Europe from around AD 800 to 1100. Viking warriors made fierce raids on peaceful villages, they battled to win new land, they plundered treasures and snatched people to sell as slaves. Viking merchants travelled vast distances through Europe to the Middle East, selling jewellery and fine goods. Viking families set up farms in England, Ireland, Scotland and France while explorers sailed west to start new settlements in Iceland, Greenland and Russia – and were the first Europeans to reach North America, around AD 1000.

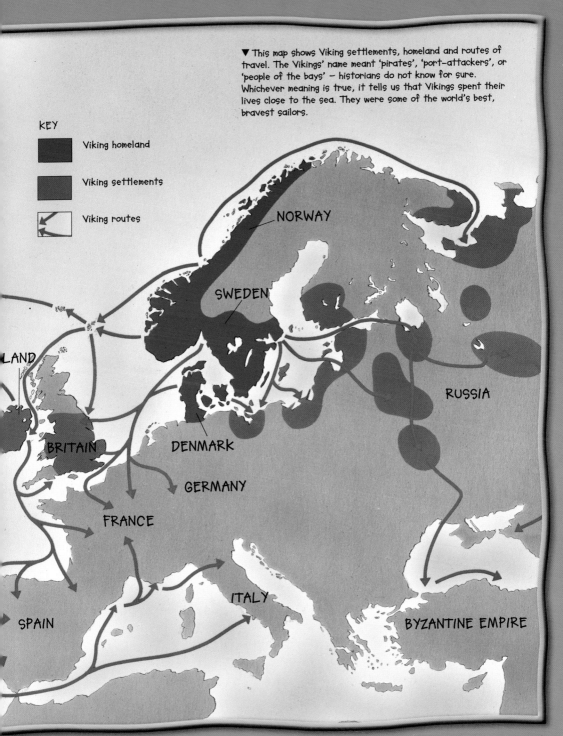

▼ This map shows Viking settlements, homeland and routes of travel. The Vikings' name meant 'pirates', 'port-attackers', or 'people of the bays' — historians do not know for sure. Whichever meaning is true, it tells us that Vikings spent their lives close to the sea. They were some of the world's best, bravest sailors.

KEY

Viking homeland

Viking settlements

Viking routes

NORWAY

SWEDEN

LAND

RUSSIA

BRITAIN

DENMARK

GERMANY

FRANCE

ITALY

SPAIN

BYZANTINE EMPIRE

Kings and people

536 Viking society had three classes. At the top were nobles (kings or chiefs). They were rich, owned land and had many servants. Freemen, the middle group, included farmers, traders, and craftworkers and their wives. Slaves were the lowest group. They worked hard for nobles and freemen and could not leave their owner.

Viking slave

Viking farmer

Viking noble warrior

▲ Slaves, farmers and warriors all worked hard to make Viking lands rich and powerful.

537 Viking warlords turned into kings. During early Viking times, local chiefs controlled large areas of land. They also had armies of freemen. Over the centuries, some became richer and more powerful than the rest by raiding and conquering lands. By AD 1050, one noble controlled each Viking country, and called himself king.

◀ Famous for his cruelty, Erik Bloodaxe was the last Viking to rule the kingdom of Northumbria, in north-east England.

538 King Erik Bloodaxe killed his brothers. When a Viking king died, each of his sons had an equal right to inherit the throne. Members of Viking royal families often had to fight among themselves for the right to rule. In AD 930, King Erik of Norway killed his brothers so that he could rule alone.

539 **King Harald Bluetooth left a magnificent memorial.** King Harald ruled Denmark from around AD 935 to 985. He was one of the first Viking kings to become a Christian. He built a church at Jelling, the ancient Danish royal burial site, and had his parents' bodies dug up and re-buried inside. He also paid for a splendid pyramid-shaped monument to be built next to the church, in memory of them. This 'Jelling Stone' was decorated with carvings in Viking and Christian designs.

▶ The Jelling stone (far right of picture) has carvings of a snake and a lion-like monster, fighting together. They symbolize the forces of good and evil.

540 **King Cnut ruled a European empire – but not the waves!** King Cnut was one of the mightiest Viking kings. By 1028 he ruled England, Denmark and Norway. However he did not want to appear too proud. So, one day, he staged a strange event on an English beach and commanded the waves to obey him! When they did not he said, 'This proves that I am weak. Only God can control the sea.'

I DON'T BELIEVE IT!

Many Viking rulers had strange or violent names, such as Svein Forkbeard, Einar Falsemouth, Magnus Barelegs, Thorfinn Skullsplitter and Sigurd the Stout.

Sailors and raiders

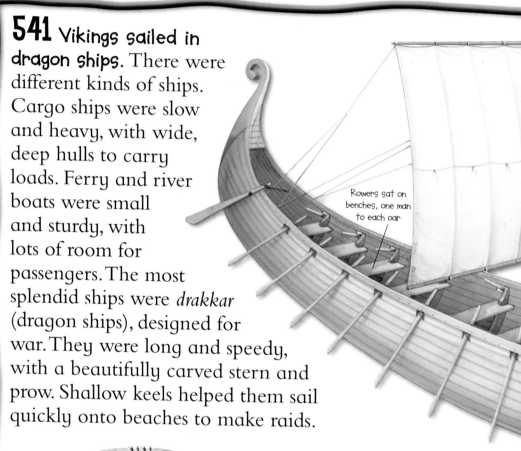

541 **Vikings sailed in dragon ships.** There were different kinds of ships. Cargo ships were slow and heavy, with wide, deep hulls to carry loads. Ferry and river boats were small and sturdy, with lots of room for passengers. The most splendid ships were *drakkar* (dragon ships), designed for war. They were long and speedy, with a beautifully carved stern and prow. Shallow keels helped them sail quickly onto beaches to make raids.

Rowers sat on benches, one man to each oar

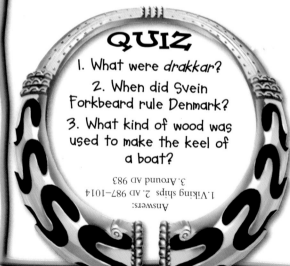

QUIZ

1. What were *drakkar*?

2. When did Svein Forkbeard rule Denmark?

3. What kind of wood was used to make the keel of a boat?

Answers:
1. Viking ships 2. AD 987–1014
3. Around AD 983

542 **Sailors steered by the stars.** The Vikings had no radio or satellite systems to help them navigate (steer a course) when they were out of sight of land. So they made observations of the Sun by day and the stars by night, to work out their position. They also studied the winds, waves and ocean currents, and the movements of fish and seabirds.

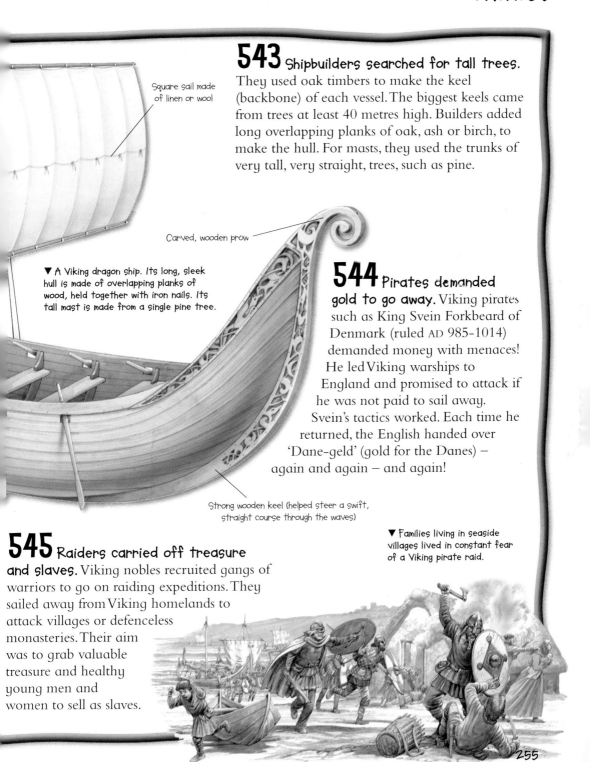

543 Shipbuilders searched for tall trees.
They used oak timbers to make the keel
(backbone) of each vessel. The biggest keels came
from trees at least 40 metres high. Builders added
long overlapping planks of oak, ash or birch, to
make the hull. For masts, they used the trunks of
very tall, very straight, trees, such as pine.

Square sail made
of linen or wool

Carved, wooden prow

▼ A Viking dragon ship. Its long, sleek
hull is made of overlapping planks of
wood, held together with iron nails. Its
tall mast is made from a single pine tree.

544 Pirates demanded
gold to go away. Viking pirates
such as King Svein Forkbeard of
Denmark (ruled AD 985-1014)
demanded money with menaces!
He led Viking warships to
England and promised to attack if
he was not paid to sail away.
Svein's tactics worked. Each time he
returned, the English handed over
'Dane-geld' (gold for the Danes) –
again and again – and again!

Strong wooden keel (helped steer a swift,
straight course through the waves)

▼ Families living in seaside
villages lived in constant fear
of a Viking pirate raid.

545 Raiders carried off treasure
and slaves. Viking nobles recruited gangs of
warriors to go on raiding expeditions. They
sailed away from Viking homelands to
attack villages or defenceless
monasteries. Their aim
was to grab valuable
treasure and healthy
young men and
women to sell as slaves.

Warriors and weapons

546 Vikings valued glory more than long life. They believed that a dead warrior's fame lived on after him, and made sure that his name would never die. Myths and legends also told how warriors who died in battle would go to Valhalla, where they feasted with the gods.

547 Berserkers were mad for battle. Berserkers ('bear-shirts') were warriors who dressed in animal skins and worked themselves into a trance before battle. They charged at the enemy, howling and growling like wolves and chewing at their shields. In this state, they were wild and fearless, and dangerous to anyone who got in their way. This is where the word 'beserk' comes from.

▲ Berserker warriors rushed madly into battle, wearing animal skins over their chain mail armour.

548 Lords led followers into war.
There were no national armies in Viking times. Each king or lord led his followers into battle against a shared enemy. A lord's followers fought to win praise, plus rich rewards, such as arm rings of silver or a share of captured loot.

549 Warriors gave names to their swords.
A good sword was a Viking warrior's most treasured possession. He often asked to be buried with it and gave it a name such as 'Sharp Biter'. Viking swords were double-edged, with strong, flexible blades made by hammering layers of iron together. Their hilts (handles) were decorated with silver and gold patterns.

550 Viking soldiers lived in camps and forts.
Wars and raids took warriors far from home. Soldiers in places such as England built camps of wooden huts, surrounded by an earth bank topped by a wooden wall.

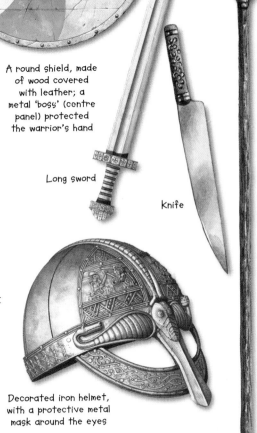

A round shield, made of wood covered with leather; a metal 'boss' (centre panel) protected the warrior's hand

Long sword

Knife

Decorated iron helmet, with a protective metal mask around the eyes

Long, sharp spear

▲ Each Viking soldier had to provide his own weapons and armour. Poor soldiers wore leather caps and tunics, and carried knives and spears. Wealthy Vikings could afford metal helmets and tunics, and fine, sharp swords.

I DON'T BELIEVE IT!

Viking women went to war but they did not fight. Instead, they nursed wounded warriors and cooked meals for hungry soldiers.

Traders, explorers, settlers

551 **Viking traders rode on camels and carried their ships!** The Vikings were brave adventurers, keen to seek new land, slaves and treasures. Some traders travelled through Russia to Constantinople (now Istanbul in Turkey), and Jerusalem (in Israel). Each journey took several years. In Russia, they carried their ships over ground between rivers. In the desert near Jerusalem, they rode on camels, like local traders.

▼ Vikings made long overland journeys in winter. The frozen ground was easier to walk across — especially when carrying heavy loads.

◀ Viking merchants carried scales and weights with them on their travels.

552 **Traders carried scales and silver.** Vikings traded with many different peoples. Some used coins for trading, others preferred to barter (swap). There were no banks in Viking times and traders could not be sure of having the right money for every business deal. So they bought and sold using pieces of silver, which they weighed out on delicate, portable scales.

553 **Traders came home with lots of shopping!** Viking merchants purchased goods, as well as selling them. They went to Britain to buy wheat and cloth and to France for wine and pottery. They bought glass in Germany, jewellery in Russia, and spices from the Middle East.

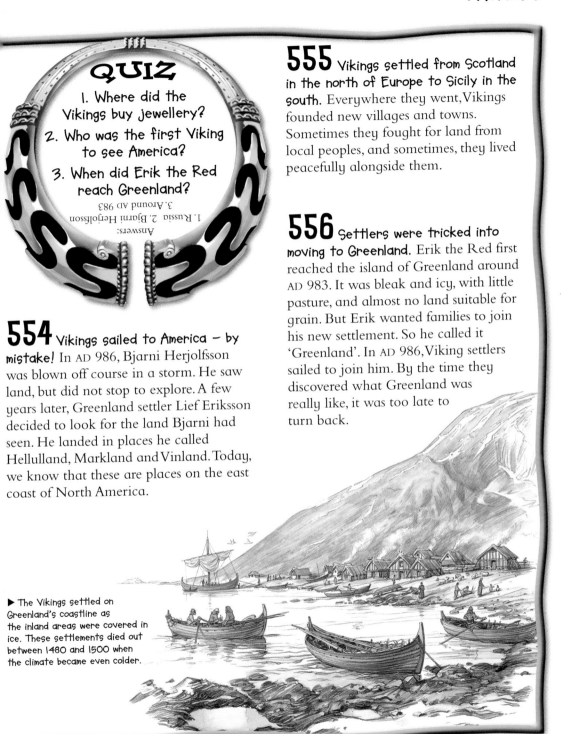

554 **Vikings sailed to America — by mistake!** In AD 986, Bjarni Herjolfsson was blown off course in a storm. He saw land, but did not stop to explore. A few years later, Greenland settler Lief Eriksson decided to look for the land Bjarni had seen. He landed in places he called Hellulland, Markland and Vinland. Today, we know that these are places on the east coast of North America.

555 **Vikings settled from Scotland in the north of Europe to Sicily in the south.** Everywhere they went, Vikings founded new villages and towns. Sometimes they fought for land from local peoples, and sometimes, they lived peacefully alongside them.

556 **Settlers were tricked into moving to Greenland.** Erik the Red first reached the island of Greenland around AD 983. It was bleak and icy, with little pasture, and almost no land suitable for grain. But Erik wanted families to join his new settlement. So he called it 'Greenland'. In AD 986, Viking settlers sailed to join him. By the time they discovered what Greenland was really like, it was too late to turn back.

▶ The Vikings settled on Greenland's coastline as the inland areas were covered in ice. These settlements died out between 1480 and 1500 when the climate became even colder.

The Vikings at home

557 In the 700s and 800s, the Vikings were some of the best craftworkers in Europe. They lived in a harsh environment, with cold, long dark winters. Buildings were needed to shelter livestock, as well as people. In towns, pigs, goats and horses were kept in sheds, but in parts of the countryside, farmers built longhouses, with rooms for the family at one end and for animals at the other.

558 Vikings built houses out of grass. In many lands where the Vikings settled, such as the Orkney Islands or Iceland, there were hardly any trees. So Viking families built homes out of slabs of turf (earth with grass growing in it), arranged on a low foundation of stone. If they could afford it, they lined the rooms with planks of wood imported from Scandinavia. Otherwise, they collected pieces of driftwood, washed up on shore.

Walls made of logs

▶ Longhouses were usually built on sloping ground so that waste from the animals ran downhill, away from human living rooms.

Animals were kept in the longhouse

Loom for weaving cloth

559 Viking homes could be unhealthy. Viking houses did not have windows – they would have let in too much cold. So homes were often damp, and full of smoke from the fire burning on the hearth. As a result, Viking people suffered from chest diseases. Some may also have been killed by a poisonous gas, called carbon monoxide, that is produced when a fire uses up all the oxygen in a room.

I DON'T BELIEVE IT!

Vikings liked living in longhouses, because heat from the animals provided a kind of central heating, keeping everyone warm.

Wooden rafters

Turf (earth with growing grass) roof

eat was smoked o preserve it

560 Homeowners sat in the high seat. Most Viking families had little furniture. Only the rich could afford beds, or tables with fixed legs. Most homes were simply furnished with trestle tables, wooden storage chests and wooden benches. The centre of one bench was marked off by two carved wooden pillars, and reserved as the 'high seat' (place of honour) for the house owner. Important guests sat facing him or her, on the bench opposite.

Outside lavatory

261

561 **Viking farmers prized pasture more than ploughed fields.** In northern lands, the soil was too thin and stony for crops such as wheat and barley to grow well. Farmers relied on sheep and cattle to provide meat and milk. These animals needed fresh grass to eat so Viking farmers valued pasture land, where grass flourished, more than stony fields.

562 Flax and hay were the most important crops. They were needed to make clothes and feed cattle. Outer garments were made of wool, and could be very itchy, so women wove smoother, finer cloth to wear next to the skin. They used the stalks of a plant called flax, which farmers planted in damp ground. Farm animals needed hay (dried grass) to eat in winter, when pastures were covered by snow. Viking farmers grew grass in well-manured meadows, then cut it, dried it and stored it for winter.

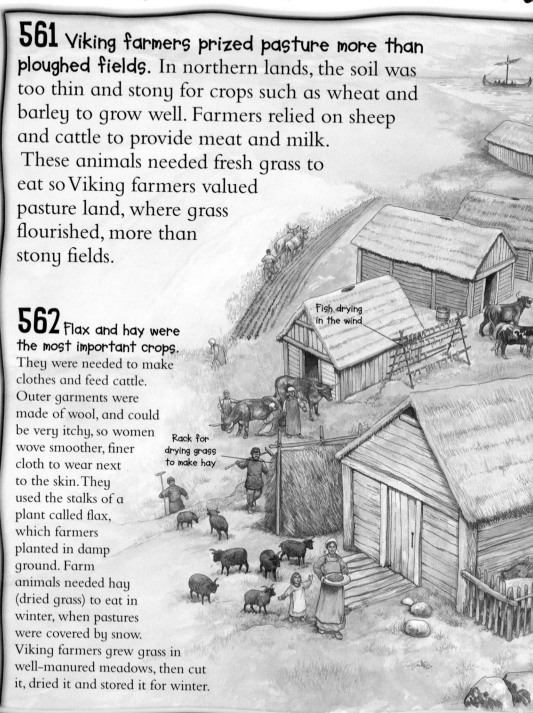

Fish drying in the wind

Rack for drying grass to make hay

Ships anchored in
a safe harbour

563 Hunters and fishermen found food
around the coast. The Vikings lived close to
some of the world's richest fishing grounds.
Fishermen used nets and traps to catch sea fish
such as cod and herring, or river fish such as
salmon, trout and eels. They gathered mussels and
oysters from the seashore, and hunted whales,
mostly for their blubber. Young men climbed
dangerous cliffs to collect seabirds and their eggs
or scrambled over skerries – little rocky islands –
to catch seals and walruses basking there.

Cutting
grass to
make hay

◀ The Vikings were not just interested in
raiding and stealing. They realized that the
British Isles provided good farmland and safe
areas for settlements.

Ploughing with oxen

564 Trappers tracked
wild animals. In Norway and
Sweden, there were many
wild animals, such as bears,
wolves and foxes. These
were hunted for their
furs, which made warm
clothes, or were sold to
rich customers. Hunters also
chased deer for their meat,
antlers and skins. Antlers were
used to make beads and combs.

Scattering grain
to feed chickens

Food and famine

565 **Vikings ate two meals a day.** First thing in the morning was the 'day meal' of barley bread or oatcakes, butter or cheese. The main meal – 'night meal' – was eaten in the early evening. It included meat or fish, plus wild berries in summer. Meals were served on wooden plates or soapstone bowls and eaten with metal knives and wood or horn spoons.

▼ Objects made from cattle horn were light but very strong – ideal for Viking traders or raiders to carry on their journeys.

Patterned silver cup used by the rich

Pottery beaker used by the poor

Drinking horn used by warriors

QUIZ

1. What did Viking warriors drink from?
2. How did the Vikings boil water?
3. What is offal?
4. How long would a feast last for?

Answers:
1. From cow horns 2. On red-hot stones 3. The heart, liver and lungs of animals 4. A week or more

566 **Warriors drunk from hollow horns.** Favourite Viking drinks were milk, whey (the liquid left over from cheese-making), ale (brewed from malted barley), and mead (honey wine). Rich people drank from glass or silver cups, but ordinary people had wooden or pottery beakers. On special occasions feasts were held, and Viking warriors drank from curved cattle horns.

567 Red-hot stones boiled water for cooking. Few Viking homes had ovens. So women and their servants boiled meat in iron cauldrons, or in water-filled pits heated by stones that were made red-hot in a fire. This was a very efficient way of cooking.

Cabbage

Beans

Garlic

Peas

Onion

▲ Viking vegetables included peas, beans, cabbages, onions and garlic.

568 The Vikings loved blood sausages. Cooks made sausages by pouring fresh animal blood and offal (heart, liver and lungs) into cleaned sheep's intestines, then boiling them. Sometimes they added garlic, cumin seeds or juniper berries as flavouring. Vikings preferred these to vegetables such as cabbages, peas and beans.

▼ Viking women and slaves cooked huge meals over open fires, and served them to feasting warriors.

569 Feasts went on for a week or more. After winning a great victory, Vikings liked to celebrate. Kings and lords held feasts to reward their warriors, and families feasted at weddings. Guests dressed in their best clothes and hosts provided food and drink. Everyone stayed in the hall until the food ran out, or they grew tired.

Women and children

570 Viking women were independent. They made household decisions, cooked, made clothes, raised children, organized slaves and managed farms and workshops while their husbands were away.

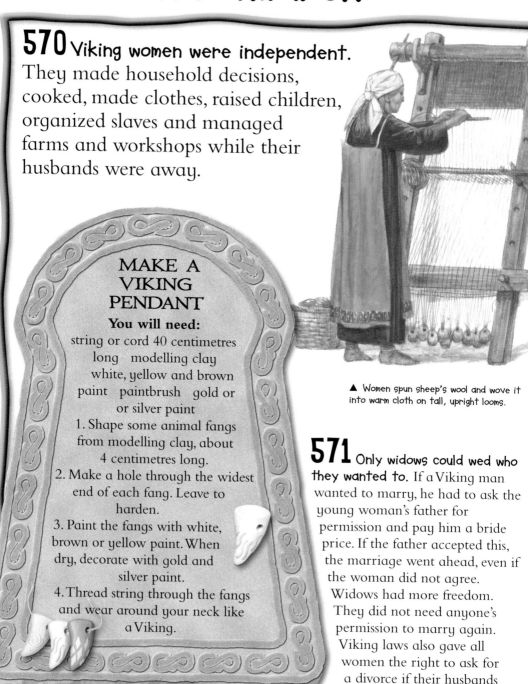

▲ Women spun sheep's wool and wove it into warm cloth on tall, upright looms.

MAKE A VIKING PENDANT

You will need:
string or cord 40 centimetres long   modelling clay
white, yellow and brown paint   paintbrush   gold or or silver paint

1. Shape some animal fangs from modelling clay, about 4 centimetres long.
2. Make a hole through the widest end of each fang. Leave to harden.
3. Paint the fangs with white, brown or yellow paint. When dry, decorate with gold and silver paint.
4. Thread string through the fangs and wear around your neck like a Viking.

571 Only widows could wed who they wanted to. If a Viking man wanted to marry, he had to ask the young woman's father for permission and pay him a bride price. If the father accepted this, the marriage went ahead, even if the woman did not agree. Widows had more freedom. They did not need anyone's permission to marry again. Viking laws also gave all women the right to ask for a divorce if their husbands treated them badly.

572 Old women won respect for wise advice. Many Viking women died young in childbirth or from infectious diseases. So older people, aged 50 or more, were a small minority in Viking society. While they were still fit, they were respected for their knowledge and experience. But if they grew sick or frail, their families saw them as a burden.

574 Viking fathers chose which children survived. Parents relied on children to care for them in old age so they wanted strong offspring. The father examined each baby after it was born. If it seemed healthy, he sprinkled it with water and named it to show it was part of his family. If the child looked sickly it was left outside to die.

◀ Feeding chickens and collecting eggs was work for Viking girls. They learnt how to grow and cook vegetables by helping their mothers.

573 Viking children did not go to school. Daughters helped their mothers with cooking and cleaning, fed farm animals, fetched water, gathered wood, nuts and berries and learned how to spin, weave and sew. Sons helped their fathers in the workshop or on the farm. They also learned how to ride horses and use weapons. Boys had to be ready to fight by the time they were fifteen or sixteen years old.

▲ Viking boys practised fighting with wooden swords and small, lightweight shields.

Clothes and jewellery

575 **Vikings wore lots of layers to keep out the cold.** Women wore a long dress made of linen or wool with a woollen over-dress. Men wore wool tunics over linen undershirts and woollen trousers. Both men and women wore gloves, cloaks, socks, and leather boots or shoes. Men added fur or sheepskin caps while women wore headscarves and shawls

▶ Viking men and women liked bright colours and patterns. They often decorated their clothes with strips of woven braid.

576 **Furs, fleeces and feathers also helped Vikings keep warm.** Vikings lined or trimmed their woollen cloaks with fur, or padded them, like quilts, with layers of goose-down. Some farmers used sheepskins to make cloaks that were hard-wearing, as well as very warm.

577 **Brooches held Viking clothes in place.** There were several different styles. Men wore big round brooches, pinned on their right shoulders, to hold their cloaks in place. Women wore pairs of brooches – one on each shoulder – to fasten the straps of their over-dresses. They might also wear another brooch at their throat, to fasten their cloak, plus a brooch with little hooks or chains, to carry their household keys.

▶ This beautiful brooch, decorated with real gold wire, was once worn by a very rich Viking nobleman.

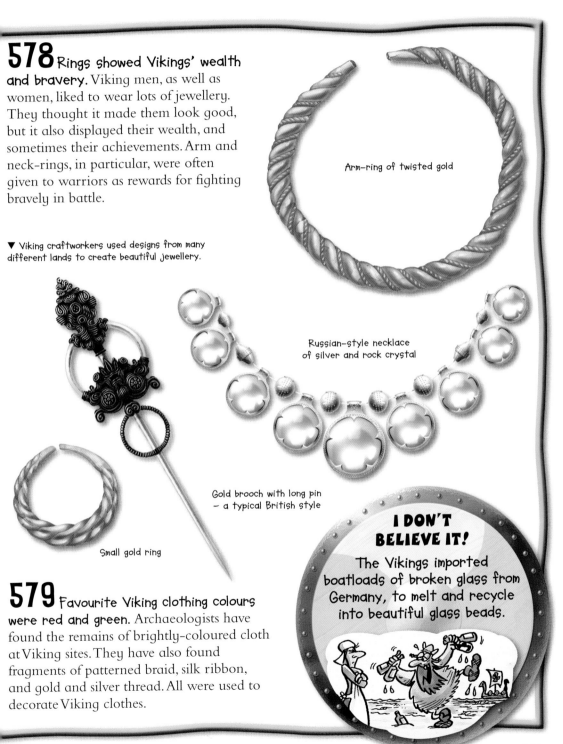

578 Rings showed Vikings' wealth and bravery. Viking men, as well as women, liked to wear lots of jewellery. They thought it made them look good, but it also displayed their wealth, and sometimes their achievements. Arm and neck-rings, in particular, were often given to warriors as rewards for fighting bravely in battle.

Arm-ring of twisted gold

▼ Viking craftworkers used designs from many different lands to create beautiful jewellery.

Russian-style necklace of silver and rock crystal

Gold brooch with long pin – a typical British style

Small gold ring

579 Favourite Viking clothing colours were red and green. Archaeologists have found the remains of brightly-coloured cloth at Viking sites. They have also found fragments of patterned braid, silk ribbon, and gold and silver thread. All were used to decorate Viking clothes.

I DON'T BELIEVE IT!

The Vikings imported boatloads of broken glass from Germany, to melt and recycle into beautiful glass beads.

Health and beauty

580 **The English complained that Vikings were too clean!** The Vikings combed their hair often, changed their clothes frequently and bathed once a week. Vikings bathed by pouring water over red-hot stones to create clouds of steam. They sat in the steam to sweat, then whipped their skin with birch twigs to help loosen the dirt. Then they jumped into a pool of cold water to rinse off.

▲ Vikings 'bathed' in clouds of steam. Similar steam baths, called saunas, are still popular in Scandinavia today.

581 Some Vikings took their swords to the lavatory. Most Viking homes had an outside lavatory, consisting of a bucket or a hole in the ground with a wooden seat on top. The lavatory walls were often made of wickerwork – panels of woven twigs. But Viking warriors in enemy lands made different arrangements. They went outside in groups of four, carrying swords to protect one another.

▲ Viking lavatories may have looked like this. Vikings used dried moss, grass or leaves as toilet paper.

582 Vikings used onions to diagnose illness. If a warrior was injured in the stomach during a battle, his comrades cooked a dish of porridge strongly flavoured with onion and gave it to him to eat. They waited, then sniffed the wound. If they could smell onions, they left the man to die. They knew that the injury had cut open the stomach, and the man would die of infection.

I DON'T BELIEVE IT!

Viking men wore make-up! They particularly liked eyeliner – probably made from soot, or crushed berries. They thought it made them look more handsome.

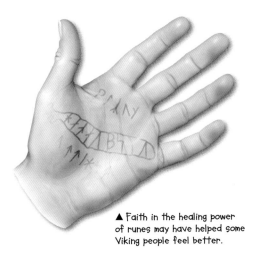

▲ Faith in the healing power of runes may have helped some Viking people feel better.

583 For painkilling power, the Vikings relied on runes. The Vikings made medicines from herbs and other plants, but they also believed that runes – their way of writing – had magic healing powers. They carved runic spells and charms on pieces of bone and left them under the heads of sleeping sick people. Runes were written on women's palms during childbirth to protect from pain.

584 Hair–care was very important. Viking women wore their hair long. They left it flowing loose until they married, then tied it in an elaborate knot at the nape of their neck. Viking men also liked fancy hairstyles. They cut their hair short at the back, but let their fringes grow very long. So that they could see where they were going, some Vikings plaited the strands that hung down either side of their face.

▲ Fashionable Viking hairstyles. Women also wove garlands of flowers to wear in their hair on special occasions.

Skilled craftworkers

585 **Vikings made most of the things they needed.** Viking families had to make – and mend – almost everything they needed, from their houses and its furniture to farm carts, children's toys and clothes. They had no machines to help them, so most of this work was done slowly and carefully, by hand.

586 **Blacksmiths travelled from farm to farm.** Many Viking men had a simple smithy at home, where they could make and mend tools. For specialized work, they relied on skilled blacksmiths, who travelled the countryside, or they made a long journey to a workshop in a town.

▶ Blacksmiths heated iron over open fires until it was soft enough to hammer into shape to make tools and weapons.

587 Bones could be beautiful. Skilled craftworkers used deer antler to make fine combs. But these were too expensive for ordinary Vikings to buy. They carved bones left over from mealtimes into combs, beads and pins, as well as name tags and weaving tablets (used to make patterned braid).

589 Craftsmen carved cups from the cliff face. Deposits of soft soapstone were found in many Viking lands. It looked good, but it was very heavy. To save taking lumps of it to their workshops, stoneworkers carved rough shapes of cups and bowls into cliffs at soapstone quarries, then took them home to finish neatly.

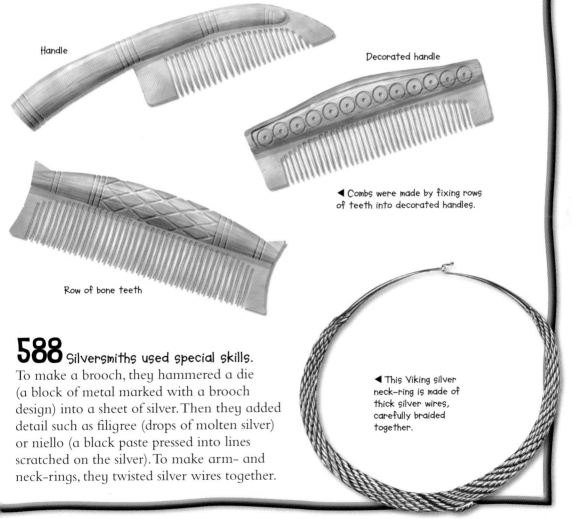

Handle

Decorated handle

◄ Combs were made by fixing rows of teeth into decorated handles.

Row of bone teeth

588 Silversmiths used special skills. To make a brooch, they hammered a die (a block of metal marked with a brooch design) into a sheet of silver. Then they added detail such as filigree (drops of molten silver) or niello (a black paste pressed into lines scratched on the silver). To make arm- and neck-rings, they twisted silver wires together.

◄ This Viking silver neck-ring is made of thick silver wires, carefully braided together.

Viking towns

590 **Kings built towns to encourage trade.** Before the Vikings grew so powerful, merchants traded at fairs held just once or twice a year. Viking kings decided to build towns so that trade could continue all year round. Taxes were collected from the people and merchants who traded there.

▶ Viking markets were often held on beaches. Farming families and travelling merchants met there to buy and sell.

591 Towns were tempting targets for attack. Pirates and raiders from Russia and north Germany sailed across the Baltic Sea to snatch valuable goods from Viking towns. So kings paid for towns to be defended with banks of earth and wooden walls. They also sent troops of warriors to guard them.

592 Houses in towns were specially designed. Space was limited inside town walls so houses were built close together. They were smaller than country homes, as people needed less space to store crops or house animals. Most town houses were made of wood with thatched roofs. Many had craft workshops and showrooms inside.

I DON'T BELIEVE IT!

The first Russians were Vikings! The name 'Russia' comes from the word, 'Rus', used by people living east of the Baltic Sea to describe Viking traders who settled there.

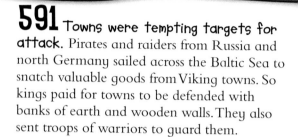

593 Towns made the first Viking coins.

As far as we know, there were no coins in Scandinavia before the Viking age. Traders bartered (swapped) goods, or paid for them using bits of silver, weighed out on tiny, portable scales. But many foreign coins came to Viking lands from overseas trading and raiding. Around AD 825, craftsmen in the Viking town of Hedeby (now in north Germany) began to copy them. Later, other towns set up mints to make coins of their own.

594 Viking traders gave Russia its name.

Adventurous Vikings visiting the eastern shores of the Baltic set up towns as bases for trade. Some of the biggest were Staraja Ladoga and Novgorod, in Russia, and Kiev in the Ukraine.

◀ This Viking coin shows a merchant ship. It comes from the town of Hedeby.

Law and order

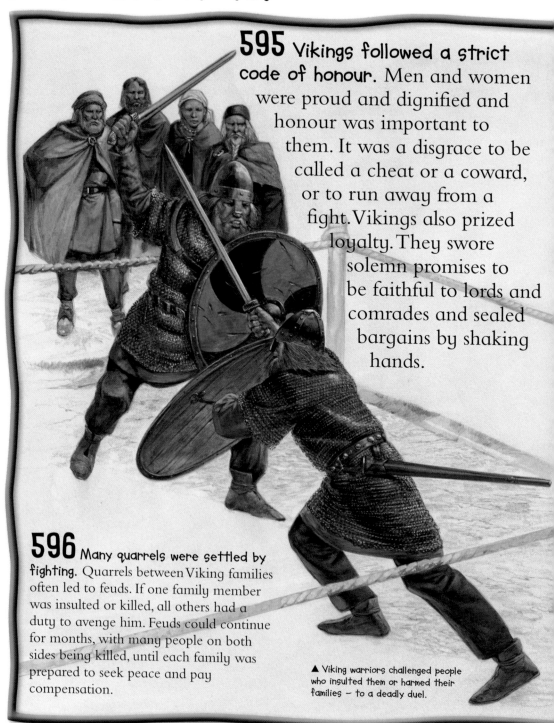

595 Vikings followed a strict code of honour. Men and women were proud and dignified and honour was important to them. It was a disgrace to be called a cheat or a coward, or to run away from a fight. Vikings also prized loyalty. They swore solemn promises to be faithful to lords and comrades and sealed bargains by shaking hands.

596 Many quarrels were settled by fighting. Quarrels between Viking families often led to feuds. If one family member was insulted or killed, all others had a duty to avenge him. Feuds could continue for months, with many people on both sides being killed, until each family was prepared to seek peace and pay compensation.

▲ Viking warriors challenged people who insulted them or harmed their families – to a deadly duel.

597 Viking laws were not written down. Instead, they were memorized by a man known as the law-speaker. He recited them out loud every year so that everyone could hear and understand them. Because of their expert knowledge, law-speakers often became advisors to kings and lords.

598 Every year, Vikings met at the Thing. This was an open-air assembly of all free men in a district. It met to punish criminals and make new laws. The most usual punishments were heavy fines. Thing meetings were great social occasions where people from remote communities had the chance to meet and exchange news. Traders also attended, setting up stalls with goods around the edge of a field.

▼ All free men — from noble chieftains to farmers — could speak and vote at a Viking Thing.

599 Ruthlessness was respected. It was tough being a Viking. Everyone had to work hard to survive and there was no room in the community for people who were weak, lazy or troublesome. Thieves were often hanged and criminals who refused to pay compensation or fines were outlawed. This was a very harsh penalty. Without a home and family, it was hard for any individual to survive.

QUIZ

1. What were the two worst Viking punishments for crimes?

2. How did the Vikings settle family feuds?

3. Why did Vikings shake hands with each other?

4. Who recited the Viking laws?

Answers:
1. Hanging and outlaw 2. By fighting — a duel 3. To seal bargains 4. The law-speaker

Gods and goddesses

600 **Vikings honoured many gods.**
The Aesir (sky gods) included Odin,
Thor and Tyr, who were gods of
war, and Loki, who was a
trickster. The Vanir (gods of
earth and water) included
Njord (god of the sea)
and Frey (the farmers'
god). He and his sister
Freyja brought pleasure
and fertility.

▼ Odin, Viking god of war, rode an
eight-legged horse. Two ravens,
called Thought and Memory, flew
by his side.

▼ Beautiful Viking goddess
Freyja rode in a chariot
pulled by cats.

601 **Animals — and people — were killed as sacrifices.**
The Vikings believed that they could win favours from the
gods by offering them gifts. Since life was the most
valuable gift, they gave the gods living sacrifices. Vikings
also cooked meals of meat — called blood-offerings —
to share with the gods.

602 **Destiny controlled the Vikings.**
According to legends, three sisters (Norns) decided
what would happen in the world. They
sat at the foot of Yggdrasil, the great
tree that supported the universe,
spinning 'the thread of destiny'. They
also visited each newborn baby to
decide its future. Once made, this
decision could not be changed.

▶ Vikings asked fierce and furious god Tyr to help them win victories.

603 **After death, Vikings went to Hel's kingdom.** Warriors who died in battle went to Valhalla or to Freyja's peaceful home. Unmarried girls also joined Freyja, and good men went to live with gods in the sky. Most Vikings who lived ordinary lives and died of illness or old age could only look forward to a future in Niflheim. This was a gloomy place, shrouded in freezing fog, ruled by a fierce goddess called Hel.

604 **Towards the end of the Viking age, many people became Christians.** Missionaries from England, Germany and France visited Viking lands from around AD 725. The Vikings continued to worship their own gods for the next 300 years. Around AD 1000, Viking kings, such as Harald Bluetooth and Olaf Tryggvason decided to follow the Christian faith as it helped strengthen their power. They built churches and encouraged people to be Christians.

▼ Njord was god of the sea. He married the giantess Skadi, who watched over snowy mountains.

QUIZ

1. Who was Loki?
2. What tree supported the universe?
3. Where did warriors go when they died?

Answers:
1. A trickster god
2. Yggdrasil 3. Valhalla

Heroes, legends and sagas

605 Vikings honoured heroes who died in battle. They told stories, called 'sagas', about their adventures so that their name and fame never died. These stories were passed on by word of mouth for many years. After the end of the Viking Age, they were written down.

◀ Vikings loved sagas – stories that recorded past events and famous peoples' lives.

606 Skalds sang songs and told saga stories. Viking kings and lords employed their own personal poets, called skalds. A skald's job was to sing songs and recite poems praising his employer, and to entertain guests at feasts. Most skalds played music on harps or lyres to accompany their poems and songs.

▼ Viking legends told how the world would come to an end at the battle of Ragnarok. They also promised that a new world would be born from the ruins of the old.

607 Vikings feared that the world might end. There were many Viking stories foretelling Ragnarok – the Doom of the Gods. This would be a terrible time, when the forces of good clashed with the powers of evil. Viking gods would fight against giants and monsters – and lose. Then the world would come to an end.

608 **The Vikings believed in spirits and monsters.** They were unseen powers who lived in the natural world. Some, such as elves, were kindly and helpful. They sent good harvests and beautiful children. Others, such as giants who ate humans, were wicked or cruel. Vikings often imagined monsters as looking like huge, fierce animals. They carved these monster heads on ships and stones to scare evil spirits away.

▲ Vikings believed that Valkyries — wild warrior women — carried men who had died in battle to live with Odin in Valhalla (the hall of brave dead).

◀ A Viking silver amulet (lucky charm), shaped like Thor's hammer.

QUIZ

1. What did Vikings call the end of the world?

2. Who did skalds praise?

3. Why did farmers wear hammers round their necks?

4. What did giants eat?

Answers:
1. Ragnarok 2. Their employer 3. To bring fertility to fields and animals 4. Humans

609 **Lucky charms protected warriors and farmers.** They wore amulets shaped like the god Thor's magic hammer as pendants around their necks. Warriors believed that these little hammers would give them extra strength in battle. Farmers hoped they would bring fertility to their fields and animals.

Death and burial

610 **Early Vikings burned their dead.** At the start of the Viking age, the bodies of dead people were cremated (burned) on big wood fires. After this, their ashes were collected and buried in pottery urns. Between AD 800 and 900, people in some Viking lands began to bury unburned dead bodies in the ground.

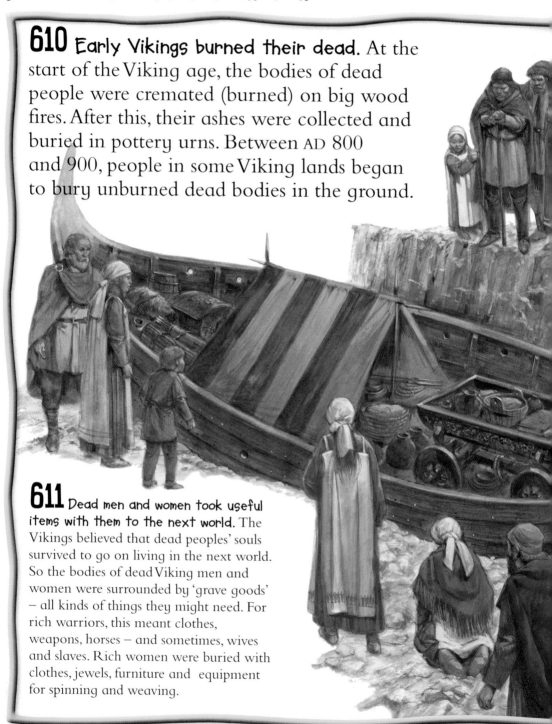

611 Dead men and women took useful items with them to the next world. The Vikings believed that dead peoples' souls survived to go on living in the next world. So the bodies of dead Viking men and women were surrounded by 'grave goods' – all kinds of things they might need. For rich warriors, this meant clothes, weapons, horses – and sometimes, wives and slaves. Rich women were buried with clothes, jewels, furniture and equipment for spinning and weaving.

612 Viking graves have survived for hundreds of years. Archaeologists have discovered many collections of grave contents, in remarkably good condition. Some, such as jewellery, pottery and stone carvings, are made of materials that do not rot. Some, such as clothing, have survived by chance. Others, such as ship burials, have been preserved underwater. All have provided valuable evidence about life in Viking times.

▲ These stones arranged in the shape of a ship's hull mark an ancient Viking burial ground.

◄ The dead were laid to rest in cloth-covered shelters on board real ships. Then the ships were set on fire so that their souls could 'sail away' to the next world.

613 Vikings hoped that ships might carry their souls away. So they surrounded buried cremation urns with ship-shaped enclosures of stones. Some enclosures were very large – up to 80 metres long – and were probably also used as places of worship. Very important Viking men and women were cremated or buried in real wooden ships, along with valuable grave-goods.

614 Vikings treated dead bodies with great respect. They washed them, dressed them and wrapped them in cloth or birch bark before burying them or cremating them. This was because the Vikings believed that dead people might come back to haunt them if they were not treated carefully.

I DON'T BELIEVE IT!

Some Viking skeletons and wooden ships that were buried in acid soils have been completely eaten away. But they have left 'shadows' in the ground, which archaeologists can use to find out more about them.

Writing and picture stories

615 **Many ordinary Vikings could not read or write.** They relied on the spoken word to communicate and on memory to preserve details of land, family histories and important events. At the beginning of the Viking Age, all Vikings spoke the *donsk tunga* (Danish Tongue). But after AD 1000, different dialects developed.

▲ Viking runes. From top left, these symbols stand for the sounds: F U Th A R K H N I A S T B M L R.

616 **Viking scribes wrote in 'runes'.** There were 16 letters, called runes, in the Viking alphabet. They were used for labelling valuable items with the owner's name, for recording accounts, keeping calendars and for sending messages. Runes were written in straight lines only. This made them easier to carve on wood and stone. The Vikings did not have paper!

▼ Vikings used sharp metal points to carve runes on useful or valuable items.

Deer antler with runes carved on it

Viking calendar

Comb with runes showing owner's name

617 **Runes were used to cast magic spells.** Sometimes, runes were used to write messages in secret code, or even magic spells. These supposedly gave the objects they were carved on special power. Some secret Viking writings in runes still have not been deciphered today.

618 Rune stones told stories. Wealthy families paid for expert rune masters to carve runic inscriptions on stones, praising and commemorating dead parents and children. Some boastful people also had stones carved with details of their own achievements. When the carvings were completed, the rune stones were raised up in public places where everyone could see them.

◄ Rune stones were written records of Viking citizens.

619 Picture stones told of great adventures. In some Viking lands, people carved memorial stones with pictures, instead of runes. These show scenes from the dead person's life and details of their adventures, together with pictures of gods, giants and monsters.

▲ Some picture stones told of people's achievements, others commemorated loved ones who had died.

WRITE YOUR NAME IN RUNES

Use the chart on page 284 to try to write your name in runes. The Viking alphabet was called 'futhark', after its first six letters. It had a special letter for the sound 'th' and no letters for the sounds 'e' and 'o'. Even the Vikings found it difficult to write some names and words!

The end of the Vikings

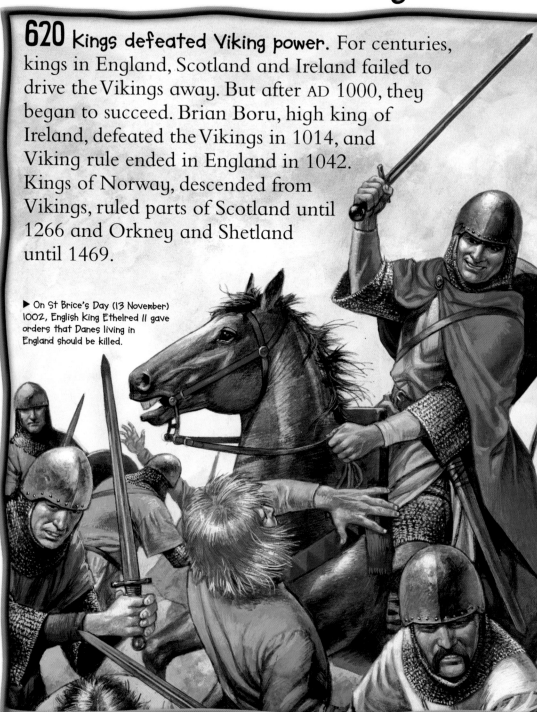

620 **Kings defeated Viking power.** For centuries, kings in England, Scotland and Ireland failed to drive the Vikings away. But after AD 1000, they began to succeed. Brian Boru, high king of Ireland, defeated the Vikings in 1014, and Viking rule ended in England in 1042. Kings of Norway, descended from Vikings, ruled parts of Scotland until 1266 and Orkney and Shetland until 1469.

▶ On St Brice's Day (13 November) 1002, English King Ethelred II gave orders that Danes living in England should be killed.

621 **Vikings learned to live alongside other peoples.** In most places where Vikings settled, they married local women and worked with local people. Some of their words and customs blended with local ones, but many disappeared. Viking traditions only survived if the place where they settled was uninhabited, such as Iceland, or the Orkney Islands, off the north of Scotland.

▲ In 1066, the Normans – descendants of Vikings who had settled in Normandy, France – invaded and conquered England. This scene from the huge Bayeux Tapestry (embroidered wall-hanging) shows their Viking-style ships.

622 **Christianity destroyed faith in Viking gods.** The Vikings believed their gods would punish them if they did not worship them, and would kill Christian missionaries. But the missionaries survived. So did Vikings who became Christians. This made other Vikings wonder if their gods had any powers, at all.

◀ Christians living in Scandinavia after the end of the Viking age made statues of Jesus Christ to stand in their churches, as symbols of their faith.

623 **Vikings set up new kingdoms outside Viking lands.** In places far away from the Viking homelands, such as Novgorod in Russia, or Normandy, in northern France, Viking warlords set up kingdoms that developed independently. Over the years, they lost touch with their Viking origins, and created new customs, laws and lifestyles of their own.

624 **Viking settlers abandoned America.** Soon after AD 1000, Thorfinn Karlsefni, a Viking merchant from Iceland, led over 100 Viking men and women to settle at Vinland – the site in North America where Lief Eriksson landed. They stayed there for two years, but left because the Native North Americans attacked them and drove them away.

Knights and Castles

Sharpen your sword, pick up your shield
and prepare to do battle as a knight!

Building a castle • Kings • Peasants • Battle
Training • Coats of arms • Feasts • Jousting
Attackers • Defenders • Crusades • Famous knights
Eastern warriors • St George

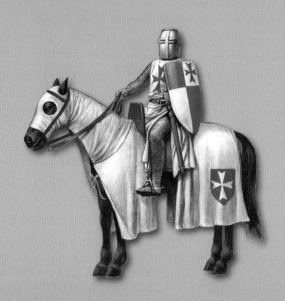

Castle life

625 **A castle was both a home and a fortress in the Middle Ages.** It provided shelter for a king or a lord and his family, and it allowed him to defend his lands. Castles were also places where soldiers were stationed, wrong-doers were imprisoned, courts settled disputes, weapons and armour were made and great banquets and tournaments were held.

In the beginning

626 **The first castles were mostly built from wood on top of a hill.** Sometimes castle builders piled up soil to make the hill artificially. On top of the hill, called a motte, stood a wooden tower, or keep. This was the central part of the castle and the easiest part to defend.

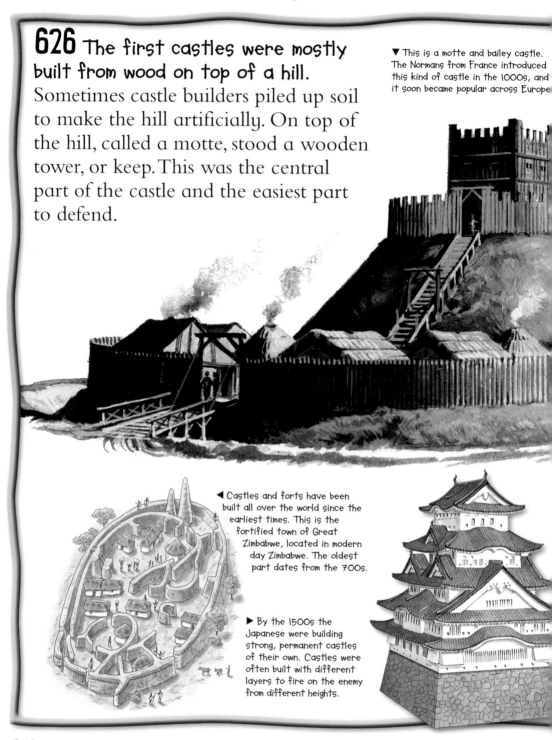

▼ This is a motte and bailey castle. The Normans from France introduced this kind of castle in the 1000s, and it soon became popular across Europe

◄ Castles and forts have been built all over the world since the earliest times. This is the fortified town of Great Zimbabwe, located in modern day Zimbabwe. The oldest part dates from the 700s.

► By the 1500s the Japanese were building strong, permanent castles of their own. Castles were often built with different layers to fire on the enemy from different heights.

627 At the bottom of the motte was a courtyard called a bailey. It was usually surrounded by a wooden fence. Castle builders dug a deep ditch, called a moat, all around the outside of the motte and bailey. They often filled the moat with water. Moats were designed to stop attackers reaching the castle walls.

I DON'T BELIEVE IT!

The builders of the early wooden castles covered the walls with wet leather – to stop them from burning down.

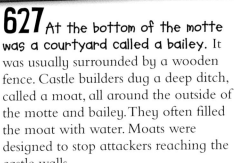

◀ For extra protection, a wooden fence was often built around the top of the motte. The top of each wooden plank was shaped into a point to make it harder for the enemy to climb over.

628 Wooden castles were not very strong – and they caught fire easily. From around 1100 onwards, people began to build castles in stone. A stone castle gave better protection against attack, fire and cold rainy weather.

gatehouse

inner defensive wall

outer defensive wall

turret

Keep

▶ Sometimes an extra wall was built on the inside of the strong outer wall. Archers could stand on the inner wall and fire down onto the outer wall if it was captured.

Building a castle

629 The best place to build a castle was on top of a hill. A hilltop position gave good views over the surrounding countryside, and made it harder for an enemy to launch a surprise attack. Sometimes a castle was built on the banks of a river or lake, and its waters were used to create a moat.

KEY
1. Scaffolding was made of wood, and was slotted into openings in the stonework.
2. The main walls of a castle were packed with stone rubble and flints mixed with mortar. This gave extra strength.
3. A master mason was hired to design the castle and take charge of the building work.
4. Directly underneath him were freemasons who cut and carved the stone, and roughmasons who built the walls.
5. Heavy stones were raised by a treadwheel crane.

630 The lord of the castle and his family lived in the safest part of the castle – the keep.
The walls of the keep were built to be very strong, and at least 3.5 metres thick in some castles. Inside the keep were large rooms for receiving visitors and holding banquets, as well as smaller storerooms and guardrooms. The family's bedrooms were on the top floor of the keep. All these rooms and defences made building a castle very slow and expensive.

DESIGN YOUR OWN CASTLE

Imagine you have been asked to design a castle for your local lord. It is important that he can defend his castle and his family against attacks by his enemies.

Draw a plan of your ideal castle, making sure it has plenty of defences. And don't forget the drawbridge to let the lord and his family in and out of their castle.

Who's who in the castle

631 **A castle was the home of an important and powerful person, such as a king, a lord or a knight.** The lord of the castle controlled the castle itself, as well as the lands and people around it. The lady of the castle was in charge of the day-to-day running of the castle. She controlled the kitchens and gave the servants their orders for feasts and banquets.

▶ Lord and lady of the manor

632 **The constable was in charge of defending the castle.** He was usually a fierce and ruthless man. He trained his soldiers to guard the castle properly and organized the rota of guards and watchmen. The constable was in charge of the whole castle when the lord was away.

633 **Many servants lived and worked inside the castle, looking after the lord and his family.** They cooked, cleaned, served at the table, worked as maids and servants and ran errands. A man called the steward was in charge of all the servants.

Servants   Steward   Cooks

634 Inside the castle walls were many workshops where goods were made and repaired. The castle blacksmith was kept busy making shoes for all the horses. The armourer made weapons and armour.

Blacksmith

Armourer

▶ The master of the horse had to look after the lord's horses.

635 Local villagers would shelter in the castle when their lands were under attack. They were not allowed to shelter inside the keep itself, so they stayed inside the bailey with their families and all their animals.

From kings to peasants

636 In medieval times, the king or queen was the most important person in the country. The king gave land to his barons and other noblemen. In return, they supplied the king with soldiers, horses and weapons to fight wars. This system of giving away land in return for services was known as feudalism.

▶ This bishop is having a meeting, called an audience, with the king and queen. In medieval times there was often conflict between the Church and the king. Both were very powerful, and they had to try to work together.

637 The Church was very powerful in the Middle Ages. It controlled large areas of land, and grew rich from the taxes paid by the peasants who worked on these lands. Peasant farmers had to give the church a tithe, one-tenth of everything they produced.

638 The barons were the most powerful noblemen. A wealthy baron might supply the king with around 5000 fighting men. Some barons also had their own private army to keep control over their own lands.

639 The wealthier lords and barons often gave away some of their lands to professional fighters called knights. Knights were skilled soldiers who rode into battle on horseback.

640 At the very bottom of the feudal system was the poor peasant. In the Middle Ages over 90 per cent of people living in Europe worked on the land. Everything in their lives – their land, animals, food, even their clothes – belonged to the local lord.

How to be a good knight

641 *It took about 14 years of training to become a knight.* The son of a noble joined a lord's household aged seven. He learned how to ride, to shoot a bow and arrow and how to behave in front of nobles. He then became a squire, where he learned how to fight with a sword, and he looked after his master's armour and weapons. If he was successful, he became a knight at 21.

642 *The ceremony of making a new knight was known as dubbing.* A knight had to spend a whole night in church before his dubbing ceremony took place. This all-night watch was called a vigil. First, he had a cold bath and dressed in a plain white tunic. Then he spent the night on his knees in church, praying and confessing his sins.

643 The dubbing ceremony changed over time. In the beginning a knight was struck on the back of the neck. Later, dubbing involved a tap on the knight's shoulder with a sword.

644 Knights had to behave according to a set of rules, known as the 'code of chivalry'. The code involved being brave and honourable on the battlefield, and treating the enemy politely and fairly. It also instructed knights how to behave towards women.

645 A knight who behaved badly was disgraced and punished. A knight in disgrace had either behaved in a cowardly way on the battlefield, cheated in a tournament or treated another knight badly.

646 A rich knight would have three horses. He rode his heaviest horse for fighting and tournaments. He also had a horse for riding, and a baggage horse. The best horses were warhorses from Italy and Spain. They were quick but strong and sturdy.

Ready for battle

647 Knights wore a long-sleeved tunic made of linen or wool, with a cloak over the top. By the 1200s knights had started to wear long hooded coats called surcoats. Knights nearly always wore bright colours, and some even wore fancy items such as shoes with curled pointed toes, and hats decorated with sparkling jewels.

◀ A knight was dressed for battle from the feet upwards. The last item of armour to be put on him was his helmet.

648 Early knights wore a type of armour called chainmail. It was made of thousands of tiny iron rings joined onto each other. A piece of chainmail looked a bit like knitting, except it was made of metal, not wool. But a knight also wore a padded jacket under his chainmail to make sure he wasn't cut by his own armour!

649 Gradually, knights began to wear more and more armour. They added solid metal plates shaped to fit their body. By the 1400s knights were wearing full suits of steel armour. They wore metal gloves, called gauntlets, and even metal shoes!

650 A knight had two main weapons: his sword and his shield. The sword was double edged and was sharp enough to pierce chainmail. Knights also fought with lances, daggers and axes.

◀ These knights are fighting in battle. The knight on the right has the usual weapons of a sword and shield. The knight on the left has a morning star. This was a spiked ball on the end of a chain.

I DON'T BELIEVE IT!

Soldiers called 'retrievers' had to run into the middle of the battle and collect up all the spare arrows!

651 Between 1337 and 1453 England and France were almost continually at war with each other, in what we now know as the Hundred Years' War. The English armies won important battles against the French in 1356 and at Agincourt in 1415. The skilled English and Welsh longbowmen, who could fire as many as 12 arrows every minute, helped to stop the French knights.

652 A Swiss foot soldier's main weapon was a halberd. This was a combined spear and battleaxe, and was a particularly nasty, but very effective, way of a foot soldier getting a knight off his horse.

Colours and coats of arms

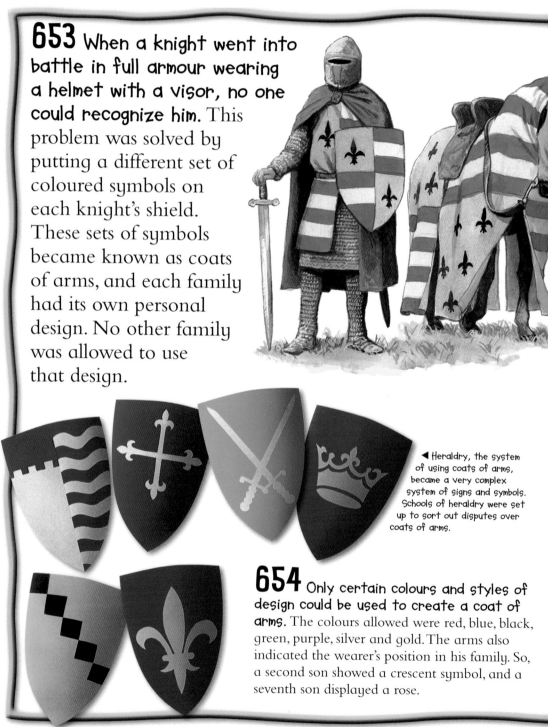

653 When a knight went into battle in full armour wearing a helmet with a visor, no one could recognize him. This problem was solved by putting a different set of coloured symbols on each knight's shield. These sets of symbols became known as coats of arms, and each family had its own personal design. No other family was allowed to use that design.

◀ Heraldry, the system of using coats of arms, became a very complex system of signs and symbols. Schools of heraldry were set up to sort out disputes over coats of arms.

654 Only certain colours and styles of design could be used to create a coat of arms. The colours allowed were red, blue, black, green, purple, silver and gold. The arms also indicated the wearer's position in his family. So, a second son showed a crescent symbol, and a seventh son displayed a rose.

655 On the battlefield, each nobleman had his own banner around which his knights and other soldiers could meet. The nobleman's colours and coat of arms were displayed on the banner. Banners decorated with coats of arms also made a colourful display at tournaments and parades.

◀ The banner of a nobleman was a very important symbol during battle. If the person holding the banner was killed in battle, someone had to pick the banner up and raise it straight away.

656 Messengers called heralds carried messages between knights during battle. They had to be able to recognize each individual knight quickly. After coats of arms were introduced, the heralds became experts at identifying them. The system of using coats of arms became known as heraldry.

▲ After a battle, it was the sad job of a herald to walk around the battlefield and identify the dead by their coats of arms.

DESIGN YOUR OWN COAT OF ARMS

Would you like your own personal coat of arms? You can design one by following the basic rules of heraldry explained on these pages. You will need the seven paint colours listed opposite, a paintbrush, a fine-tipped black felt pen, a ruler and some thick white paper. Good luck!

Famous knights

657 Roland was a brave, loyal knight who died in the service of his master. Roland served King Charles the Great – Charlemagne – who ruled much of France and Germany in the 800s. Roland had to protect Charlemagne and his army from Muslim attackers as they crossed from Spain into France. But Roland was betrayed and died fighting for his king.

▲ Famous stories of old knights have been recorded in old books, like this one bound in leather.

658 The Spanish knight Rodrigo Díaz de Vivar had the nickname 'El Cid'. This comes from the Arabic for 'the Lord'. El Cid fought against the Moors from North Africa. He was exiled by his lord, King Alfonso VI, after the knight's enemies turned the king against him.

▼ Don Quixote charged at windmills because he thought they were giants.

Rodrigo Díaz de Vivar, 'El Cid'

659 The book 'Don Quixote' tells the story of an old man who dreams about past deeds of bravery and chivalry. It was written in the 1500s by a Spaniard called Miguel de Cervantes. After reading about the knights of old, Don Quixote dresses in armour and sets off on horseback to become famous. He takes a peasant called Sancho Panzo with him as his squire, and it is his squire who gets Don Quixote out of trouble during his travels.

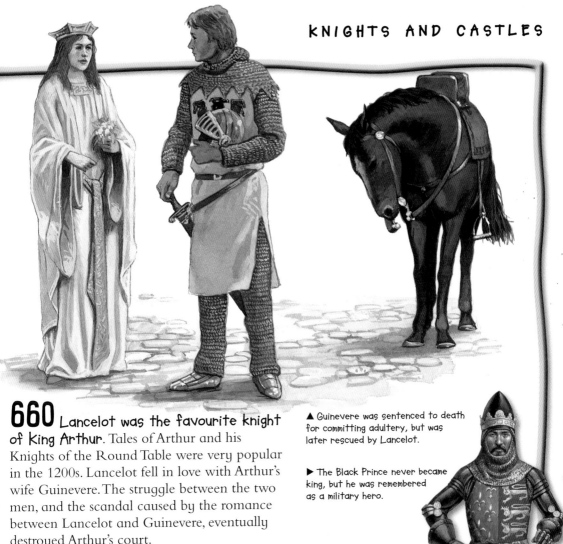

660 Lancelot was the favourite knight of King Arthur. Tales of Arthur and his Knights of the Round Table were very popular in the 1200s. Lancelot fell in love with Arthur's wife Guinevere. The struggle between the two men, and the scandal caused by the romance between Lancelot and Guinevere, eventually destroyed Arthur's court.

▲ Guinevere was sentenced to death for committing adultery, but was later rescued by Lancelot.

▶ The Black Prince never became king, but he was remembered as a military hero.

I DON'T BELIEVE IT!

During his travels Don Quixote mistakes flocks of farmyard animals for enemy armies!

661 The Black Prince was the nickname of Edward, the oldest son of Edward III of England. The Black Prince was a great warrior who captured the French king, John II, at the battle of Poitiers in 1356.

A castle tour

662 Stone castles were cold, damp places with lots of draughts. A castle was not exactly a luxury home. Cold winds blew through the windows, which had no glass.

▶ The lord of the castle and his family were the only people who slept in beds. Most people slept on wooden pallets covered with straw.

▶ Almost all castles also had a well within their walls. This was essential as a source of water if someone laid siege to the castle.

▶ The kitchens were often built in a separate part of the castle, away from the keep, in case they caught fire.

▼ Castles had no central heating and no running water. Wool hangings and tapestries on the walls, and rugs on the floor, helped to warm the rooms. Roaring fires burned in the huge fireplaces.

663 There were many workshops and other buildings inside the safety of the castle walls. They included an armoury, a smithy, stables, kennels, a mill for making flour and a chapel. There were sometimes even gardens and orchards.

664 Medieval castles had no toilets! Instead people sat on wooden seats called 'garderobes'. These were built over a very long chute. Waste from the toilet fell down the chute into the moat.

◀ Every castle had a cold, dark and often slimy dungeon for keeping prisoners. The dungeon was usually located beneath one of the gatehouse towers. Prisoners would be locked inside a small airless cell.

Feasts and fun

665 **The Great Hall was the centre of castle life.** The lord and his family ate their meals here and carried out their daily business. Colourful banners and coats of arms and shiny pieces of armour hung from the walls of the Great Hall. The hall was sometimes turned into a courtroom to try local law-breakers.

666 **Musicians entertained the lord and his guests at banquets in the Great Hall.** They played instruments such as pipes, drums, fiddles and lutes.

667 **Jesters, jugglers and acrobats performed for the diners between courses.** Sometimes a dancing bear might brought in to entertain the guests.

BAKE A 'TARTE OF APPLES AND ORANGES'

You will need:

1 packet of shortcrust pastry
4 eating apples
4 oranges
juice of ½ lemon
3 cups of water
1 cup of honey

½ cup of brown sugar
¼ tsp cinnamon
pinch of dried ginger
a little milk
a little caster sugar

Ask an adult to help you. Line a pie dish with pastry and bake for 10 minutes in a medium-hot oven. Slice the oranges thinly. Boil the water, honey and lemon juice, add the oranges. Cover and simmer for 2 hours, then drain. Peel, core and slice the apples and mix with the sugar, cinnamon and ginger. Place a layer of apples in the bottom of the dish followed by a layer of oranges, then alternate layers until the fruit is used up. Place a pastry lid over the top and brush with a little milk. Make small slits in the lid. Bake in a medium-hot oven for about 45 minutes.

668 Huge amounts of exotic–looking and delicious foods were served at banquets. Roast meats included stuffed peacock and swan, as well as venison, beef, goose, duck and wild boar. Whole roasted fish were also served. These foods were followed by dishes made from spices brought from Asia, and then fruit and nuts.

669 The lord, his family and important guests sat at the high table on a platform called a dais. From their raised position they could look down over the rest of the diners. The most important guests such as priests and noblemen sat next to the lord.

670 Important guests drank fine wine out of glasses. Cup-bearers poured the wine out of decorated pottery jugs. Less important diners drank ale or wine from mugs or tankards made of wood, pewter or leather.

Knights and dragons

671 **The legend of St George tells how the brave knight killed a fierce dragon.** The dragon was terrorizing the people of Lydia (part of modern Turkey). The king offered his daughter to the dragon if the it left his people alone. St George arrived and said he would kill their dragon if they became Christians like him. Thousands accepted his offer, and George killed the dragon.

▲ St George was adopted as the patron saint of England in the 1300s.

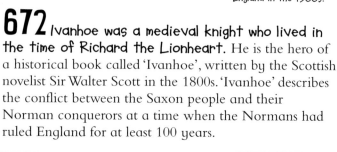

672 **Ivanhoe was a medieval knight who lived in the time of Richard the Lionheart.** He is the hero of a historical book called 'Ivanhoe', written by the Scottish novelist Sir Walter Scott in the 1800s. 'Ivanhoe' describes the conflict between the Saxon people and their Norman conquerors at a time when the Normans had ruled England for at least 100 years.

673 Legend says that King Arthur became king after pulling a magic sword called Excalibur out of a stone. This act proved that he was the right person to rule Britain. People have written stories about Arthur and his followers, the Knights of the Round Table, for more than 1000 years.

◄ No one really knows who the real Arthur was, but he may have been a Celtic warrior who lived about 1400 years ago.

675 In the 1300s an Englishman called Geoffrey Chaucer wrote 'The Canterbury Tales'. These stories were about a group of pilgrims travelling from a London inn to a religious site in Canterbury. The pilgrims included a priest, a nun, a merchant, a cook, a ploughman and a knight and his squire.

674 King Arthur had many castle homes but his favourite was Camelot. Historians think that Camelot was really an English castle called Tintagel. When Arthur heard that his best friend and favourite knight, Sir Lancelot, had fallen in love with his wife, Queen Guinevere, Arthur banished Lancelot from his court at Camelot.

Quiz

1. What is a minstrel?
2. Whose job was it to fill everyone's glass at a banquet?
3. What did a troubadour do?
4. Who were the Knights of the Round Table?
5. What is the name of King Arthur's favourite castle?

Answers:
1. A wandering musician
2. The cup-bearer 3. Write songs about knights and courtly love
4. The followers of King Arthur
5. Camelot

Practice for battle

676 In a tournament, knights divided into two sides and fought each other as if in a proper battle. Tournaments were good practice for the real thing – war. The idea for these mock battles, called tourneys, probably started in France in the 12th century.

▼ Jousting knights charged at each other at top speed. Each one tried to knock his opponent off his horse with a blow from a long wooden lance.

▲ Edward I of England was a keen supporter of tournaments and jousts. He banned spectators from carrying weapons themselves because this caused too much trouble among the watching crowds.

677 Tournaments took place under strict rules. There were safe areas where knights could rest without being attacked by the other side. Knights were not meant to kill their opponents but they often did. Several kings became so angry at losing their best knights that all tournaments were banned unless the king had given his permission.

I DON'T BELIEVE IT!
Some knights cheated in jousts by wearing special armour that was fixed onto the horse's saddle!

680 Sometimes the knights carried on fighting on the ground with their swords. The problem was that this was as dangerous as a tourney!

678 Jousting was introduced because so many knights were being killed or wounded during tournaments. More than 60 knights were killed in a single tourney in Cologne, Germany. Jousting was a fight between two knights on horseback. Each knight tried to win by knocking the other off his horse. Knights were protected by armour, and their lances were not sharp.

681 A joust gave a knight the chance to prove himself in front of the woman he loved. Jousts were very social events watched by ladies of the court as well as ordinary people. Knights could show off their skills and bravery to impress the spectators.

679 A knight's code of chivalry did not allow him to win a tournament by cheating. It was better to lose with honour than to win in disgrace.

Friend or enemy?

682 When Edward the Confessor died in 1066, Duke William of Normandy, his cousin, claimed that he had been promised the throne of England. William and his knights invaded England and defeated Harold, the English king, at the Battle of Hastings.

▲ The Bayeux Tapestry records the story of the Norman invasion of England. It shows William and his knights landing along the English coast, and also shows the moment when England's King Harold was killed at the Battle of Hastings.

▲ Here you can see the route that William the Conqueror took to London.

683 On and off between 1337 and 1453 the neighbouring countries of England and France were at war. The Hundred Years' War, as it was called, carried on through the reigns of five English kings and five French ones. The two countries fought each other to decide who should control France. In the end the French were victorious, and England lost control of all her lands in France apart from the port of Calais.

684 One of the major battles of the Hundred Years' War was fought at Crécy in 1346. English soldiers defeated a much larger French army, killing almost half the French soldiers. During the battle, the English army used gunpowder and cannons for possibly the first time.

685 Deadly weapons called caltrops were used in the Hundred Years' War. A caltrop was a star-shaped piece of metal. These were scattered along the ground in front of an attacking army. They stopped both horses and footsoldiers in their tracks.

686 A young French girl called Joan of Arc led the French army against the English, who had surrounded the city of Orléans. After 10 days the English were defeated. Joan was later captured, accused of being a witch, and burned to death.

I DON'T BELIEVE IT!

If you captured a knight alive during battle, you could offer him back to his family in return for a generous ransom!

Under attack

687 An attacking enemy had to break through a castle's defences to get inside its walls. One method was to break down the castle gates with giant battering rams. Attackers and defenders also used siege engines to hurl boulders at each other.

688 A siege is when an enemy surrounds a castle and stops all supplies from reaching the people inside. The idea is to starve the castle occupants until they surrender or die.

689 A riskier way of trying to get inside a castle was to climb over the walls. Attackers either used ladders or moved wooden towers with men hidden inside them into position beside the walls.

690
Giant catapults were sometimes uses to fire stones or burning pieces of wood inside the castle. The Romans were some of the first people to use catapults in warfare.

▲ This siege engine was called a trebuchet. It had a long wooden arm with a heavy weight at one end and a sling at the other. A heavy stone was placed inside the sling. As the weight dropped, the stone was hurled towards the castle walls, sometimes travelling as far as 300 metres.

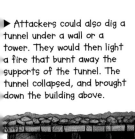

► Attackers could also dig a tunnel under a wall or a tower. They would then light a fire that burnt away the supports of the tunnel. The tunnel collapsed, and brought down the building above.

I DON'T BELIEVE IT!
The ropes used to wind up siege catapults were made from plaits of human hair!

691
The enemy sometimes succeeded in tunnelling beneath the castle walls. They surprised the defenders when they appeared inside the castle itself.

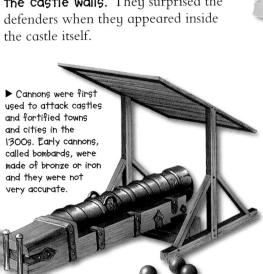

► Cannons were first used to attack castles and fortified towns and cities in the 1300s. Early cannons, called bombards, were made of bronze or iron and they were not very accurate.

692
The invention of cannons and gunpowder brought the building of castle strongholds almost to an end. It marked the end of warrior knights too. Castle walls could not stand up to the powerful cannonballs that exploded against them. Guns and cannons were now used on the battlefield, so armies no longer needed the services of brave armoured knights on horseback.

Defending a castle

693 When the enemy was spotted approaching a castle, its defenders first pulled up the castle drawbridge. They also lowered an iron grate, called a portcullis, to form an extra barrier behind the drawbridge.

694 The castle archers fired their arrows through narrow slits in the thick castle walls. They also fired through the gaps in the battlements.

▶ Soldiers could use a longbow while the enemy was still a long way away.

▶ Crossbows were far slower to aim and fire than longbows.

695 In the middle of the night, a raiding party might leave a besieged castle to surprise the enemy camped outside. The raiders would move along secret passages and climb out through hidden gates or doorways.

696 Defenders poured boiling-hot water onto the heads of the enemy as they tried to climb the castle walls. Quicklime was also poured over the enemy soldiers, making their skin burn.

▶ Water was poured onto the enemy's heads through holes in the stonework of the battlements.

697 Heavy stones and other missiles often rained down from the battlements onto the enemy below. Hidden from view by the high battlements, the defenders stood on wooden platforms to throw the missiles.

Quiz

1. What is the name of the mock battles held between large numbers of knights?

2. Which weapon did jousting knights use when on horseback?

3. Which two countries fought a war that lasted 100 years?

4. In what year was the battle of Agincourt?

5. Which machine was used to break down castle walls and gates?

Answers:
1. Tourneys
2. A lance 3. England and France 4. 1415 5. a battering ram

Off to the crusades

698 The crusades were military expeditions from Europe to Palestine. The aim for European Christians was to recapture Palestine, at the eastern end of the Mediterranean Sea, from the Muslim Turks who had seized control of it. The First Crusade set off from Europe in 1096. Between 1096 and 1204 there were four separate crusades.

699 The crusaders built huge castles to defend their lands against the much larger Muslim armies. Many of these castles were big enough to house thousands of soldiers as well as their servants and horses. In the port of Acre the crusaders had constructed a vast underground fortress.

700 Thousands of young boys and girls set off for the Holy Land in 1212 in one of the strangest crusades — the Children's Crusade. Many died of cold or hunger while marching to the Mediterranean ports. Others drowned during the sea crossing, and some were sold as slaves along the way.

701 The Muslim leader Saladin fought against the knights of the Third Crusade. Saladin had already defeated the Christian armies and seized the city of Jerusalem. The Third Crusade was meant to recapture Jerusalem. It was led by an emperor and two kings: Emperor Frederick I of Germany, Richard the Lionheart of England and Philip II of France, but the crusaders failed to regain Jerusalem.

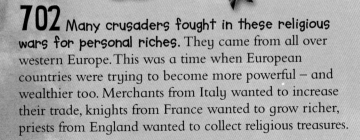

I DON'T BELIEVE IT!

A crusader knight would share his tent with his beloved horse — it must have been a bit of a squeeze!

702 Many crusaders fought in these religious wars for personal riches. They came from all over western Europe. This was a time when European countries were trying to become more powerful — and wealthier too. Merchants from Italy wanted to increase their trade, knights from France wanted to grow richer, priests from England wanted to collect religious treasures.

Garters and elephants

703 A group of Christian knights living in the Holy Land were in charge of protecting pilgrims on their way to and from Palestine. They were the Templar knights, or Templars. Their headquarters were in the Aqsa Mosque in the city of Jerusalem. The Templars grew very rich during their time in the Holy Land, but their organization was eventually broken up.

704 The Knights of St John looked after the safety and health of pilgrims while they were in the Holy Land. The knights lived like monks and followed strict rules, but they also continued to provide soldiers to fight the Muslims.

705 Medieval knights began to band together to form special groups called orders. Each order had its own badge showing the symbol chosen by the order. It was considered an honour to be asked to join an order. New orders began to appear in many countries across Europe. The Order of the Golden Fleece, for example, was started in France by Philip the Good.

▶ The Knights of St John had been monks who cared for sick people before becoming religious knights. They were often referred to as the Hospitallers.

▶ Knights wore the badge of their order on a chain around the neck. Knights from the Order of the Golden Fleece wore a badge depicting a golden sheep.

706 The Order of the Bath was founded in Britain in the early 1400s. Knights who belonged to an order swore loyalty to their king or queen, and promised to fight against their enemies.

707 The Order of the Garter is the oldest and most important order in Britain. According to the story, Edward III was dancing with a countess when she lost her garter. As the king gave it back to her, he heard the people near him laughing and joking about what they had seen. Angry, the king said that anyone who had evil thoughts should be ashamed. This is still the motto of the order.

Quiz

1. Which Muslim warrior fought against the knights of the Third Crusade?

2. By what other name is Richard I of England known?

3. In which city can you find important Muslim and Christian sites?

4. What do knights of the Order of the Golden Fleece wear around their necks?

Answers:
1. Saladin
2. Richard the Lionheart
3. Jerusalem 4. A golden sheep

▼ The emblem of the Order of the Garter is a dark-blue garter trimmed with gold. Knights of the order wear it on their left leg at important ceremonies.

708 The Order of the Elephant from Denmark is more than 500 years old. Members of the order wear a badge that features an elephant waving its trunk in the air.

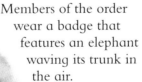

Warriors from the East

709 Warrior knights in Japan in the Middle Ages were known as samurai. People in Japan were also divided into different feudal groups, where people in each group served someone in a higher-ranking group. The samurai, like European knights, served a lord. They usually fought on horseback but later on they began to fight more on foot.

▼ The Seljuk Turks were named after their first leader, Seljuk.

710 A long curving sword was a samurai warrior's most treasured possession. Samurai warriors wore armour on the bodies, arms and legs, a helmet and often a crest made up of a pair of horns.

711 The fierce Seljuk Turks fought against Christian knights during the crusades. The Seljuks swept across southwest Asia in the 1000s and 1100s. They conquered many lands, including Syria, Palestine, Asia Minor (modern Turkey) and Persia (modern Iran).

712 Fierce Mongol warriors from the East terrified the enemy in battle. The Mongols were expert horsemen who controlled their horses with their feet while standing up in their stirrups. This way of riding left both hands free to shoot a bow and arrow.

▼ Each Mongol warrior had a team of five horses ready for battle. As well as being skilled archers, the Mongols were highly trained spear-throwers.

713 Genghis Khan was the greatest of the Mongol leaders. He became leader of his tribe when he was just 13 years old. He united all the Mongol tribes, and went on to conquer northern China, Korea, northern India, Afghanistan, Persia and parts of Russia.

I DON'T BELIEVE IT!

The Turks fought with gold pieces in their mouth, to stop the crusader knights from stealing their gold. If a Turkish warrior thought he was going to die, he swallowed the gold.

Explorers

Begin a voyage of discovery with
world-famous explorers.

Marco Polo • River Nile • Charles Darwin
Archaeology • Ibn Battuta • Conquistadors • Arctic
Africa • Captain Cook • America • Mount Everest
Australia • Ferdinand Magellan • China

The first explorers

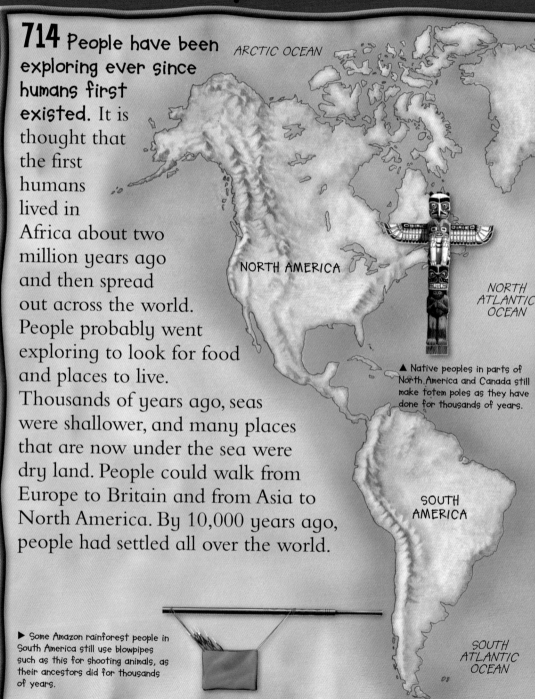

714 People have been
exploring ever since
humans first
existed. It is
thought that
the first
humans
lived in
Africa about two
million years ago
and then spread
out across the world.
People probably went
exploring to look for food
and places to live.
Thousands of years ago, seas
were shallower, and many places
that are now under the sea were
dry land. People could walk from
Europe to Britain and from Asia to
North America. By 10,000 years ago,
people had settled all over the world.

ARCTIC OCEAN

NORTH AMERICA

NORTH
ATLANTIC
OCEAN

▲ Native peoples in parts of
North America and Canada still
make totem poles as they have
done for thousands of years.

SOUTH
AMERICA

▶ Some Amazon rainforest people in
South America still use blowpipes
such as this for shooting animals, as
their ancestors did for thousands
of years.

SOUTH
ATLANTIC
OCEAN

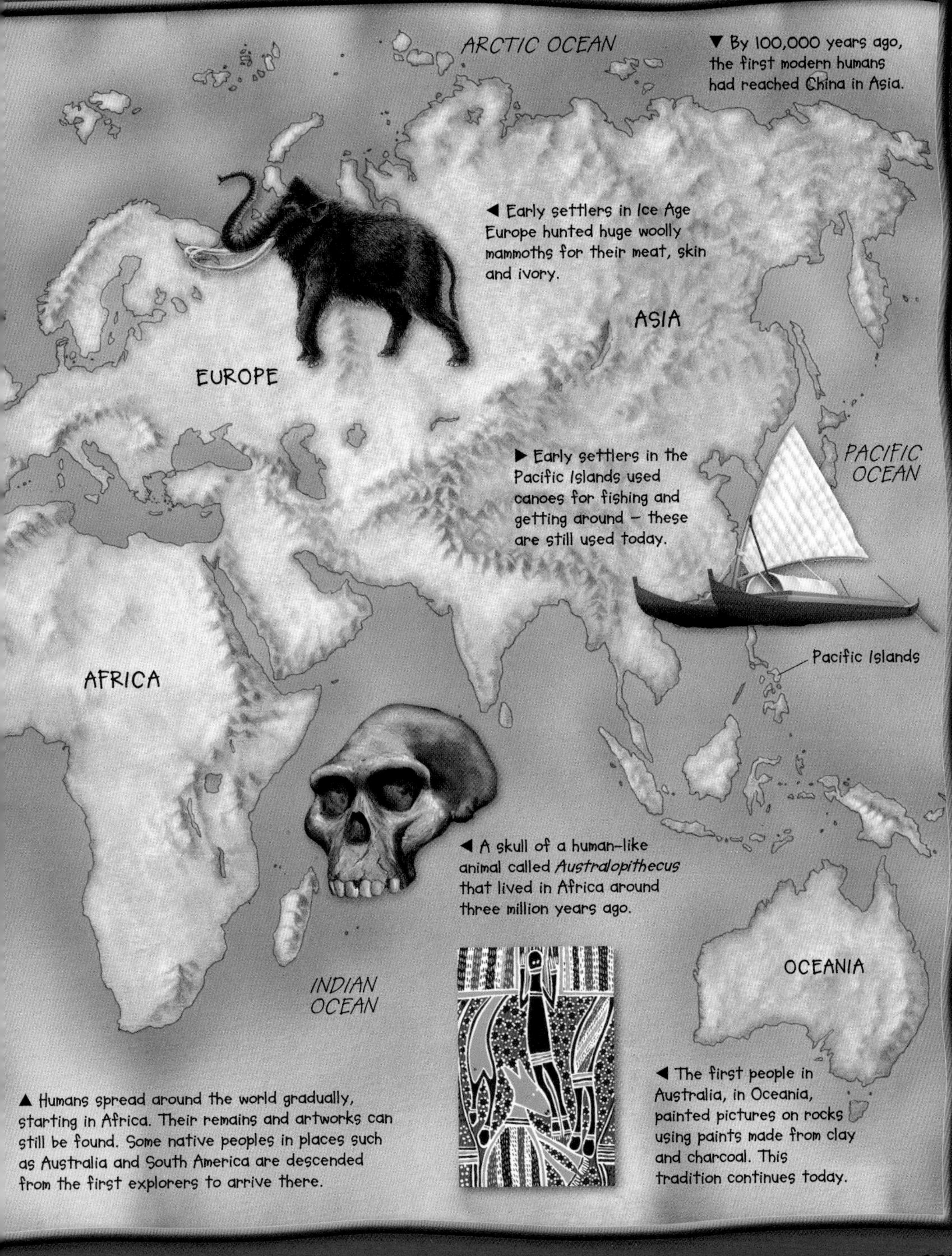

ARCTIC OCEAN

▼ By 100,000 years ago, the first modern humans had reached China in Asia.

◄ Early settlers in Ice Age Europe hunted huge woolly mammoths for their meat, skin and ivory.

ASIA

EUROPE

▶ Early settlers in the Pacific Islands used canoes for fishing and getting around — these are still used today.

PACIFIC OCEAN

Pacific Islands

AFRICA

◄ A skull of a human-like animal called *Australopithecus* that lived in Africa around three million years ago.

INDIAN OCEAN

OCEANIA

▲ Humans spread around the world gradually, starting in Africa. Their remains and artworks can still be found. Some native peoples in places such as Australia and South America are descended from the first explorers to arrive there.

◄ The first people in Australia, in Oceania, painted pictures on rocks using paints made from clay and charcoal. This tradition continues today.

331

Ancient adventurers

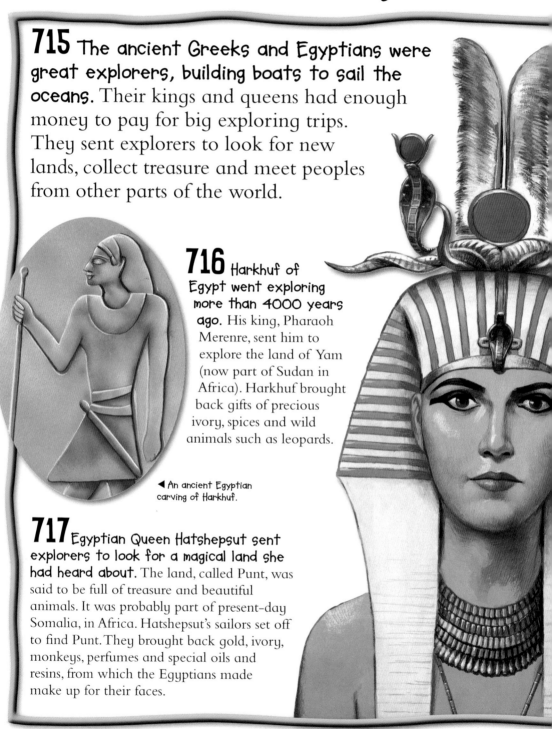

715 The ancient Greeks and Egyptians were great explorers, building boats to sail the oceans. Their kings and queens had enough money to pay for big exploring trips. They sent explorers to look for new lands, collect treasure and meet peoples from other parts of the world.

716 Harkhuf of Egypt went exploring more than 4000 years ago. His king, Pharaoh Merenre, sent him to explore the land of Yam (now part of Sudan in Africa). Harkhuf brought back gifts of precious ivory, spices and wild animals such as leopards.

◀ An ancient Egyptian carving of Harkhuf.

717 Egyptian Queen Hatshepsut sent explorers to look for a magical land she had heard about. The land, called Punt, was said to be full of treasure and beautiful animals. It was probably part of present-day Somalia, in Africa. Hatshepsut's sailors set off to find Punt. They brought back gold, ivory, monkeys, perfumes and special oils and resins, from which the Egyptians made make up for their faces.

718 In ancient times, the best sailors of all were the Phoenicians (say 'fuh-nee-shuns').
They came from what is now Syria and Lebanon and sailed all over the Mediterranean Sea. In 600 BC, an Egyptian king, Pharaoh Necho II, asked a crew of Phoenicians to see if they could sail all the way around Africa. The trip took them three years. It was 2000 years before anyone sailed around Africa again. The Phoenicians used the stars to help them navigate (find their way).

▼ For long-distance journeys, the Phoenicians used ships with both sails and oars.

719 Pytheas was an ancient Greek who explored the icy north between 380 and 310 BC. He sailed out of the Mediterranean Sea, past Spain and Britain, and discovered a cold land he named Thule. This might have been Iceland, or part of Norway. Pytheas was the first Greek to see icebergs, the northern lights, and the Sun shining at midnight. However, when he returned to Greece, few people believed his stories.

◄ Hatshepsut stayed at home attending to her duties as queen, while her sailors set off to look for Punt.

I DON'T BELIEVE IT!

When Pytheas sailed past Scotland, he was amazed to see fish the size of boats. In fact they weren't fish at all — they were whales!

Marco Polo

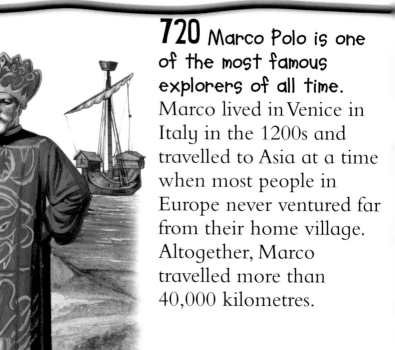

720 Marco Polo is one of the most famous explorers of all time. Marco lived in Venice in Italy in the 1200s and travelled to Asia at a time when most people in Europe never ventured far from their home village. Altogether, Marco travelled more than 40,000 kilometres.

◀ When Marco Polo visited Far Eastern lands such as China, hardly anyone in Europe had ever been there.

◀ This map shows Marco Polo's route across Asia. The journey home took three years.

Venice

CHINA

INDIA

INDIAN OCEAN

722 In China, the Polos stayed with a mighty emperor called **Kublai Khan**. He had enormous palaces, rooms full of treasure, and many wives and servants. Kublai Khan gave Marco the job of travelling around his lands to bring him news. Marco went all over China and Southeast Asia.

721 Marco Polo started exploring when he was just 17 years old. His father and uncle were merchants who went to the Far East on business. When Marco was old enough, they took him with them. In 1271, they all set off for China – a journey that took them three years.

◀ Coal, fireworks, eyeglasses, ice cream, pasta and paper money were some of the things Marco saw for the first time on his travels.

724 After 20 years away, the Polos were ready to go home. They sailed most of the way in a junk – a Chinese sailing ship. More than 600 passengers and crew died of diseases on the way, but the Polos got safely home to Venice in 1295.

725 Later, there was a war in Italy and Marco Polo was captured. He ended up sharing a prison cell with a writer, and told him his life story. The writer wrote down Marco's tales of travel to make a book called *The Travels of Marco Polo*. It became a bestseller!

723 On his travels through Asia, Marco Polo discovered all kinds of amazing inventions. He saw fireworks, coal, paper money, pasta, ice cream and eyeglasses for the first time. He was also impressed to find that the Chinese had a postage system and could post each other letters.

TRUE OR FALSE?
1. In Indonesia, Marco met human beings with tails.
2. A junk is a type of carriage.
3. Christopher Columbus loved reading Marco Polo's book.
4. Marco discovered pizza in China.

Answers:
1. FALSE In his book, Marco said men with tails existed, but he never saw them himself. Now we know it was just an old wives' tale. 2. FALSE It is a type of ship. 3. TRUE Reading Marco Polo's book inspired Columbus to become an explorer. 4. FALSE He discovered pasta, not pizza.

Ibn Battuta

726 Ibn Battuta became an explorer because of a dream. Battuta was visiting Mecca, the Muslim holy city, in 1325. There he dreamed that a giant bird picked him up and carried him away. Battuta thought the dream was a message from God, telling him to go exploring. Since he was a Muslim, he decided to visit every Muslim country in the world.

727 Ibn Battuta set off on his travels, and kept going for nearly 30 years! He visited more than 40 countries, including present-day Kenya, Iran, Turkey, India and China. Just as he had planned, he visited every Muslim land that existed at the time. Altogether, he travelled more than 120,000 kilometres.

▶ India's Sultan, Muhammad Tughluq, was violent and cruel.

728 Ibn Battuta stayed in India for seven years, working for the Sultan. Battuta's job was to be a judge, deciding whether people charged with crimes were innocent or guilty. Battuta was afraid of the Sultan, who was cruel. If anyone disagreed with him, he would have them boiled, beheaded or skinned alive. Once, he nearly beheaded Battuta for being friends with a man he didn't like.

▼ Ibn Battuta's travels began after he dreamt of setting off to the East, carried by a giant bird.

730 Ibn Battuta was lucky to finish his travels alive. During his journey, Battuta was attacked by robbers in India, kept prisoner in the Maldives, chased by pirates in Sri Lanka and shipwrecked several times. At the end of his journey, he saw people suffering from the Black Death, a terrible and deadly disease. Fortunately Battuta managed to avoid catching it.

729 At last, Ibn Battuta went home to Morocco, his own country. When the Sultan heard about his adventures, he asked Battuta to write them all down for him. Battuta didn't have to do the writing himself, though. Instead, he told his story to a scribe (writer) who wrote it all down for him. The finished book was called the *Rihala*, meaning the travels.

I DON'T BELIEVE IT!

In many of the places he visited, Ibn Battuta got married. He had several wives and children in different parts of the world.

Chinese explorers

▲ The Silk Road reached across Asia, from Europe to China.

731 **Some of the greatest ever explorers came from China.** The first was a soldier, Zhang Qian, who lived around 114 BC. The Chinese emporer sent him to find a tribe called the Yueh-Chih, who they hoped would help them fight their enemies, the Huns. On their journey, the Zhang Qian was captured by the Huns and put in prison for ten years. When he finally escaped and found the Yueh-Chih, they said they didn't want to help!

732 **The explorer Xuan Zang was banned from going exploring, but he went anyway.** The Chinese emperor wanted him to work in a temple but Xuan Zang wanted to go to India to learn about his religion, Buddhism. In the year 629, he sneaked out of China and followed the Silk Road to Afghanistan. Then he went south to India. Xuan Zang returned 16 years later, with a collection of Buddhist holy books and statues. The emperor was so pleased, he forgave Xuan Zang and gave him a royal welcome.

MAKE A COMPASS

On his travels, Zheng He used a compass to find his way about.

You will need:
magnet   water   large bowl
piece of wood   compass

1. Half-fill the large bowl with water.
2. Place the wood in the water with the magnet on top, making sure they do not touch the sides.
3. When the wood is still, the magnet will be pointing to the North and South Poles. You can even check the position with a real compass.

◀ A junk was a giant Chinese sailing ship, bigger than any other ships built at the time.

733 **By the 1400s, the Chinese were exploring the world.** Their best explorer was a sailor named Zheng He. Zheng He used huge Chinese junks to sail right across the Indian Ocean as far as Africa. Wherever he went, Zheng He collected all kinds of precious stones, plants and animals to take back to China to show the emperor. The present that the emperor liked most was a giraffe from East Africa.

◀ The Chinese emperor was thrilled when Zheng He presented him with a live giraffe.

734 **Zheng He's junks were the largest sailing ships on Earth.** The biggest was 130 metres long and 60 metres wide. On a typical expedition, Zheng He would take 300 ships and more than 1000 crew members, as well as doctors, map-makers, writers, blacksmiths and gardeners. The gardeners grew fruit and vegetables in pots on the decks, so that there would be plenty of food for everyone.

Sailing around Africa

▼ Spices are cheap today, but in the Middle Ages they were worth their weight in gold – at least!

Ginger

735 In Europe in the 1400s, people loved spices. They used the strong-tasting seeds and leaves to flavour food and make medicines. Nutmeg, cloves, ginger and pepper came from Asian countries such as India. The spices had to be transported on camels across Asia and Europe, which took a long time. They wanted to find a way to sail from Europe to Asia, and so make the journey easier.

Mace

Nutmeg

736 The best way to sail to Asia was around Africa. But nobody knew how. A Portuguese prince named Henry (1394–1460) started a sailing school to train sailors for the task and began sending ships around the coast of Africa. At first, the sailors were too scared to sail very far because they thought the Atlantic Ocean was too stormy and dangerous. But slowly, they sailed further and further.

I DON'T BELIEVE IT!

Sailors were afraid to sail around Africa because of a myth that said if you went too far south in the Atlantic Ocean, the sun would burn you to ashes.

◄ Henry the Navigator never went exploring himself. He just organized expeditions and paid sailors to go on them.

737 In 1488, a captain named Bartolomeu Dias sailed around the bottom of Africa into the Indian Ocean. Dias had a rough journey, so he named the southern tip of Africa The Cape of Storms. Afterwards, it was renamed The Cape of Good Hope to make sailors think it was safe.

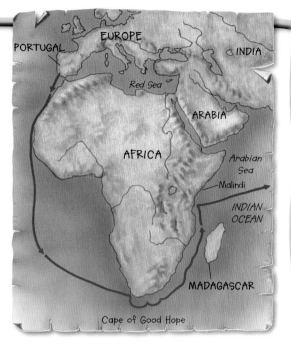

▲ Vasco da Gama sailed from Portugal, right around the southern tip of Africa and up the east coast, before crossing the Indian Ocean to India.

738 In 1497, a Portuguese sailor finally sailed around the coast of Africa. His name was Vasco da Gama. After sailing around the Cape of Good Hope, da Gama sailed up the east coast of Africa to Malindi. From there he crossed the Indian Ocean to Calicut in India. Here he hoped to buy spices, but the Rajah, Calicut's ruler, told da Gama he would have to come back with some gold. Da Gama went home empty-handed, but the king of Portugal was very happy. The sea route to Asia had been found, and many traders used it from then on.

◀ Besides being a sea captain, Vasco da Gama was a wealthy nobleman, as his grand outfit shows.

341

Discovering America

739 **Lots of people think Christopher Columbus discovered America, but he didn't.** The Vikings were the first to sail there, in around the year 1000. They found a land with lots of trees, fish and berries, and called it Vinland. They didn't stay long – they went home after getting into fights with the native Americans. After that, many people forgot that Vinland existed.

▶ The *Santa Maria* was the leader of Columbus' fleet of ships. She was about 23 metres long and had three masts and five sails.

740 **Almost 500 years later, Christopher Columbus found America – by mistake!** Columbus set sail from Spain in 1492, with three ships called the *Santa Maria*, the *Nina* and the *Pinta*. Columbus wasn't looking for a new land. Instead, he wanted to sail right around the Earth to find a new route to Asia, where he planned to buy spices. Although he was Italian, it was Queen Isabella of Spain who gave Columbus money for his trip.

741 **When Columbus found land, he was sure he'd sailed to Japan.** In fact, Columbus had found the Bahamas, which are close to American mainland.

742 **Back in Spain, no one believed Columbus' story.** They knew he couldn't have reached China in such a short time. Instead, they realized he must have found a brand new country. People called it the New World, and many more explorers set off at once to see it for themselves.

▲ Columbus and two of his men stepping ashore on the Bahamas, to be greeted by the local people.

743 **America wasn't named after Columbus.** Instead, it was named after another famous explorer, Amerigo Vespucci. In 1507, a map-maker put Amerigo's name on a map of the New World, and changed it from Amerigo to America. The name stuck.

744 **It's thanks to Columbus that Native Americans were known as Indians.** Since he thought he was in Asia, Columbus called the lands he found the West Indies, and the people he met Indians. They are still called this today – even though America is nowhere near India.

The Conquistadors

745 'Conquistador' is a Spanish word that means conqueror. The Conquistadors were Spanish soldiers and noblemen who lived in the 1500s. After Christopher Columbus discovered America in 1492, the Conquistadors set off to explore the new continent. Many of them wanted to get rich by grabbing all the land, gold and jewels they could find in America.

▲ The Aztecs often used the precious stone turquoise in their art. This mask is covered in tiny turquoise tiles.

◀ Leoncico, Balboa's dog, was always at his master's side as he trekked through the forest.

746 Vasco Nuñez de Balboa was one of the first Conquistadors. He sailed to America in 1500 to look for treasure. In 1513, Balboa trekked through the jungle with his dog, Leoncico, and an army of soldiers. He was the first European to cross America and see the Pacific Ocean on the other side. Balboa loved his dog so much, he paid him a wage like the soldiers. But like most Conquistadors, Balboa could be cruel too – he killed many local people and stole their gold.

747 Hernan Cortes was a very cunning Conquistador. In 1519, he went to what is now Mexico, to conquer the Aztec people. When he arrived at their city, Tenochtitlan, the people thought he was a god. Cortes captured Moctezuma, their king, and took over the city. Moctezuma was killed by his own people. Then, after lots of fighting, Cortes took control of the whole Aztec empire.

QUIZ

1. What was Vasco Nuñez de Balboa's dog called?

2. What did the Aztecs do to make their gods happy?

3. What did the Inca king offer Pizarro in exchange for his freedom?

Answers:
1. Leoncico 2. Made human sacrifices 3. A roomful of gold

▼ The Spanish and the Aztecs fought fierce battles, but in the end the Spanish won — mainly because they had guns, and the Aztecs didn't.

748 To conquer the Inca people of Peru, Francisco Pizarro, another explorer, played a nasty trick. In 1532, he captured Atahuallpa, the Inca leader. Atahuallpa said that if Pizarro set him free, he would give him a room filled to the ceiling with gold. Pizarro agreed. But once Atahuallpa had handed over the gold, Pizarro killed him anyway. Then he took over Cuzco, the Inca capital city. Cuzco was high in the mountains, and Pizarro didn't like it. So he started a new capital city at Lima. Today, Lima is still the capital city of Peru.

Around the world

▲ Ferdinand Magellan was a clever man who was very good at maths and science. These skills helped him on his exploration.

749 At the start of the 1500s, no one had ever sailed around the world. Portuguese explorer Ferdinand Magellan wanted to sail past South America, and across the Pacific Ocean. It is possible that, like Columbus before him, Magellan thought he could get to Asia that way, where he could buy spices. Then he could sail home past India and Africa – a round-the-world trip.

750 Magellan fell out with the king of Portugal, but the king of Spain agreed to help him. The king paid for five ships, and Magellan set off in 1519. Magellan sailed down the coast of South America until he found a way through to the Pacific Ocean. Sailing across the Pacific, many of the crew died from a disease called scurvy. It was caused by not eating enough fresh fruit and vegetables.

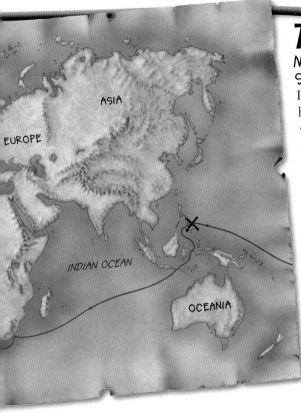

▲ Magellan set off from Spain on his round-the-world trip. X marks the spot where Magellan died, on the island of Mactan.

752 In the end, just one of Magellan's ships made it back to Spain. It picked up a cargo of spices in Indonesia and sailed home. Magellan had taken over 200 crew members with him, but less than 20 of them returned. They were the first people to have sailed all the way around the world.

753 Another 55 years went by before anyone sailed around the world again. Queen Elizabeth I asked an English privateer (a kind of pirate) named Francis Drake to try a round-the-world trip in 1577. He made money on the way by robbing Spanish ships (the Queen said he could!). After his three-year voyage, Drake returned to England. Queen Elizabeth gave him a huge reward of £10,000.

751 Magellan made it across the Pacific – but then disaster struck. After landing in the Philippines in 1521, Magellan made friends with the king of the island of Cebu. The king was fighting a war and he wanted Magellan to help him. Magellan and some of his crew went into battle, and Magellan was killed. The rest of the crew took two of the ships and escaped.

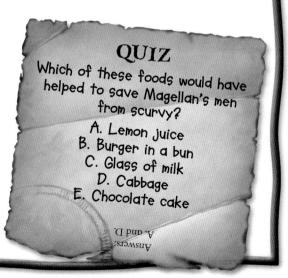

QUIZ
Which of these foods would have helped to save Magellan's men from scurvy?
A. Lemon juice
B. Burger in a bun
C. Glass of milk
D. Cabbage
E. Chocolate cake

Answers:
A. and D.

347

Captain Cook

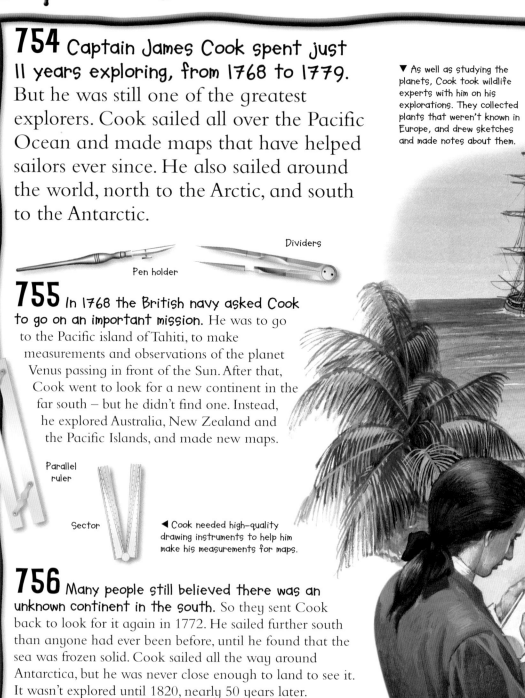

754 Captain James Cook spent just 11 years exploring, from 1768 to 1779. But he was still one of the greatest explorers. Cook sailed all over the Pacific Ocean and made maps that have helped sailors ever since. He also sailed around the world, north to the Arctic, and south to the Antarctic.

▼ As well as studying the planets, Cook took wildlife experts with him on his explorations. They collected plants that weren't known in Europe, and drew sketches and made notes about them.

Dividers

Pen holder

755 In 1768 the British navy asked Cook to go on an important mission. He was to go to the Pacific island of Tahiti, to make measurements and observations of the planet Venus passing in front of the Sun. After that, Cook went to look for a new continent in the far south – but he didn't find one. Instead, he explored Australia, New Zealand and the Pacific Islands, and made new maps.

Parallel ruler

Sector

◄ Cook needed high-quality drawing instruments to help him make his measurements for maps.

756 Many people still believed there was an unknown continent in the south. So they sent Cook back to look for it again in 1772. He sailed further south than anyone had ever been before, until he found that the sea was frozen solid. Cook sailed all the way around Antarctica, but he was never close enough to land to see it. It wasn't explored until 1820, nearly 50 years later.

757 For Cook's third voyage, he headed north. He wanted to see if he could find a sea route between the Pacific Ocean and the Atlantic Ocean, across the top of Canada. After searching for it in 1778, he went to spend the winter in Hawaii. At first, the Hawaiians thought Cook was a god named Lono!

I DON'T BELIEVE IT!

Captain Cook was the first European to discover Hawaii, in 1778. He called it the Sandwich Islands.

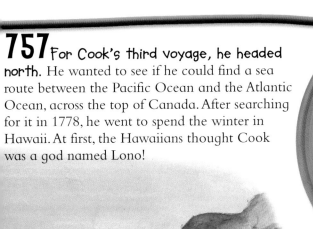

758 Cook found his way around better than any sailor before him. An inventor named John Harrison had created a new clock (called the chronometer) that could measure the time precisely, even at sea. Before that, clocks had pendulums, so they didn't work on ships. From the time that the sun went down, Cook could work out exactly how far east or west he was.

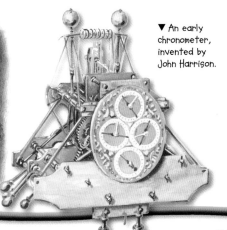

▼ An early chronometer, invented by John Harrison.

Crossing America

759 **The United States of America was created in 1776, less than 250 years ago.** At that time, there were huge parts of it that still hadn't been explored. In 1803, the third president of the USA, Thomas Jefferson, asked Meriwether Lewis to go exploring. Lewis asked his friend William Clark to go with him.

▼ After the Missouri grew too narrow for their boat, Lewis and Clark's team used canoes. Local Native American guides helped them to paddle and find their way.

760 **Lewis and Clark planned to travel all the way across America to the Pacific Ocean.** They built a special boat for sailing on rivers. The boat could be rowed, pushed along with a pole, or towed with a rope. It also had sails for catching the wind. They took a crew of about 40 men, and in May 1804, set off from the city of St Louis, sailing along the Missouri River.

▶ It's thought that Sacagawea died a few years after the Lewis and Clark expedition, aged just 25 or 26.

761 **In North Dakota, Lewis and Clark made a new friend – Sacagawea.** She was a Shoshone Native American who joined the expedition as a guide. She helped Lewis and Clark to make friends with the Native American peoples they met during their trip. She knew where to find plants that they could eat, and how to make tools. She also saved a pile of valuable papers that were about to fall into the river.

762 During the trip, Lewis and Clark were scared by bears. One day, Lewis was out hunting when a grizzly bear chased him. Lewis tried to shoot it, but he was out of bullets. The bear chased him into a river, but Lewis was in luck – the bear changed its mind and walked away.

MAKE A TOTEM POLE

You will need:
scissors   cardboard tube   paper
felt-tip pens   glue

1. Cut strips of paper long enough to wrap around the tube.
2. Draw faces, monsters and birds on the strips, then glue them around the tube.
3. Make wings from paper and glue them to the back of the tube.
4. Make a beak by cutting out a triangle, folding it in half and gluing it to the front of the tube.

764 The crew paddled in canoes along the Columbia River to the sea. They reached the Pacific Ocean in November 1805 – then turned around and trekked all the way back. When they got home, Lewis and Clark were national heroes. The president gave them money and land.

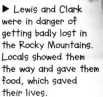

763 As they crossed the Rocky Mountains, Lewis and Clark and their men almost starved. They couldn't find any buffalo or deer to hunt and eat, so they had to eat three of their own horses. They were only saved when they met a group of Nez Perce Native Americans who gave them food.

▶ Lewis and Clark were in danger of getting badly lost in the Rocky Mountains. Locals showed them the way and gave them food, which saved their lives.

Exploring Africa

765 When Europeans began exploring Africa they found it could be deadly. In 1795, Scottish doctor Mungo Park went to explore the Niger River, in West Africa. Along the way, Park was robbed, kept prisoner, had all his clothes stolen, almost died of thirst and fell ill with a fever. However, he still went back to Africa in 1805.

Mungo Park

▶ Livingstone made many of his journeys by boat. On one occasion, his boat collided with a hippo and overturned, causing him to lose some of his equipment.

TRUE OR FALSE?

1. Victoria Falls is a giant cliff.
2. Timbuktu is in the Sahara Desert.
3. Henry Stanley found Dr Livingstone in New York.
4. David Livingstone was eaten by a lion.

Answers:
1. FALSE It's a huge waterfall.
2. TRUE 3. FALSE He found him in Tanzania, Africa.
4. FALSE A lion attacked him, but he escaped with an injured arm.

766 Dr David Livingstone was one of the most famous explorers of Africa. He went there in 1840 as a missionary, to try to teach African people to be Christians. He trekked right across the dusty Kalahari Desert with his wife and young children and discovered Lake Ngami. He was also mauled by a lion, so badly that he could never use his left arm again.

768 Dr Livingstone kept exploring and became the first European to travel all the way across Africa. On the way, he discovered a huge, beautiful waterfall on the Zambezi River. The locals called it Mosi Oa Tunya, meaning 'the smoke that thunders'. Livingstone renamed it Victoria Falls, after Britain's Queen Victoria.

769 In 1869, Dr Livingstone went missing. He had gone exploring in East Africa and no one had heard from him. Everyone thought he had died. An American writer, Henry Stanley, went to look for Livingstone. He found him in the town of Ujiji, in Tanzania. He greeted him with the words: "Dr Livingstone, I presume?"

▼ It took Henry Stanley eight months to find Dr Livingstone in Africa.

▲ At their centre, the Victoria Falls are 108 metres high.

767 French explorer René Caillié went exploring in disguise. He wanted to see the ancient city of Timbuktu in the Sahara Desert, but only Muslims were allowed in. He dressed up as an Arab trader and sneaked into the city in 1828. He was the first European to go there and return home alive.

The source of the Nile

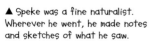
▲ Speke was a fine naturalist. Wherever he went, he made notes and sketches of what he saw.

770 In the ancient world, the Nile was an important river. It provided the Egyptians with water, and the Greeks and Romans knew about it, too. Ancient explorers tried to sail up the Nile to see where it went, but they kept getting stuck. An Egyptian named Ptolemy drew a map of the Nile, showing it flowing from a big lake in the middle of Africa.

771 In the 1800s, explorers still wanted to find the beginning, or 'source', of the Nile. In 1856, two British explorers named Richard Burton and John Speke set off to find it. They trekked across Africa to look for the big lake. Both men soon caught the disease malaria from mosquito bites. Burton became so ill he had to stop and rest.

▲ Richard Burton was an English army officer who learned to speak 29 languages.

▲ The Nile is the world's longest river. It flows across the entire length of the desert lands of Egypt.

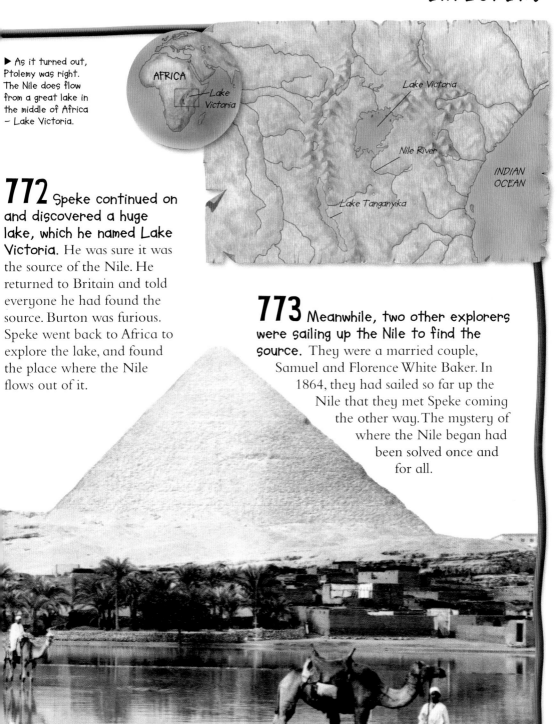

▶ As it turned out, Ptolemy was right. The Nile does flow from a great lake in the middle of Africa — Lake Victoria.

AFRICA

Lake Victoria

Lake Victoria

Nile River

INDIAN OCEAN

Lake Tanganyika

772 Speke continued on and discovered a huge lake, which he named Lake Victoria. He was sure it was the source of the Nile. He returned to Britain and told everyone he had found the source. Burton was furious. Speke went back to Africa to explore the lake, and found the place where the Nile flows out of it.

773 Meanwhile, two other explorers were sailing up the Nile to find the source. They were a married couple, Samuel and Florence White Baker. In 1864, they had sailed so far up the Nile that they met Speke coming the other way. The mystery of where the Nile began had been solved once and for all.

355

Exploring Australia

▶ The didgeridoo is a traditional musical instrument made from a hollowed out tree trunk. It is an important part of the historical culure of the aboriginal people.

774 People settled in Australia more than 50,000 years ago. The aboriginal people have lived there ever since. Just 400 years ago, in the early 1600s, sailors from Europe began to explore Australia. Britain claimed Australia for itself, and lots of British people went to live there.

775 European settlers were sure there was a huge sea in the middle of Australia. In 1844, a soldier named Charles Sturt went to look for the sea. He found that the middle of Australia was a hot, dry desert (now called the outback). His men got sunburn and scurvy, and their fingernails crumbled to dust. Sturt himself nearly went blind. But he had proved the mythical sea did not exist.

▼ Burke and Wills took more than 40 horses and camels on their expedition. The camels were from India, as they were well suited to Australia's dry climate.

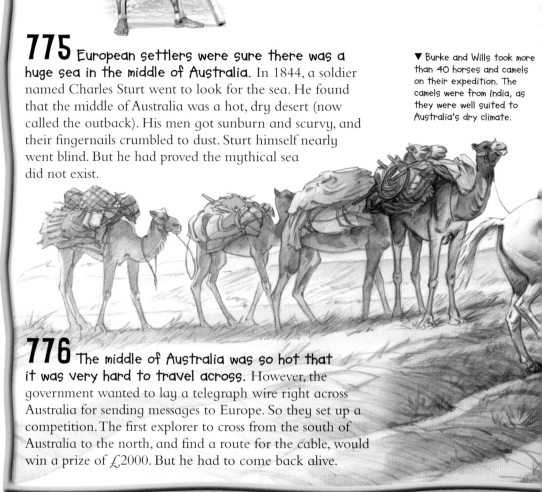

776 The middle of Australia was so hot that it was very hard to travel across. However, the government wanted to lay a telegraph wire right across Australia for sending messages to Europe. So they set up a competition. The first explorer to cross from the south of Australia to the north, and find a route for the cable, would win a prize of £2000. But he had to come back alive.

777 Irishman Robert Burke decided to try for the prize. He set off in 1860 with a team of horses and camels. Four men – Burke, William Wills, and two others – made it all the way across Australia. On the way back one man died, and they stopped to bury him. The rest of the team, waiting to meet them, gave up and went home. The three survivors were left alone in the desert, and Burke and Wills starved to death. Only one man lived – he was rescued by Aborigines.

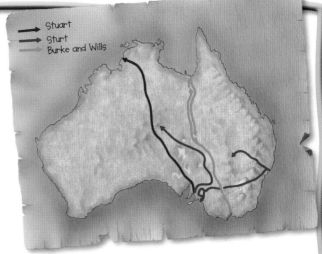

Stuart
Sturt
Burke and Wills

▲ Only Stuart's expedition was completely successful. His journey opened up the interior of Australia for settlement and farming.

778 Meanwhile, another explorer was racing Burke for the prize. John McDouall Stuart took a different route across Australia, further west than Burke's. Unlike Burke, Stuart made it back alive – but he almost died. When he came home to Adelaide to claim his prize, he was so sick he had to be carried on a stretcher.

QUIZ

The Aborigines could survive in the outback because they knew what foods to eat and where to find them. Which of these foods could Burke's men have eaten?

1. Bunya nut
2. Wichetty grub (a kind of baby insect)
3. Seaweed
4. Ostrich eggs
5. Wild honey

Answers:
1, 2 and 5. Not ostrich eggs, as ostriches are only found in Africa. Not seaweed, as it is only found in the sea.

Arctic adventures

779 **The Arctic is the land and sea around the North Pole.** Explorers first went there to search for the Northwest Passage – the sea-route leading from the Atlantic Ocean to the Pacific Ocean. They spent 400 years trying to find it, and many explorers died of cold or drowned in the Arctic Ocean.

780 **Norwegian explorer Roald Amundsen was the first to sail through the Northwest Passage.** Amundsen used a small fishing boat that made it easier to sail along shallow channels and between chunks of floating ice. But the journey still took him three years – from 1903 to 1906. Amundsen learnt a lot about surviving in the cold from local peoples he met on the way.

781 **There was still part of the Arctic where no one had been – the North Pole.** Another Norwegian explorer, Fridtjof Nansen, built a ship called the *Fram*, which was designed to get stuck in the ice without being damaged. As the ice moved, it carried the *Fram* nearer to the Pole. In 1895, Nansen almost reached the Pole – but not quite.

782 Next, an American named Robert Peary and his assistant Matthew Henson, set off for the North Pole. Peary had always wanted to be the first to get there. After two failed attempts, Peary used dogsleds and Inuit guides to help him reach the pole in the year 1909.

783 When Peary announced that he had been to the Pole, he was in for a shock. Another explorer, Frederick Cook, who had been Peary's friend, said he had got there first! The two men argued about this. Then it was revealed that Cook had lied about another expedition. After that, nobody believed he had been to the North Pole either.

▲ Peary and Henson used traditional sealskin clothes for their journey, and paid local Inuit people to make their clothes and equipment.

◄ Fridtjof Nansen's boat, the *Fram*, was specially shaped so that when it was squeezed by ice, it lifted up instead of getting crushed. This allowed the ship to move safely with the ice towards the North Pole.

I DON'T BELIEVE IT!

Some experts think Peary didn't actually reach the North Pole. If this is true then the first person at the North Pole was Wally Herbert, who walked there in 1969.

Antarctic adventures

784 Antarctica was explored less than 200 years ago. This large and mountainous continent is at the southern tip of the Earth. It is even colder than the Arctic and very dangerous. In the early 1900s, explorers such as Robert Scott and Ernest Shackleton tried to reach the South Pole and failed. In 1909, Shackleton came within 155 kilometres of the South Pole, but had to turn back.

785 In 1910, British explorer Robert Scott decided to set off for the South Pole again. He took motor sleds and ponies to carry all his supplies. He decided that when his men got near the Pole, they would pull their own sleds. In Antarctica, he also wanted to collect rock samples to study.

786 Meanwhile, Roald Amundsen was on his way to try to reach the North Pole. But when he heard that Robert Peary had already got there, he decided to race Scott to the South Pole instead. Amundsen used different methods from Scott – sleds pulled by husky dogs carried supplies.

▶ Amundsen's team used lightweight dogsleds. If a dog died or became too weak to go on, it was fed to the other dogs. This reduced the amount of food the men had to carry.

787 In 1911, both Scott and Amundsen reached Antarctica, and set off for the South Pole. Amundsen left first and got there quickly with his dogs. Scott's motor sleds broke down and his ponies died. His team trudged to the Pole, only to find Amundsen had been there first. On the way back, Scott's men got stuck in a blizzard. They ran out of food, and died of cold and hunger.

▲ When Scott's team reached the South Pole, they took photos of each other, but their faces showed how upset they were not to be there first.

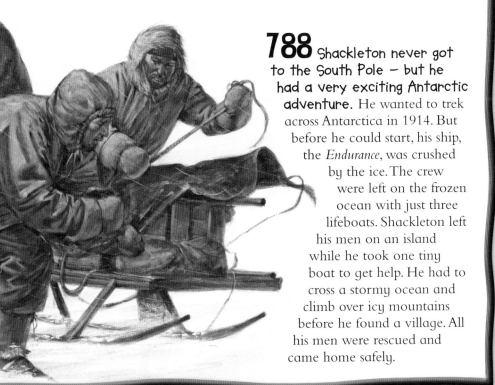

788 Shackleton never got to the South Pole — but he had a very exciting Antarctic adventure. He wanted to trek across Antarctica in 1914. But before he could start, his ship, the *Endurance*, was crushed by the ice. The crew were left on the frozen ocean with just three lifeboats. Shackleton left his men on an island while he took one tiny boat to get help. He had to cross a stormy ocean and climb over icy mountains before he found a village. All his men were rescued and came home safely.

Scientific searches

789 **Lots of great explorers were scientists.** Some went exploring to find rocks and minerals, or to study mountains or seas. Some were looking for new species (types) of plants and animals. Today, scientists explore in jungles, deserts and oceans to look for things no one else has found before.

▲ Darwin studied the many different types of finch on the Galapagos Islands.

790 Charles Darwin went on a round-the-world voyage on a ship called the *Beagle*, from 1831 to 1836. As the ship's naturalist (nature expert), it was Darwin's job to collect new species. He found all kinds of birds, plants, lizards, insects and other living things. He found many strange fossils, too. Back in England, Darwin wrote lots of important books about the natural world.

▲ Darwin made notes about his findings. He believed that plants and animals changed to suit their surroundings.

▼ The horses we know today developed gradually from smaller horse-like animals over a period of about 55 million years. Darwin called this process of gradual change evolution.

Eohippus   Mesohippus   Parahippus   Merychippus   Pliohippus   Equus

791 **Henry Bates' favourite animals were bugs.** In 1848, Bates went to the Amazon rainforest to study butterflies, beetles and other insects. He found more than 8000 species that no one had known about before. He also discovered that some harmless animals look like poisonous animals to stay safe. Today, this is called 'Batesian mimicry' (mimicry means copying).

◄ The hornet moth is an example of 'Batesian mimicry'. It is harmless but it mimics the hornet, which has a painful sting. This helps to scare predators away.

Hornet moth

Hornet

TRUE OR FALSE?

1. Henry Bates discovered more than 8000 species of insects.
2. Aimé Bonpland was an expert on local medicines.
3. Darwin's ship was called the *Basset*.
4. Mary Kingsley became caught in an animal trap.

Answers:
1. TRUE 2. FALSE Aimé Bonpland was a plant expert.
3. FALSE Darwin's ship was called the *Beagle*.
4. TRUE

792 **German scientist Alexander von Humboldt wanted to understand everything in the world.** He and his friend, French plant expert Aimé Bonpland, explored South America for five years between 1799 and 1804. They studied all kinds of things – poisonous plants, local medicines, ocean currents, rocks, rivers, mountains, and the stars at night. Later, Humboldt wrote a book, *Kosmos*, all about nature.

► Von Humboldt studied landscape extensively. The cold sea current that flows up the west coast of South America is named in his honour.

793 **Mary Kingsley loved exploring rivers in Africa.** She searched for new species, especially river fish, and studied the way of life of local rainforest people. On her travels, Kingsley fell into an animal trap full of spikes, got caught in a tornado, was cornered by an angry hippo and had a crocodile climb into her canoe.

Archaeological adventures

▲ The Nabataean people built many beautiful temples on the small plain at Petra.

794 Old ruined cities, palaces and tombs can stay hidden for centuries. Some get buried or covered with desert sand. Some are in faraway places where no one goes any more. When an explorer finds an ancient ruin, it can reveal lots of secrets about how people used to live long ago. Finding things out from ancient ruins is called archaeology.

795 Swiss explorer Johann Ludwig Burckhardt wanted to explore Africa. First he went to the Middle East to learn Arabic for his African trip. In 1812, in what is now Jordan, he discovered an amazing ruined city, carved out of red and yellow rock. It was Petra, the capital of the Nabataean people, built in the 2nd century. Burckhardt was the first European to go there.

796 The city of Troy, which you can read about in Greek myths, really existed. In 1870, German archaeologist Heinrich Schliemann travelled to Turkey to see if he could find Troy. He discovered the ruins of nine cities, one of which he thought was Troy. He found it had been destroyed and rebuilt many times. Schliemann also dug up piles of beautiful gold jewellery from the ruins.

797 In 1911, American explorer Hiram Bingham found a lost city, high on a mountain in Peru. The local people knew about it, and called it Machu Picchu, meaning 'old mountain', but the outside world had no idea it was there. Bingham wrote a book about his discovery, and today, half a million tourists visit it every year.

◀ Schliemann's wife, Sophia, wearing some of the jewels found in the ruins uncovered by her husband.

▲ The cave paintings at Lascaux depict animals such as bison, deer and horses.

MAKE A CAVE PAINTING

You will need:
paper (rough beige paper looks best)
red and black paint   twigs
To make your painting look like real Lascaux cave art, use a twig dipped in paint to draw stick figures and animals such as cows, deer and cats. You can also try making patterns of spots using your fingertips.

798 Four teenagers exploring a cave stumbled upon some of the world's most important cave paintings. The cave was in Lascaux, France, and the four boys found it in 1940 after a tree fell down, leaving a hole in the ground. Inside were passages leading to several rooms. The walls were covered with paintings of wild animals and humans who had lived 17,000 years ago.

The highest mountains

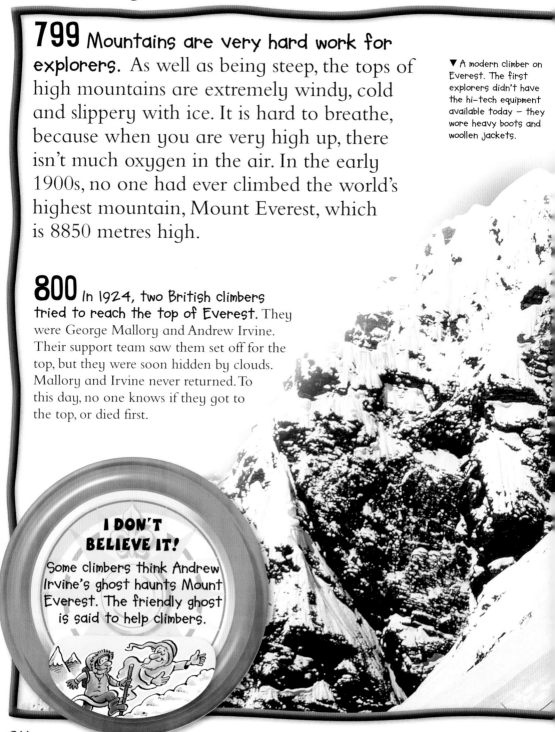

799 Mountains are very hard work for explorers. As well as being steep, the tops of high mountains are extremely windy, cold and slippery with ice. It is hard to breathe, because when you are very high up, there isn't much oxygen in the air. In the early 1900s, no one had ever climbed the world's highest mountain, Mount Everest, which is 8850 metres high.

▼ A modern climber on Everest. The first explorers didn't have the hi-tech equipment available today – they wore heavy boots and woollen jackets.

800 In 1924, two British climbers tried to reach the top of Everest. They were George Mallory and Andrew Irvine. Their support team saw them set off for the top, but they were soon hidden by clouds. Mallory and Irvine never returned. To this day, no one knows if they got to the top, or died first.

I DON'T BELIEVE IT!

Some climbers think Andrew Irvine's ghost haunts Mount Everest. The friendly ghost is said to help climbers.

801 In the 1950s, many countries were trying to send climbers to the top of Everest. A Swiss expedition nearly made it in 1952. In 1953, a British team set off. Two climbers, Evans and Bourdillon, climbed to within 90 metres of the summit, but had to turn back when an oxygen tank broke. Then, another two climbers tried. Their names were Edmund Hillary and Tenzing Norgay.

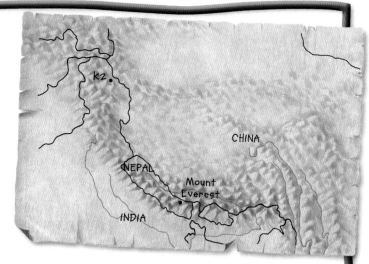

▲ Hillary and Norgay started their approach to Everest from its south side, which had been called unclimbable.

802 At 11:30 a.m. on 28 May, 1953, Tenzing and Hillary stood on top of Mount Everest. They hugged each other and took photos. They couldn't stay long, as they had to get back to their camp before their oxygen ran out. Hillary and Tenzing made it home safely, but many people have died trying to come back down Mount Everest after reaching the top.

803 There was still a mighty mountain yet to be climbed. K2, the world's second-highest mountain, is even more dangerous than Everest. People had been trying to climb it since 1902, and many had died. At last, in 1954, an Italian team succeeded. Lino Lacedelli and Achille Compagnoni were chosen to go to the top. Their oxygen ran out, but they kept going and reached the summit.

Under the sea

804 In 1872, a ship set out to explore a new world — the bottom of the sea. But the HMS *Challenger* wasn't a submarine. It measured the seabed, using ropes to find out the depth of the ocean. On its round-the-world voyage, *Challenger*'s crew also found many new species of sea creatures.

▲▶ HMS *Challenger* and some of the equipment her crew used to measure the shape and depth of the seabed all around the world.

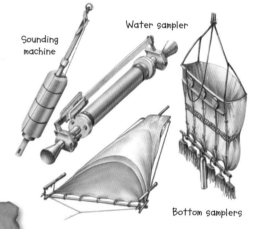

Sounding machine

Water sampler

Bottom samplers

805 Lots of people still wanted to explore the seabed themselves. In 1928, an engineer, Otis Barton, and a wildlife professor, William Beebe, built the bathysphere, a round steel ball that could be lowered into the sea. In 1934, Beebe and Barton climbed inside and dived 923 metres down into the Atlantic Ocean.

806 Another inventor, Auguste Piccard, invented a craft called the bathyscaphe. It wasn't lowered from a ship, but could travel about by itself. In 1960, a bathyscaphe named *Trieste* took two passengers to the deepest part of the sea, Challenger Deep, in the Pacific Ocean. It is more than 10,900 metres deep.

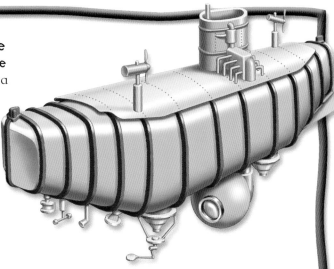

▼ Chimney-shaped hydrothermal vents surrounded by giant tubeworms, which can grow more than one metre long.

▲ The *Trieste*'s two passengers crouched inside the round part that you can see hanging below the main section.

807 In 1977, scientists discovered strange chimneys on the seabed and named them hydrothermal vents. Hot water from inside the Earth flowed out of these vents. The hot water contained minerals that living things could feed on. All around the vents were weird sea creatures that no one had ever seen before, such as giant tubeworms and giant clams.

808 The seas and oceans are so big, that parts of the undersea world are still unknown. There could be all kinds of strange sea caves and underwater objects we haven't found. Scientists think there could also be many new sea creatures, such as giant squid, sharks and whales, still waiting to be discovered.

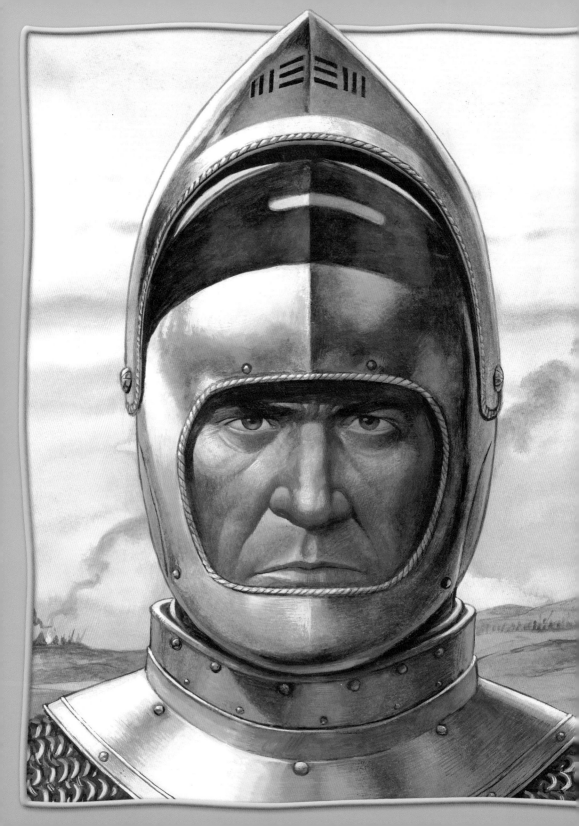

Arms and Armour

Be as brave as a knight and get to
grips with all sorts of weapons.

Shields • Mail armour • Crossbows • Hoplites
Barbarians • Roman legions • Knights • Archers
Chinese troops • Indian soldiers • Swords • Arrows
Guns • Boomerangs • Spears

Weapons of war

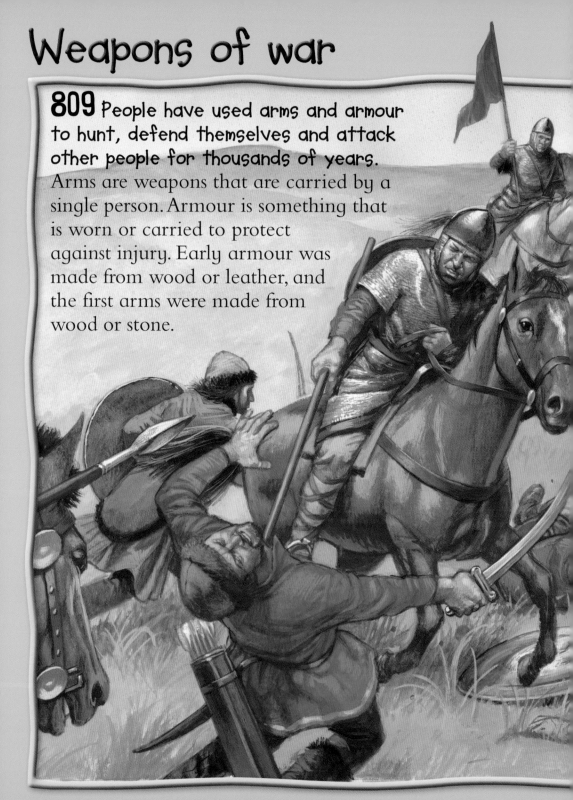

809 People have used arms and armour to hunt, defend themselves and attack other people for thousands of years. Arms are weapons that are carried by a single person. Armour is something that is worn or carried to protect against injury. Early armour was made from wood or leather, and the first arms were made from wood or stone.

▼ At the battle of Lechfeld in AD 955 the Germans crushed the much larger army of Magyars. The Germans succeeded because they were wearing suits of mail armour and carrying new weapons.

The first arms

810 **Some of the first arms were made from stone.** The earliest humans lived hundreds of thousands of years ago. Archaeologists (scientists who study the remains of ancient humans) have found weapons made of sharpened stone that were created by these ancient people.

▲ This handaxe is made from a single piece of stone. It was held in the hand and used with a chopping motion.

811 **Early weapons were used for both hunting and fighting.** Archaeologists have found bones from cattle, deer and mammoths, and discovered that these animals were hunted and killed by ancient people using stone weapons.

▶ Around 75,000 years ago, spears were made from a stone point, which was attached to a wooden handle with leather straps.

812 **The first warriors did not use armour.** It is thought that early tribes of people fought each other to get control of the best hunting grounds or sources of water. These men may not have used armour, relying instead on dodging out of the way of enemy weapons.

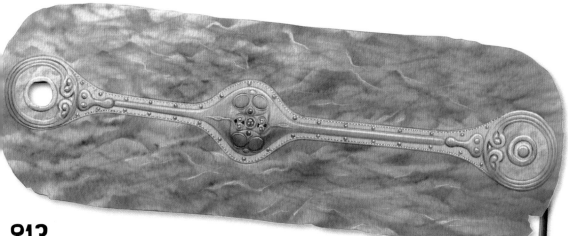

813 Shields were an early form of defence. A thrust from a spear could be stopped by holding a piece of wood in the way. People soon began to produce shields made of flat pieces of wood with a handle on the back. Over the years, shields came to be produced in many different shapes, and from a wide range of materials including metal, wood and leather.

▲ By about 300 BC, the Celts of Europe were producing beautiful shields decorated with bronze and colourful enamel. Some, like this one found in London, may have been used in ceremonies.

▶ Flint is a hard stone that can be chipped and flaked into a wide variety of shapes to produce different types of weapons, such as these points or tips for arrows.

814 Spears were the first effective weapons. Many early spears consisted of a stone point mounted on the end of a wooden pole. With a spear, a man could reach his enemy while still out of reach of the opponent's hand-held weapons. The earliest known spears are 400,000 years old, and were found in Germany.

I DON'T BELIEVE IT!

The oldest signs of warfare come from Krapina, Croatia. Human bones over 120,000 years old have been found there that show marks caused by stone spearheads.

Ancient civilizations

815 **Early Egyptians may have used their hair as armour.** Some ancient Egyptians grew their hair very long, then plaited it thickly and wrapped it around their heads when going into battle. It is thought that this may have helped protect their heads.

▲ The Egyptian pharaoh Tutankhamun is shown firing a bow while riding in a chariot to attack the enemies of Egypt.

816 Some Egyptian soldiers had shields that were as big as themselves. Around 1800 BC, soldiers carried shields that were the height of a man. They hid behind their shields as the enemy attacked, then leapt out to use their spears.

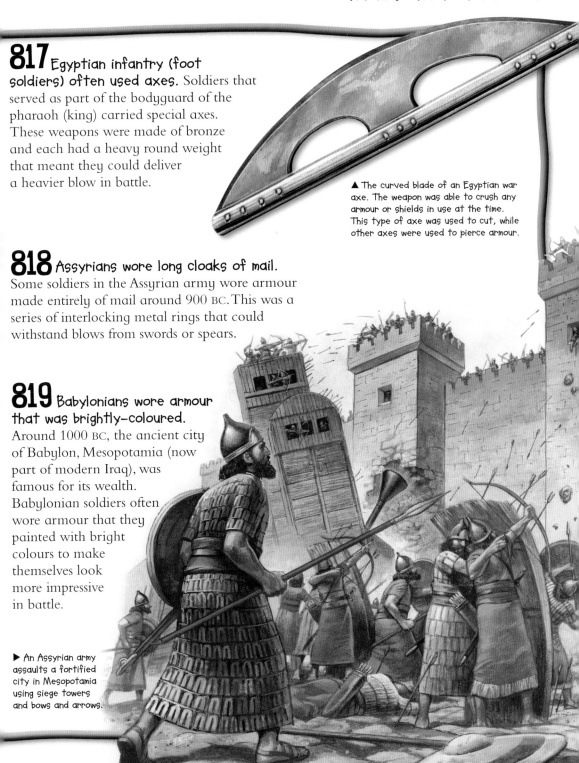

817 Egyptian infantry (foot soldiers) often used axes. Soldiers that served as part of the bodyguard of the pharaoh (king) carried special axes. These weapons were made of bronze and each had a heavy round weight that meant they could deliver a heavier blow in battle.

▲ The curved blade of an Egyptian war axe. The weapon was able to crush any armour or shields in use at the time. This type of axe was used to cut, while other axes were used to pierce armour.

818 Assyrians wore long cloaks of mail. Some soldiers in the Assyrian army wore armour made entirely of mail around 900 BC. This was a series of interlocking metal rings that could withstand blows from swords or spears.

819 Babylonians wore armour that was brightly-coloured. Around 1000 BC, the ancient city of Babylon, Mesopotamia (now part of modern Iraq), was famous for its wealth. Babylonian soldiers often wore armour that they painted with bright colours to make themselves look more impressive in battle.

▶ An Assyrian army assaults a fortified city in Mesopotamia using siege towers and bows and arrows.

Hoplites and phalanxes

820 Hoplites were armoured infantry. From about 700 BC Greek infantry (foot soldiers) were equipped with a shield, helmet, spear and sword. They were called 'hoplites' ('armoured men'). Each hoplite used his own weapons and armour.

821 A Greek who lost his shield was a coward. The shield carried by hoplites was over one metre across and made of wood and bronze. It was very heavy, and anyone trying to run away from an enemy would throw it away, so men who lost their shields in battle were often accused of cowardice.

822 Hoplites fought in formations called phalanxes. When going into battle, hoplites stood shoulder to shoulder so that their shields overlapped, and pointed their spears forwards over the shields. A phalanx was made up of six or more ranks of hoplites, one behind the other.

▶ The success of Greek soldiers in battle depended on them keeping tightly in formation so that enemy soldiers could not get past the line of shields.

I DON'T BELIEVE IT!

Spartan hoplites were so tough that they reckoned they could win any battle, even if they were outnumbered by as many as five to one!

378

823 **Greek spears had a 'lizard stabber'.** Hoplite spears had a bronze spike at the bottom end. This was used to stick the spear upright into the ground and was called a 'sauroter', meaning 'lizard stabber'.

824 **The best helmets were made from a single sheet of metal.** Skilled metalworkers in the Greek city of Corinth invented a way to make a helmet by beating a single sheet of bronze into shape. This produced a helmet that was much stronger than one made of several pieces of metal. The helmets were called 'Corinthian'.

Roman legions

▲ A Roman legion marches out of a border fortress supervised by the legate, who commands the legion.

825 **Armoured infantry formed legions.** The main fighting formation of the Roman army was the legion. Most were equipped with body armour, a helmet, a large rectangular shield, a sword and a throwing spear.

826 Roman armour was made of metal strips. At the height of the Roman Empire, around AD 50 to AD 250, legionaries wore armour called *lorica segmentata*. It was made up of strips of metal that were bent to fit the body, and held together by straps and buckles.

▶ The armour of a legionary was made up of several pieces, each of which could be replaced if it was damaged.

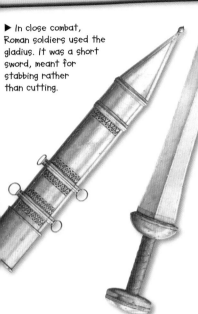

▶ In close combat, Roman soldiers used the gladius. It was a short sword, meant for stabbing rather than cutting.

829 Roman swords were copied from the Spanish. After 200 BC, Roman soldiers carried swords with straight blades and sharp points. They were copied from swords used by Spanish soldiers who had defeated the Romans in battle.

▶ An auxiliary soldier wearing a short mail tunic and helmet, and carrying an oval shield. He has a gladius and javelin as weapons.

827 Roman auxiliaries wore cheaper armour. Every Roman legion included soldiers called auxiliaries (soldiers from places other than Rome). These units had to provide their own armour, often wearing tunics covered with mail or scale armour, which was made up of lots of small metal plates.

828 Roman shields could form a 'tortoise'. One tactic used by the Romans was called the 'testudo', or 'tortoise'. Soldiers formed short lines close together, holding their shields so they interlocked on all sides and overhead, just like the shell of a tortoise. In this formation they could advance on an enemy, safe from spears or arrows.

The fall of Rome

830 Roman infantry later abandoned armour. By around AD 350, Roman legions preferred to fight by moving quickly around the battlefield. They stopped wearing heavy armour and relied upon large shields and metal helmets for protection.

831 Later Roman armies also used mercenary archers. Roman commanders found that archers were useful for attacking barbarian tribesmen. Few Romans were skilled at archery, so the Romans hired soldiers from other countries (mercenaries) to fight as archers in the Roman army.

832 Roman shields were brightly coloured. Each unit in the late Roman army had its own design of shield. Some were decorated with pictures of eagles, scorpions or dolphins, while others had lightning bolts or spirals.

◄ Late Roman shields were brightly decorated with impressive designs, but were also very important as a form of defence in battle.

833 The eagle was a sacred standard.

Each Roman legion had an eagle standard, the *aquila* – a bronze eagle covered in gold leaf mounted on top of a pole about 3 metres long. The *aquila* was thought to be sacred, and it was a great humiliation if it was captured by the enemy.

▼ By about AD 350, Roman armies had large numbers of cavalry that were used to fight fast-moving campaigns.

▶ A Roman *aquilifer* (standard bearer) carrying an eagle standard. Units of cavalry and auxiliaries carried standards of other animals instead of an eagle.

834 Later Roman cavalry had enormous shields.

One later group of Roman mounted soldiers was the *scutati*. These men wore coats of mail, and carried enormous shields with which they were expected to defend themselves and their horses. They would gallop towards the enemy army, throw javelins and then ride away before the enemy could strike back.

I DON'T BELIEVE IT!

Alaric the Goth and his men looted Rome in AD 410. Alaric was famously known to carry a sword with a handle made of solid gold.

The Barbarians

835 Celts used chariots to intimidate the enemy. Battles between rival Celtic tribes often began with famous warriors riding in chariots and performing tricks to show how skilled they were.

836 The Huns were lightly equipped. Around the year AD 370 the Huns swept into Europe from Asia. They fought on horseback with bows and spears, but wore no armour. They moved quickly, and showed no mercy.

837 The Dacian falx was a terrible weapon. The Dacians lived in what is now Romania around AD 400–600 and fought mostly on foot. Some Dacian warriors carried a long, curved sword with a broad blade that was called a falx. This weapon was so sharp and heavy, it could slice a person in half.

▶ The speed and accuracy of mounted Hun archers terrified the Romans.

838 The Franks were named after their favourite weapon. One tribe of Germans who lived around AD 300–600 were famous for using small throwing axes. These weapons had a short haft and a small, square-shaped head and were called 'francisca'. The men who used them became known as Franks, and soon the entire tribe took the name. They later gave the name to the country France.

◀ A Dacian warrior carrying a falx. Dacians were a people who lived outside the Roman Empire and often fought the Romans.

▼ A helmet belonging to an Anglo-Saxon king who ruled in East Anglia, England, about AD 625. It was made of iron and decorated with gold and silver.

839 Many barbarians wore armour decorated with gold, silver and precious stones. 'Barbarian' was the Roman name for uncivilized peoples outside the Roman Empire. They loved to show how rich they were, and did this to emphasise their status within their tribe.

The Heavenly Kingdom

840 Chinese troops wore armour made of dozens of metal plates. The plates were about 8 centimetres by 6 centimetres, and were sewn onto a leather garment or held together by leather thongs. Around 221 BC the various Chinese states were united. The Chinese believed this unity was the basis of their power and wealth.

841 Silk shirts helped protect against arrows. Many Chinese soldiers wore silk shirts under their armour. If an arrow pierced the armour it would drag the silk shirt into the wound without tearing it. By gently pulling on the shirt, the arrow could be extracted cleanly.

▼ A patrol of Chinese soldiers guarding the Great Wall around AD 200.

842 Crossbows were first used in China.

They were more powerful than the bows used by nomadic tribesmen living north of China, so they were often used by troops manning the northern frontier. Crossbows consist of a short, powerful bow mounted on a wooden shaft and operated by a trigger.

843 Infantry used sharp weapons mounted on spears.

Chinese infantry often carried spears around 2 metres in length. Often an axe-like chopping weapon, a slicing blade or a side spike replaced the spearhead. These weapons allowed the infantry to attack their enemies with a variety of actions.

844 Chinese cavalry were heavily armed.

When patrolling border regions, the Chinese cavalry operated in large formations that could defeat any tribal force causing trouble. The men were equipped with iron helmets and body armour, together with wooden shields and long lances tipped with iron.

QUIZ

1. In what year was China first united?
2. What did Chinese soldiers wear as protection against arrows?
3. Did the nomadic tribesmen live north or south of China?

Answers:
1. 221 BC 2. Silk shirts
3. North of China

The Dark Ages

845 The Dark Ages followed the fall of Rome in AD 410. Barbarian peoples took over the Western Roman Empire, and ancient culture and skills were lost. The Eastern Roman Empire lost power and lands to barbarians, but survived to become the Byzantine Empire. The Byzantines continued to use Roman-style arms and armour.

▲ English warriors patrol the great dyke built by King Offa of Mercia to define the border with Wales in AD 784.

846 Ordinary Englishmen did not wear armour. Britain was invaded and settled by Germanic tribes from around AD 450, and by around AD 700 they ruled most of the island. Only the richest Englishmen wore body armour. Most went into battle armed with a spear and sword, and carrying a round shield and a helmet as armour.

847 Berserkers wore animal skins instead of armour. Some Viking warriors were known as 'berserkers', meaning 'bear-shirts', from their habit of wearing bear or wolf skins in battle.

◄ A Viking berserker attacks dressed in a bear skin. These warriors would work themselves into a terrible rage before battle, and seemed to ignore all danger.

848 The battleaxe was a terrible weapon. Many Scandinavian peoples used a battleaxe that had a handle up to 2 metres long and a blade more than 30 centimetres across. It was used with both hands. In the hands of an expert, it could kill a horse and rider with a single blow.

◀ A Viking raiding party wielding battleaxes attacks a group of Englishmen.

849 Knights ruled the battlefield. In AD 955 a small army of German knights destroyed the larger Magyar cavalry at the Battle of Lechfeld, in Germany. Knights (mounted men in armour carrying a spear and sword) were recognized as the most effective type of soldier.

Early knights

850 **The first knights wore mail armour.** Around the year 1000, most body armour in Europe was made of mail. This was flexible to wear and could stop a sword blow with ease. Such armour was expensive to make so only richer men could afford to wear it.

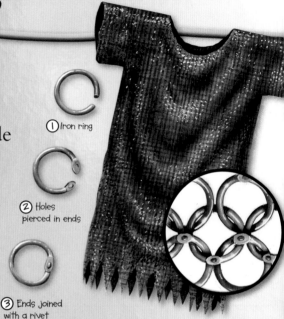

① Iron ring

② Holes pierced in ends

③ Ends joined with a rivet

▲ Mail armour was made by linking together hundreds of small iron rings. The rings could be linked in a number of different ways, just like knitting a jumper.

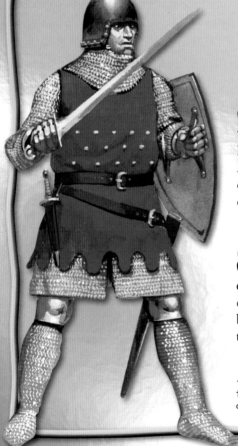

851 **Shields were decorated to identify their owners.** From about 1150, knights wore helmets that covered their faces for extra protection. Around the same time, they began to paint heraldic designs (coats of arms) on their shields so that they could recognize each other in battle.

852 **Early knights sometimes used leather armour.** Mail armour was effective, but heavy and expensive, so some knights wore armour made of boiled, hardened leather. This was lighter and easier to wear, and was still some defence against attack.

◀ A knight in about 1100. He wears a shirt and trousers made of mail and a helmet shaped from a sheet of steel. His shield is made of wood.

853 **Plate armour gave better protection than mail.** By about 1300, new types of arrows and swords had developed to pierce mail armour. This led to the development of plate armour, made of sheets of steel shaped to fit the body, which arrows and swords could not easily penetrate.

854 **The mace could smash armour to pieces.** The most effective of the crushing weapons developed to destroy plate armour, the mace had a big metal head on a long shaft. A blow from a mace crushed plate armour, breaking the bones of the person wearing it.

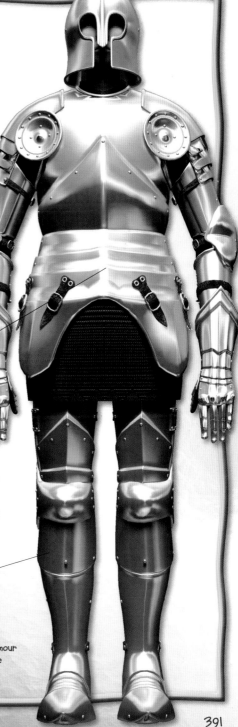

The armour around the stomach and groin had to be flexible enough to allow bending and twisting movements

The most complicated section of plate armour was the gauntlet that covered the hands. It might contain 30 pieces of metal

The legs and feet were protected by armour that covered the limbs entirely

▶ A suit of plate armour made in Europe in the early 14th century.

QUIZ

1. Why did knights paint coats of arms on their shields?

2. How was leather armour treated to make it tough?

3. Which was the most effective crushing weapon?

Answers:
1. So that they could recognize each other in battle 2. It was boiled 3. The mace

Archers and peasants

855 Infantry were usually poorly armed. Around 1000 years ago, ordinary farmers or craftsmen would turn out to protect their homes against an enemy army. Such men could not afford armour, and usually carried just a spear with a large knife or an axe. They usually guarded castles and towns.

▼ A Welsh spearman in about 1350. He carries a spear and sword, but has no armour at all.

◄ An English archer in about 1400. He wears a metal helmet and has quilted body armour.

856 The longbow was a deadly weapon. From about 1320 the English included thousands of archers in their armies. The archers were trained to shoot up to eight arrows each minute, producing a deadly rain of arrows that could slaughter an enemy force at a distance.

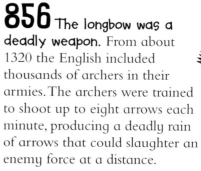

857 Some weapons were based on farming tools.

Many soldiers used weapons that were simply specialized forms of farming tools. The bill was based on a hedge-trimmer but could be used to pull a knight from his horse, and then smash through his plate armour.

▲ The heads of an English bill (left) and Dutch godendag (right). Both were pole weapons used by infantrymen.

858 Crossbows were used in some countries.

Soldiers from Italy, the Low Countries (now Belgium and the Netherlands) and some other areas of Europe preferred to use the crossbow instead of the bow. It could not shoot as quickly, but was easier to learn how to use, and was much more powerful.

859 Some foot soldiers wore armour.

Infantrymen sent to war by wealthy towns or cities were often equipped with armour. They usually formed solid formations with their long spears pointing forward, and could be highly effective in battle.

◄ A crossbowman would hide behind a large shield called a pavise while reloading his weapon.

Make a castle bookmark

You will need:
card   scissors   crayons   sticky tape

1. Draw a tower 12 centimetres tall on card and cut it out.

2. Draw the top half of a soldier holding a shield on card and cut it out.

3. Colour in the tower and soldier.

4. Place the soldier so that his body is behind the tower and his shield in front.

5. Tape the soldier's body to the back of the tower to hold it in place.

Your bookmark is ready to use!

Later knights

860 **Armoured knights were the most important troops.** Knights had the best arms and armour and were the most experienced men in any army, so they were often put in command.

861 Knights sometimes fought on foot, instead of on horseback. English knights fought on foot after about 1300. This enabled them to hold a position more securely and co-operate more effectively with other soldiers.

▶ The bascinet helmet had a visor that could be lifted so the wearer could see and breathe.

I DON'T BELIEVE IT!

At the Battle of Agincourt in France in 1415, the English killed 10,000 Frenchmen, but only about 100 Englishmen lost their lives.

862 Horse armour made of metal and leather was introduced to protect horses. By about 1300, knights began to dress their horses in various sorts of armour. Horses without armour could be killed or injured by enemy arrows or spears, leaving the knight open to attack. Men with armoured horses were put in the front rank during battle.

▶ Horse armour was shaped to fit the horse's head and neck, then was left loose to dangle down over the legs.

863 The flail was a difficult weapon to use. It consisted of a big metal ball studded with spikes and attached to a chain on a handle. It could inflict terrible injuries, but also swing back unexpectedly, so only men who practised with it for hours each day could use it properly.

▲ The flail was often used by knights who fought on foot.

864 Each man had his place in battle. Before each battle, the commander would position his men to ensure that the abilities of each were put to best use. The men with the best armour were placed where the enemy was expected to attack, while archers were positioned on the flank (left or right side) where they could shoot across the battlefield. Lightly armoured men were held in the rear, ready to chase enemy soldiers if they began to retreat.

Desert warfare

865 **Bows were made of many materials.** In the desert areas of the Middle East, soldiers used bows made from layers of animal horn, bone and sinew that were stuck tightly together and then carved into shape. These were called 'composite bows', and fired arrows with much greater force than longbows.

▲ A recurved bow was short, but powerful.

866 **The Mongols wore light armour.** A tribe from central Asia called the Mongols were led by Genghis Khan (1162–1227). Their armour was light because there was a lack of iron in Central Asia. As a result, they developed tactics based on fast-moving cavalry attacks.

867 Curved swords were known as scimitars.

Armourers working in the city of Damascus, Syria, invented a new way to make swords around the year 1100. This involved folding the steel over on itself several times while the metal was white-hot. The new type of steel was used to make curved swords that were both light in weight and incredibly sharp, called scimitars.

◄ A Saracen warrior with a scimitar and recurved bow. The Saracens wore flowing cloaks and turbans to help combat the heat of the desert.

868 Teneke armour was made up of a mail coat onto which were fixed overlapping pieces of flat metal.

These pieces were about 6 centimetres by 2 centimetres. The plates were loosely hinged so that air could pass through easily but blows from a sword could not. The armour was light, comfortable and effective, but it was also expensive.

QUIZ

1. Who led the Mongols?
2. What were curved swords known as?
3. Why did the Saracens wear cloaks and turbans?

Answers:
1. Genghis Khan 2. Scimitars
3. To help them combat the heat of the desert

869 Armour was light because of the desert heat.

The plate armour in use in Europe was not worn in the deserts of the Middle East. The plates of metal stopped air circulating around the body and were very uncomfortable to wear. Instead desert fighters in the 13th to 15th centuries wore loose robes and light pieces of armour.

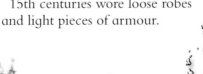

◄ A Mongol army attacks men from the city of Kiev, Ukraine. Although designed for grasslands and deserts, Mongol weaponry was effective in cold forests as well.

Indian arms

▼ An Indian soldier who wears no armour, but carries a shield and a pata sword.

▶ Indian shields often had intricate designs to make them look more impressive.

870 India had a unique tradition of making arms. Between 1650 and 1800 the vast lands south of the Himalayas, modern India, Pakistan and Bangladesh, were divided into lots of small states. Each state had its own army, and made great efforts to have impressive weapons.

871 The khanda was a sword with a long, straight blade. These swords had heavy, double-edged blades that often had handles big enough to allow them to be held in both hands. Larger khanda were slung from a belt over the shoulder so that they hung down the user's back.

872 Indian soldiers used the pata. This was an iron glove (gauntlet) that extended almost to the elbow, attached to a sword blade. It was very useful for thrusting, especially when attacking infantry from horseback, but was less effective at cutting.

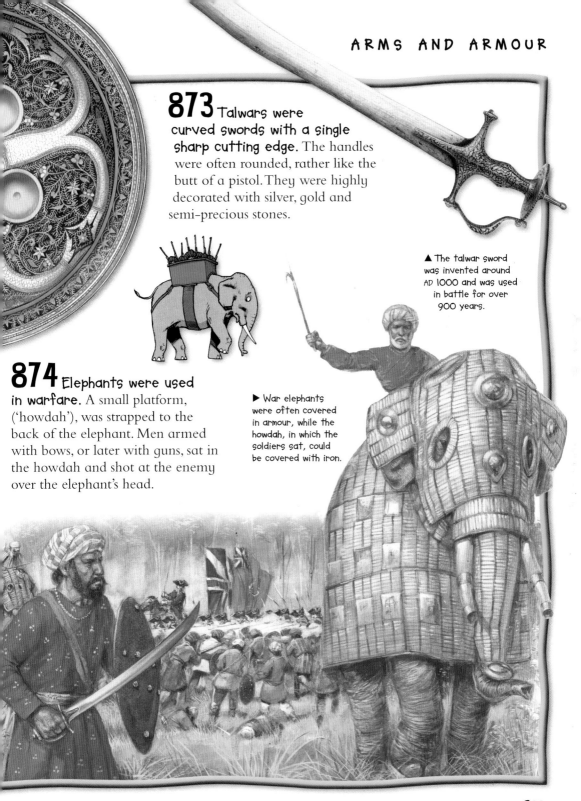

873 Talwars were curved swords with a single sharp cutting edge. The handles were often rounded, rather like the butt of a pistol. They were highly decorated with silver, gold and semi-precious stones.

▲ The talwar sword was invented around AD 1000 and was used in battle for over 900 years.

874 Elephants were used in warfare. A small platform, ('howdah'), was strapped to the back of the elephant. Men armed with bows, or later with guns, sat in the howdah and shot at the enemy over the elephant's head.

▶ War elephants were often covered in armour, while the howdah, in which the soldiers sat, could be covered with iron.

Island wars

875 **Polynesians fought without armour or shields.** The islands in the Pacific Ocean were home to people of the Polynesian culture. Before contact with Europeans around 1750, the Polynesians made their weapons from natural materials. They preferred to rely on skill and movement in battle rather than armour, though some men wore thick shirts of plaited coconut fibres as protection.

876 **Shark teeth were made into swords.** In western Polynesia, shark teeth were added to the sides of long clubs to produce a weapon called the tebutje. This was used to cut as well as smash, and was a vicious close-combat weapon.

▼ A Polynesian war canoe on its way to a raid on another island. The warriors paddling the canoe kept their weapons beside them.

▲ Boomerangs often had decorative carvings or were brightly painted.

877 The boomerang didn't always come back.

Native Australian people used spears and bows and arrows, as well as the boomerang. This heavy throwing stick was shaped so that it spun round in the air and could be thrown with accuracy. Only the lighter boomerangs, used for hunting birds, were designed to come back to the thrower.

878 War clubs were favoured weapons.

Clubs were carved from single pieces of wood, and were over one metre in length. They had wide, heavy heads that were often elaborately carved with shapes and patterns.

▶ A Maori mere, or short club. These weapons were made from very hard woods.

879 The Maori used wooden weapons.

The Polynesian people who lived in New Zealand were known as the Maori. They produced unique types of club. One type was the mere, which had a short handle and a wide curved blade that could be used for slashing at the enemy. The Maori still live in New Zealand today.

I DON'T BELIEVE IT!

In the Fiji islands warriors would often use a wooden club shaped like a pineapple to attack their victims.

African arms

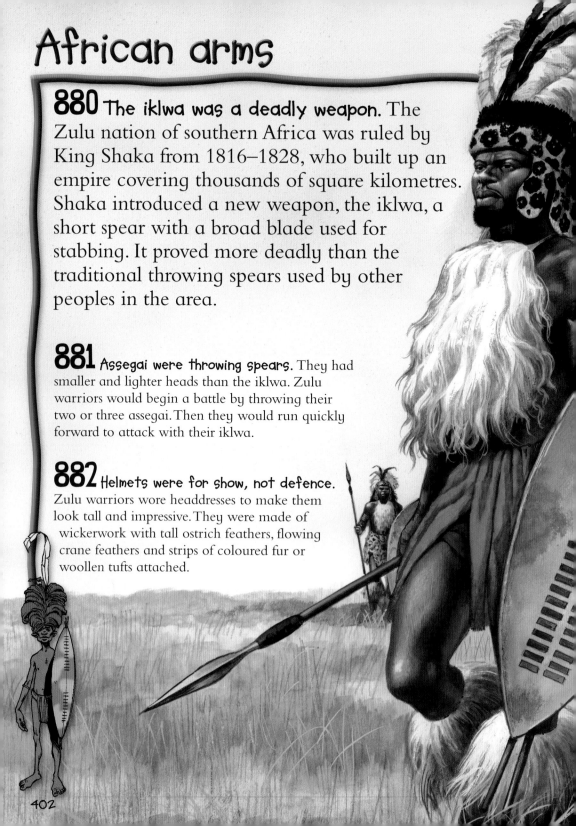

880 **The iklwa was a deadly weapon.** The Zulu nation of southern Africa was ruled by King Shaka from 1816–1828, who built up an empire covering thousands of square kilometres. Shaka introduced a new weapon, the iklwa, a short spear with a broad blade used for stabbing. It proved more deadly than the traditional throwing spears used by other peoples in the area.

881 **Assegai were throwing spears.** They had smaller and lighter heads than the iklwa. Zulu warriors would begin a battle by throwing their two or three assegai. Then they would run quickly forward to attack with their iklwa.

882 **Helmets were for show, not defence.** Zulu warriors wore headdresses to make them look tall and impressive. They were made of wickerwork with tall ostrich feathers, flowing crane feathers and strips of coloured fur or woollen tufts attached.

883 Knobkerries could crush skulls. Many Zulu warriors carried a heavy wooden club, or knobkerrie, as well as the iklwa. If the iklwa was lost, the knobkerrie could be used for close fighting.

884 Shields were made of cowhide. Zulu shields were nearly 2 metres in length, and were cut from cowhide, which was laced onto a central wooden pole with strips of leather.

Make Zulu puppets

You will need:
card   ice-lolly sticks
crayons   glue

1. Draw some Zulu warriors onto card.

2. Cut out each of the warriors and colour them in.

3. Glue an ice-lolly stick to the back of each warrior.

4. If you make enough Zulus, glue the lolly sticks to a straight piece of wood so that the warriors form a rank.

◀ A Zulu impi, or army, on the march. Boys followed the warriors carrying bedding, food and spare weapons.

The Americas

885 **In South America, spears were thrown at the start of a battle.** The Aztec people built up a large empire in what is now Mexico between 1400 and 1510. Their warriors won a series of battles against other American peoples. Each battle began with men on both sides throwing light javelins at the enemy. Then the men would charge at each other to fight in close quarters.

◀ A jaguar battle mask. In battle, some Aztec warriors wore masks and costumes of eagles, jaguars and other fierce animals.

886 Obsidian stone was razor sharp. The Aztec, Maya and other peoples of South America did not know how to make iron or bronze, so they made their weapons from natural materials. The most effective weapons were edged with slivers of obsidian, a hard, glass–like stone that has a very sharp edge when first broken.

887 **Clubs were used to knock enemies unconscious.** One of the main purposes of warfare among the Maya and Aztec people was to capture prisoners. The prisoners were then taken to temples to be sacrificed to gods such as Huitzilopochtli, the god of war, by having their hearts cut out while still beating.

888 **Shields were highly decorated.** The shields used by Aztec and Maya warriors were made of wood, and covered with brightly coloured animal skins and feathers. They often had strings of feathers or fur dangling down underneath to deflect javelins.

◄ The Maya tried to capture enemy noblemen and rulers for sacrifices to the gods.

889 **The tomahawk was a famous weapon of the North American tribes.** This was a short-handled axe with a heavy head. The first tomahawks were made with stone heads, but after Europeans reached North America, the tribes began buying steel–headed tomahawks.

▶ The native peoples of the eastern areas of North America used spears and special axes, known as tomahawks.

The end of an era

◀ A wheel-lock pistol from about 1650. The wheel-lock was the first reliable firing mechanism.

890 **The first guns could not penetrate heavy armour.** Early forms of gunpowder were not powerful enough to shoot a bullet from a hand-held gun with much force. By 1600, armourers were producing helmets and breastplates that were bulletproof.

892 Cavalry continued to wear body armour. Until 1914, cavalry engaged in fast-moving fights could not usually reload their guns once they had been fired. As a result cavalrymen often fought using swords and lances, so armour was still useful.

891 Cannons could destroy armour. Large cannons fired iron or stone balls that weighed up to 25 kilograms. They were designed to knock down stone walls, but were also used in battle. No armour could survive being hit by such a weapon.

◀ A musketeer in about 1660. Each cartridge on his belt holds a bullet and powder to fire it.

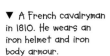

▼ A French cavalryman in 1810. He wears an iron helmet and iron body armour.

893 Infantry officers wore gorget armour. This was one of the last kinds of armour to be worn. It was a small piece of armour that fitted under the front of the helmet and protected the neck. Gorgets were often used to show the rank of the man wearing them, so they continued to be worn long after helmets were abandoned. They were used until 1914 in some countries.

▶ A musketeer in about 1770. He is using a ramrod to push the bullet and gunpowder down the barrel of a gun before firing it.

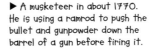

894 By 1850 most soldiers no longer wore armour. As guns became more effective, they were able to fire bullets with greater accuracy over longer distances, and with more power. By 1850 most infantry were armed with guns that could shoot through any type of armour, so most soldiers stopped wearing armour.

I DON'T BELIEVE IT!

As late as 1914 some French cavalry went to war wearing armour, despite the fact that they had to face artillery and machine guns.

Modern arms and armour

895 **The first modern use of chemical weapons was in World War I.** In April 1915, the Germans used poison gas against French soldiers. It worked by irritating the lining of the lungs and throat. Soldiers then began to wear anti-gas uniforms as protection.

▲ A British cavalryman charges in 1916. Both the man and horse wear gasmasks to protect them against poison gas.

▶ A British infantryman in 1944. He wears a steel helmet and is carrying a Sten gun – a light machine gun.

896 Modern soldiers always wear helmets. Exploding shells and rockets often throw out sharp splinters of metal called shrapnel. Soldiers take cover in trenches or holes. Metal helmets protect the head, the most likely part of the body to be hit by shrapnel.

▶ A Main Battle Tank (MBT) advances through the desert. The arrival of tanks and other armoured vehicles has transformed modern warfare.

897
Modern armoured warfare involves tanks. The armour needed to stop modern shells and rockets is too heavy for a person to carry, but it can be mounted on a vehicle, such as a tank or an armoured personnel carrier (APC). These vehicles are the key feature of a modern army, as the armoured knights were in the middle ages.

898
The best armour makes you disappear. Camouflage conceals soldiers by using colours that blend into the background of plants, sky or sand. Helmets often have a strap that can be used to attach vegetation for extra camouflage.

▼ An American soldier in Iraq. He wears bulletproof body armour as well as a helmet.

899
Bomb disposal soldiers use special armour. Designed to give protection against blast waves, the armour covers as much of the body as possible while still allowing the soldier to use his hands to defuse the bomb.

Warriors

March into battle and learn more about
the greatest fighters of all time.

Alexander the Great • Julius Caesar • Mesopotamia
William the Conqueror • Richard the Lionheart
Napoleon • Genghis Khan • Joan of Arc • Boudicca
Moctezuma • Ramses II

World of warriors

900 Warriors are people who fight in battles. A warrior is often a soldier or trained fighter who has shown great courage. Great warriors have the power to capture our imagination. Throughout history to the present day, the cry of the warrior has been heard around the world.

▼ The ancient Greeks believed that a war was fought in the 1200s BC between the Greeks and the Trojans. In the story, Hector, a Trojan warrior, killed Patroclus, a Greek hero.

The first warriors

901 **The earliest warriors lived in prehistoric times.** Archaeologists divide prehistory into three ages. First the Stone Age, when stone was used to make tools and weapons. Then the Bronze Age, when metal was first used. After this came the Iron Age, when iron took over from bronze.

▲ The first axes were made from stone, such as flint. Flint axes were shaped from large blocks, and had very sharp cutting edges.

902 **Prehistoric people used a range of weapons.** Many axes, sling stones, arrows, swords and daggers survive today, but weapons made of perishable materials, such as wood, rotted away long ago. From the weapons that have survived, we can tell that prehistoric people lived in violent times.

903 **The first warriors must have been brave.** A fighter may have had to prove his bravery before becoming a warrior. He could have been set challenges to test his courage, or have been made to perform tasks in a ceremony. Only by passing the tests would he have been accepted as a warrior by the rest of his group.

◄ ► Weapons of prehistoric warriors – a spear, an axe and a sword.

Iron sword

Stone spear

Bronze axe

QUIZ

1. What are the three ages of prehistory?
2. Which metal took over from bronze?
3. How many arrowheads were found at Crickley Hill?

Answers:
1. Stone Age, Bronze Age, Iron Age
2. Iron 3. More than 400

PREHISTORIC TIMELINE

The division of prehistory into three main ages is based on the technology of each period.

1,000,000–8500 BC	8500–7000 BC	7000–2750 BC	2750–750 BC	750–50 BC
Palaeolithic or Old Stone Age	Mesolithic or Middle Stone Age	Neolithic or New Stone Age	Bronze Age	Iron Age

904 **Prehistoric battles were fought for many reasons.** Rivalries between groups might have been a good reason to go to war, so arguments over who owned land and other property may have led to battles. If different people in a group wanted to be the leader, the only way to decide may have been to fight it out.

905 **An arrow battle was fought in prehistoric times at Crickley Hill, in Gloucestershire, England.** On top of the hill is a Neolithic (New Stone Age) camp. Archaeologists found more than 400 flint arrowheads scattered around the two entrances to the camp. It seems the camp was the site of a full-scale arrow battle, about 4500 years ago.

▶ A prehistoric hunting party equipped with bows and spears.

Warriors of Mesopotamia

906 The first armies were in Mesopotamia – a region of the Middle East where present-day Iran and Iraq are found. Here, men were first organized into fighting forces around 4500 years ago. Kings wanted to show power, and controlling an army was a way to do this. King Sargon (2334–2279 BC) was the first Mesopotamian ruler to have a full-time army.

▲ Mesopotamia was an area of the Middle East between the rivers Euphrates and Tigris.

I DON'T BELIEVE IT!

Using a composite bow, a Mesopotamian archer could fire an arrow up to about 245 metres.

907 Mesopotamian armies had hundreds of thousands of troops. They were organized into foot soldiers (infantry), horse soldiers (cavalry) and the most feared of all – charioteers. Chariots were wheeled, horse-drawn platforms used for archers to shoot from. Some battles involved hundreds of chariots.

▲ Mounted archers were a rapid strike force of Assyrian armies. Assyria was a kingdom of northern Mesopotamia.

909 **The Battle of Carchemish was fought in 605 BC.** The battle was between the Babylonians (one of the peoples of Mesopotamia) and the ancient Egyptians. The Babylonian army destroyed the Egyptian army, and the surviving Egyptian forces fled. The Babylonians gave chase, and a second battle took place near the Sea of Galilee, in Palestine. The Egyptians were defeated again, and retreated into Egypt.

910 **Mesopotamian myths tell of warrior heroes.** The greatest was Gilgamesh who, according to legend, defeated evil monsters. On a quest for immortality (eternal life), Gilgamesh was set a test to stay awake for seven nights. But he fell asleep, failing the test, and so never became immortal.

▶In the legend of Gilgamesh, the warrior killed a hideous giant called Humbaba.

908 **The Mesopotamian warrior's main weapon was the bow.** At first, bows were made from single pieces of wood, but then people discovered how to make bows from layers of wood and bone glued together. These were called composite bows, and they fired arrows further than one-piece bows.

Ramses II

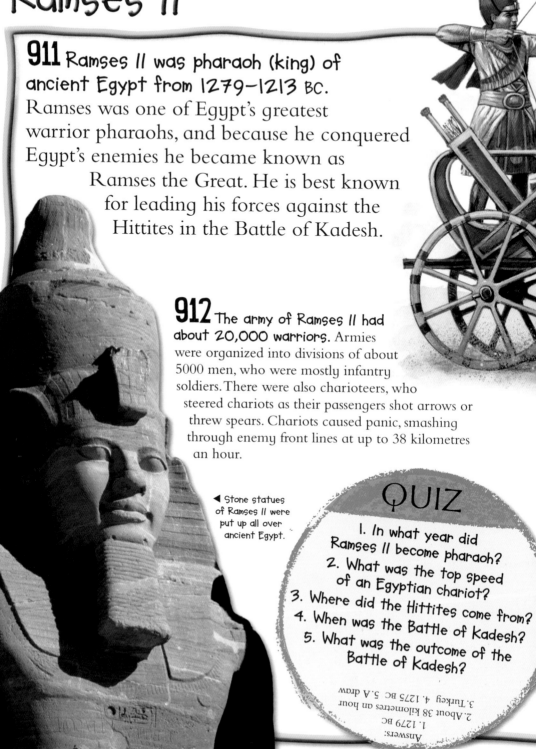

911 Ramses II was pharaoh (king) of ancient Egypt from 1279–1213 BC. Ramses was one of Egypt's greatest warrior pharaohs, and because he conquered Egypt's enemies he became known as Ramses the Great. He is best known for leading his forces against the Hittites in the Battle of Kadesh.

912 The army of Ramses II had about 20,000 warriors. Armies were organized into divisions of about 5000 men, who were mostly infantry soldiers. There were also charioteers, who steered chariots as their passengers shot arrows or threw spears. Chariots caused panic, smashing through enemy front lines at up to 38 kilometres an hour.

◄ Stone statues of Ramses II were put up all over ancient Egypt.

QUIZ

1. In what year did Ramses II become pharaoh?
2. What was the top speed of an Egyptian chariot?
3. Where did the Hittites come from?
4. When was the Battle of Kadesh?
5. What was the outcome of the Battle of Kadesh?

Answers:
1. 1279 BC
2. About 38 kilometres an hour
3. Turkey 4. 1275 BC 5. A draw

◀ Egyptian charioteers were skilled warriors and struck fear into the enemy.

913 Egyptian infantry soldiers fought with spears, axes, curved swords and daggers. Archers used powerful bows that shot arrows tipped with points of chipped stone. Instead of wearing armour, warriors protected themselves with leather or wooden shields.

914 Before Ramses II, Thutmose III waged war against Egypt's neighbours to the north-east. Thutmose was very successful, but the Hittites (a war-like people from an area that is now Turkey) also wanted to control this region, and they became Egypt's bitter enemies.

915 Ramses II fought the Hittites in 1275 BC at Kadesh (in modern-day Syria) because the Hittites were threatening to invade Egypt. It was probably the largest chariot battle ever fought, involving 5000–6000 chariots. At first, the Hittites were winning, and the Egyptians retreated. Then Ramses stopped the panic among his troops and fought back. The Hittites retreated back into the city of Kadesh. Both sides claimed they had won.

▶ The Egyptian Empire stretched to the borders of present-day Turkey.

HITTITE EMPIRE

KADESH

MEDITERRANEAN SEA

MEMPHIS · HELIOPOLIS

HERAKLEOPOLIS · ARABIA

LIBYA NILE

THEBES ·

EGYPTIAN EMPIRE

ABU SIMBEL ·

RED SEA

Warriors of ancient Greece

916 Foot soldiers formed the core of every ancient Greek army. Each of the city-states of Greece had its own army of fighting men. Rival cities went to war on many occasions, but they also came together to fight a common enemy, usually the Persians.

GREECE

OLYMPIA • CORINTH • ATHENS

IONIAN SEA

• SPARTA

▲ Ancient Greece was divided into city-states. Each one was a city and the surrounding territory.

▶ A hoplite was named after his *hoplon* (shield).

Helmet

Spear

Linen corselet

Short sword

Shield (hoplon)

Greave

917 A hoplite carried a large round shield, a long spear and a short sword. His body armour was a bronze helmet, a stiff linen corselet (tunic), and bronze greaves (leg guards). This was the standard equipment for all hoplites, regardless of their city-state.

918 Battles took place on flat, open plains. Hoplite ranks stood in a formation called a phalanx. It was six or more ranks deep, with hundreds of men in each rank. The phalanxes marched towards each other, with the first three ranks holding their spears level, pointing at the enemy.

◀ When armies met, the front soldiers thrust their spears into each other's phalanx, while the men at the back pushed their comrades forward.

919 In the city-state of Sparta all men were raised to be warriors. Training began in childhood. Children went about barefoot and were lightly dressed, even in winter. This was supposed to toughen them up. At 20 they were sent away to join other soldiers. The key to Spartan success on the battlefield was discipline.

▶ The warrior Achilles, as seen in the film *Troy* (Warner Brothers, 2004). He was one of the greatest heroes of ancient Greece.

920 Achilles was a mythological Greek warrior. As a baby, his mother took him by the heel and dipped him in the River Styx. The only part of him untouched by the water was his heel. The river's magical waters gave him great strength but his undipped heel was his weak spot. Achilles fought in the war against the Trojans. He defeated Hector, their champion fighter, and seemed unstoppable. He was only killed when an arrow struck him in the heel.

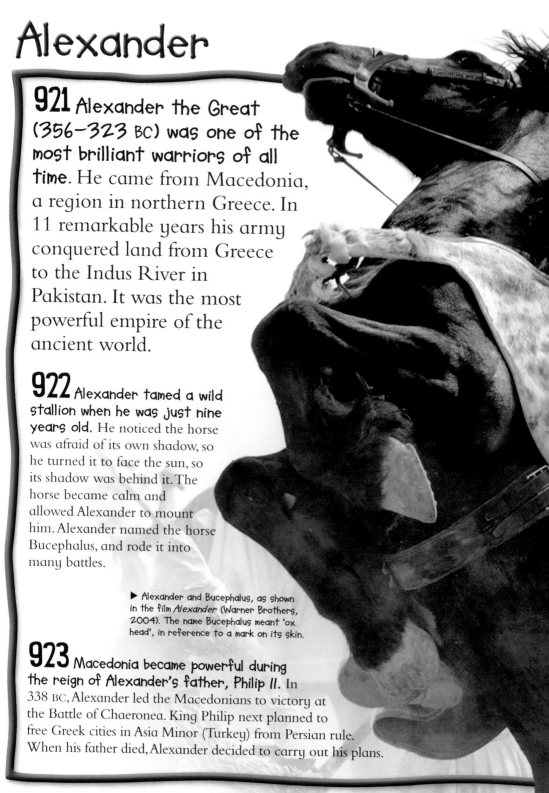

Alexander

921 Alexander the Great (356–323 BC) was one of the most brilliant warriors of all time. He came from Macedonia, a region in northern Greece. In 11 remarkable years his army conquered land from Greece to the Indus River in Pakistan. It was the most powerful empire of the ancient world.

922 Alexander tamed a wild stallion when he was just nine years old. He noticed the horse was afraid of its own shadow, so he turned it to face the sun, so its shadow was behind it. The horse became calm and allowed Alexander to mount him. Alexander named the horse Bucephalus, and rode it into many battles.

▶ Alexander and Bucephalus, as shown in the film *Alexander* (Warner Brothers, 2004). The name Bucephalus meant 'ox head', in reference to a mark on its skin.

923 Macedonia became powerful during the reign of Alexander's father, Philip II. In 338 BC, Alexander led the Macedonians to victory at the Battle of Chaeronea. King Philip next planned to free Greek cities in Asia Minor (Turkey) from Persian rule. When his father died, Alexander decided to carry out his plans.

924 Alexander raised an army of 43,000 hoplites and 5500 cavalry. Soon after entering the Persian Empire, Alexander's army defeated a Persian army at the Battle of the Granicus River (334 BC). This opened the way to the Greek cities of Asia Minor, which Alexander freed from Persian control.

▶ The Battle of the Granicus River was fought in present-day Turkey.

925 Alexander's greatest battle against the Persians was the Battle of Issus in 333 BC. His army of 35,000 troops met the army of Darius III, king of Persia, at Issus, in modern-day southern Turkey. Alexander's army was victorious, despite being outnumbered two to one. Later that year he defeated them at the Battle of Gaugamela (in present-day Iraq). Then Alexander led his army into the heart of the Persian Empire, taking city after city.

▶ A mosaic of the Battle of Issus, showing Darius III and his army.

I DON'T BELIEVE IT!

Alexander the Great marched a massive total of around 32,000 kilometres over the course of his 11-year battle campaign.

Julius Caesar

▼ A Roman warship was a long, thin galley ship. It used oarsmen to row it through the water.

926 Julius Caesar (100–44 BC) was the greatest Roman general. He was highly successful, defeating the Gauls (tribes that lived in present-day France and Belgium) and invading Britain in 55 BC and 54 BC. Caesar then led his troops into Italy and fought a civil war to rule the Roman world. He won, and was made 'dictator for life', but was stabbed to death in 44 BC.

927 As a young man, Caesar was captured by pirates. He was caught when sailing to the Mediterranean island of Rhodes. The pirates held him until a ransom was paid. Caesar vowed to hunt the pirates down. All of them were found and executed on his orders.

I DON'T BELIEVE IT!

A skeleton from Maiden Castle in Dorset, England, had a ballista bolt in its spine – evidence of a battle between Britons and Romans.

928 Caesar led the best army of the time. Roman soldiers (legionaries) were armed with a dagger, a short sword and a javelin. They wore helmets and armour made from metal and leather, and carried shields. For long-distance fighting, a *ballista* fired big arrows with iron tips. In siege warfare an *onager* hurled rocks onto enemy defences.

▶ Caesar's plan at Alesia was to starve the Gauls into surrender. It worked.

Key

1 Hilltop fort of Alesia

2 First ditch and wall traps Gauls

3 Roman camps

4 Roman look-out points

5 Second ditch and wall keeps Romans safe

▼ Roman legionaries (soldiers) preparing a ballista to fire a bolt.

929 Caesar led his army into Gaul, planning to make it part of the Roman world. For seven years, battles were fought between the Romans and the Gallic tribes. When a group of tribes (led by the Gallic chief Vercingetorix) rebelled, Caesar took action to end the revolt.

930 Vercingetorix led an army of Gauls against the Romans in 52 BC. The Romans forced the Gauls back to their hilltop fortress at Alesia, France. Caesar's troops encircled the hill with huge ditches. One kept the Gauls trapped inside, and the other protected the Romans from the Gauls' allies. Realizing that he could not win, Vercingetorix surrendered.

Boudicca

931 Boudicca was a warrior queen. She was from a Celtic tribe called the Iceni, which lived in the east of Britain. A Roman writer described Boudicca as tall, with long red hair, and wearing a large gold necklace. Boudicca is famous for leading an uprising against the Romans.

932 Boudicca's husband, King Prasutagus, died around AD 60. He left half his kingdom to the Romans and the other half to Boudicca. The Romans wanted all of it, and set about taking it by force. So during AD 60 and AD 61, Boudicca led the Iceni and other British tribes in a rebellion against the Romans.

933 Boudicca is said to have led more than 100,000 warriors against the Romans. Known as the Britons, they fought with swords and spears, and protected themselves with shields. Some rode into battle in chariots. They were brave warriors, but were not as organized as the Romans.

► Boudicca, warrior queen of the Iceni, fought the Romans in Britain.

934 Boudicca's warriors went south to fight, to the Roman towns of south-east Britain. They burned the towns of Camulodunum (Colchester), Londinium (London) and Verulamium (St Albans), killing some 70,000 civilians and destroying the Roman IXth Legion.

935 Boudicca's last battle was somewhere in the English Midlands. As many as 230,000 Britons fought a smaller Roman force. However, the Romans had better tactics and weapons, and 80,000 Britons are said to have died. The Romans won, and Boudicca died soon after, possibly by ending her own life with poison.

Ivar the Boneless

936 Ivar Ragnarsson was a Viking warrior from Scandinavia, in northern Europe. His nickname was 'Ivar the Boneless', which may have been linked to a Viking story about a man whose bones shrivelled because he had done something really bad. Ivar was a leader of the Great Army, a force of Vikings that invaded England in AD 865.

937 Ivar the Boneless was a berserker – the bravest of all Viking warriors. Berserkers worked themselves up in preparation for battle by shouting and biting the edges of their shields. They wore no armour and felt they had the strength of wild beasts. The word 'beserker' is the origin of the expression 'to go berserk'.

938 Viking warbands struck fear into the people of western and northern Europe. In November AD 866, the Viking Great Army captured the Anglo-Saxon town of York in northern England. Ivar was probably one of the warriors who helped take the town. York became the capital of the Viking kingdom in England.

▲ A figure of a berserker biting his shield.

▼ Viking warriors travelled in longships. These could be rowed inland along rivers.

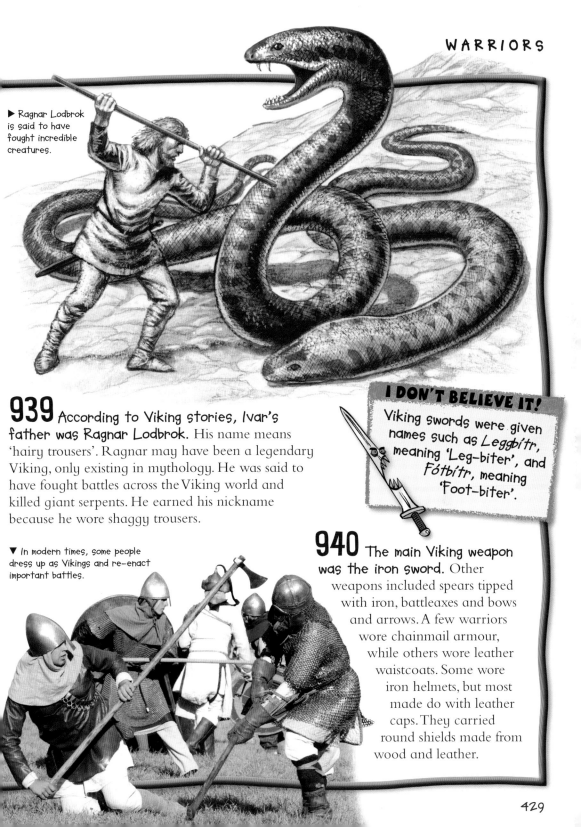

▶ Ragnar Lodbrok is said to have fought incredible creatures.

939 According to Viking stories, Ivar's father was Ragnar Lodbrok. His name means 'hairy trousers'. Ragnar may have been a legendary Viking, only existing in mythology. He was said to have fought battles across the Viking world and killed giant serpents. He earned his nickname because he wore shaggy trousers.

▼ In modern times, some people dress up as Vikings and re-enact important battles.

I DON'T BELIEVE IT!
Viking swords were given names such as *Leggbítr*, meaning 'Leg-biter', and *Fótbítr*, meaning 'Foot-biter'.

940 The main Viking weapon was the iron sword. Other weapons included spears tipped with iron, battleaxes and bows and arrows. A few warriors wore chainmail armour, while others wore leather waistcoats. Some wore iron helmets, but most made do with leather caps. They carried round shields made from wood and leather.

Norman warriors

941 In AD 911, a Viking warband led by Rollo arrived in northern France. At first the region was known as *Nordmannia* ('Northman's Land'). The Vikings settled in the area and it became known as Normandy. The warriors who came from this area were the Normans.

▲ In 1066, the Normans departed from St Valery in northern France and landed at Pevensey in southern England, ready to do battle.

942 The Normans were skilled fighters, organizers and builders. In the AD 1000s Norman armies conquered England, much of France, southern Italy and Sicily. They also took part in the Crusades to the Holy Land (Palestine).

943 A Norman army was made up of many foot soldiers. They fought with spears, axes, and bows. The cavalry was the strongest part of the army. Cavalry soldiers owned their own horses and went to war in the hope of being rewarded for their service.

944 In battle, Norman foot soldiers formed themselves into defensive shield walls or war hedges. The front ranks held their long shields close together, forming a solid barrier that protected the warriors behind it from missiles. The shield wall came apart to allow the fighters to use their weapons, and for the cavalry to charge through.

945 On 28 September 1066, William, Duke of Normandy, invaded England. He led about 750 ships across the English Channel from France. Onboard was an army of 10,000 men and 3000 horses. On 14 October 1066, the Normans defeated the English in the Battle of Hastings. Harold, the king of England, was killed, and William became the first Norman king of England. He was known as William the Conqueror.

◄ At Senlac Hill, near Hastings, Norman soldiers charged uphill to attack the English.

QUIZ

1. What area of France did the Normans come from?
2. What was the strongest part of a Norman army?
3. In what year was the Battle of Hastings?

Answers:
1. Normandy
2. The cavalry 3. 1066

Saladin

946 Saladin (1137–1193) was a Muslim warrior. He led a religious war (*jihad*) in the Middle East. Saladin (or Salah ad-Din Yuseuf) became a soldier at 14, and for many years fought against other Muslims in Egypt. By 1187, he had become the sultan (ruler) of Egypt and Syria, and decided to drive Christians out of the holy city of Jerusalem.

▲ Both sides used mounted troops in their battles.

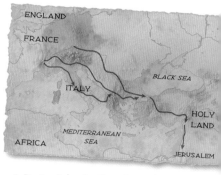

▲ Routes taken by Crusader armies as they travelled to the Holy Land.

947 The Battle of Hattin was fought in July 1187. It was a major battle between Muslims, led by Saladin, and Christians, led by Guy of Lusignan, and took place near Lake Tiberias in northern Palestine. Guy had about 20,000 troops, but Saladin's army was half as big again. Perhaps as few as 3000 Christian warriors survived the battle. It was an important victory for Saladin.

◄ Muslim warriors were lightly armoured and fought with curved swords.

948 The series of religious wars fought in the Holy Land (Palestine) between Muslims and Christians were called Crusades. Between 1096 and 1291, Christian soldiers travelled from Europe to the Holy Land, where they fought to curb the spread of Islam, save Jerusalem, and protect Christian pilgrims who went there.

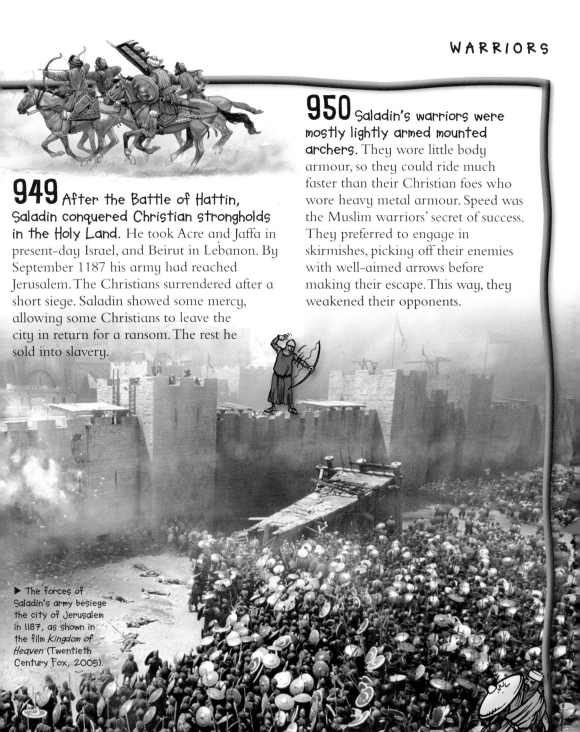

949 After the Battle of Hattin, Saladin conquered Christian strongholds in the Holy Land. He took Acre and Jaffa in present-day Israel, and Beirut in Lebanon. By September 1187 his army had reached Jerusalem. The Christians surrendered after a short siege. Saladin showed some mercy, allowing some Christians to leave the city in return for a ransom. The rest he sold into slavery.

950 Saladin's warriors were mostly lightly armed mounted archers. They wore little body armour, so they could ride much faster than their Christian foes who wore heavy metal armour. Speed was the Muslim warriors' secret of success. They preferred to engage in skirmishes, picking off their enemies with well-aimed arrows before making their escape. This way, they weakened their opponents.

▶ The forces of Saladin's army besiege the city of Jerusalem in 1187, as shown in the film *Kingdom of Heaven* (Twentieth Century Fox, 2005).

Richard the Lionheart

951 King Richard I (1157–1199) was king of England for ten years, from 1189 to 1199. He was known as *Coeur de Lion*, or Richard the Lionheart, because of his success as a military leader and warrior.

▶ King Richard I led an army of crusaders to the Holy Land.

952 Richard, the Holy Roman Emperor Frederick I (king of Germany and Italy), and King Philip II of France organized a crusade to free Jerusalem from Saladin. This was the Third Crusade, and lasted from 1189 to 1192. On reaching the Holy Land, the first action of Richard's knights was to capture the city of Acre from the Muslims. He did this in July 1191, with the use of battering rams and catapults.

953 After taking Acre, Richard marched towards Jerusalem. His progress was stopped in September 1191, when he fought Saladin at the Battle of Arsuf. The Christian and Muslim armies each had about 20,000 warriors, and although the battle was a victory for Richard, Saladin's army was able to regroup and continue with its hit-and-run skirmishes.

▼ King Richard's army besieged the city of Acre for about six weeks.

Siege tower

Trebuchet

Battering ram

Catapult

954 Richard came to within about 19 kilometres of Jerusalem. He was unable to attack it as his supplies were low and Saladin's constant skirmishes had picked off too many of his troops. The two leaders made peace, and in return for Richard agreeing to leave, Saladin allowed Christian pilgrims to visit Jerusalem, ending the Third Crusade.

955 The crusaders set sail for home, but Richard's adventures weren't over. While travelling overland from Venice, he was captured by an Austrian enemy, and handed over to Henry VI of Germany. A ransom of 150,000 silver marks (a unit of currency) was demanded for his release. After being held for over a year, the ransom was paid, and Richard returned home.

Warrior monks

956 **Crusader armies were composed of foot soldiers and mounted knights.** Among the knights were warriors who belonged to religious groups or orders. They followed strict rules, and were organized in a similar way to monks in monasteries. These 'warrior monks' were anything but peaceful.

DESIGN A SHIELD

Medieval knights carried shields made of wood and covered with coloured leather. They had pictures or patterns (coats of arms) on them so knights could recognize their friends in battle. Look for pictures of shields in books or on the Internet. Then have a go at drawing and colouring a design of your own.

957 **The Knights Hospitaller were founded in Jerusalem in 1099.** At first their role was to provide safe lodgings for Christian pilgrims to the city, and to care for the sick and wounded in their hospital. This gradually became a sizeable military force, acting as armed guards for pilgrims and crusaders. The Knights Hospitaller were also known as the Knights of St John.

▶ The symbol of the Knights Templar — two knights on one horse.

958 **The Knights Templar were founded in Jerusalem in 1119 by nine French knights.** They were called Templars because their headquarters was on the site of the Temple of Solomon. The Knights Templar were the most disciplined and bravest crusaders. They were also the richest, thanks to donations from Christians in Europe.

959 The German Teutonic Knights were founded at Acre in 1198. They were formed to protect Christian pilgrims, but took up arms against Muslims and built castles. Active in the Holy Land until the 1290s, their main work was carried out later in the Baltic region, fighting in Lithuania.

◄ Knights took part in jousting tournaments, charging at each other with lances.

960 The armoured knight was the elite warrior of medieval Europe. In childhood he was taught to ride and to use a sword and lance. As a knight, he took part in tournaments to improve his fighting skills, ready for when he went to war.

► Knights marched with colourful pennants (triangular flags).

Genghis Khan

961 Mongol warrior Genghis Khan (1162–1227) ruled with great discipline. He was born in Mongolia, and given the name Temujin. The Mongols were one of many tribes that lived on the grassy plains (steppe) of central Asia. They were horsemen who followed their herds of animals.

▲ Genghis Khan was a fearless warrior who led his Mongol troops to victory.

962 The Mongol tribes were constantly at war with each other. Temujin set about uniting the tribes, and in 1206 he became ruler (*khan*) of them all. From then on he was known as Genghis Khan, meaning 'Ruler of the Earth'. His armies conquered almost all of China. By the time he died, his empire stretched from the Black Sea to the Pacific Ocean – it was the largest empire in history.

963 Mongol warriors wore leather armour and helmets, and fired arrows from powerful bows as they rode. Soldiers also carried swords, maces, axes and sometimes short spears with hooks on their points. Mongol warriors each had a string of horses, and changed their mounts often, so as not to tire them.

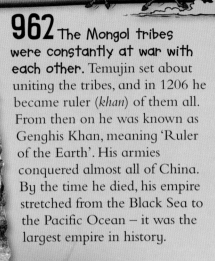

RUSSIA

BLACK SEA

MONGOLIA

CHINA

PERSIAN GULF

ARABIAN SEA

PACIFIC OCEAN

▶ The Mongol Empire covered much of Asia and beyond.

964 Mongol warriors were organized into large groups, which were divided into units of ten (an *arban*). In battle, they would pretend to flee to make their enemy give chase. When the pursuing troops became disorganized the Mongols would turn on them, closing in to trap them.

965 The Battle of the Indus River was fought in 1221, in present-day Pakistan. A Mongol army of 10,000 faced Muslim troops of 5000 on the banks of the river. The Mongols inflicted heavy losses, and only a few Muslim soldiers crossed the river to safety.

◀ Mongol cavalrymen were expert archers. Some arrows they used made whistling noises and were used to send signals.

Joan of Arc

966 Born in France, Joan of Arc (1412–1431) lived at a time when large parts of France were controlled by the English. When Joan was about 12, she believed she had a vision in which the patron saints of France commanded her to dress as a man and lead the fight to rid France of the English.

ENGLAND
LONDON
CALAIS
ENGLISH CHANNEL
HOLY ROMAN EMPIRE
PARIS
ORLÉANS
FRANCE
BORDEAUX

▲ France, showing the area controlled by the English.

▼ Joan of Arc was easy to spot on the battlefield because she wore a suit of white armour.

967 Joan lived during the Hundred Years' War. This was a series of wars between England and France that began in 1337. The wars were fought over English claims to be the rulers of France. Joan went to see France's *Dauphin* (crown prince), who was soon to become King Charles VII, and told him of her vision.

968 Charles gave Joan permission to travel to the city of Orléans with a French army. The city was under siege from the English. The army arrived in April 1429. Joan was dressed as a knight, and carried a banner. Within a week, the English retreated. From then on, Joan was known as the 'Maid of Orléans'.

969 For the next 12 months, Joan led the French in battles against the English. She won back territory for France. In May 1430, Joan was captured by the Duke of Burgundy (a French nobleman on the side of the English). She became a prisoner-of-war, and was eventually sold to the English.

▶ Saint Joan of Arc is one of the most popular saints of the Roman Catholic Church.

970 The English put Joan on trial. She was tried as a witch and a heretic (a person who goes against the teachings of the Christian church), found guilty, and sentenced to death. In May 1431, Joan was burnt at the stake in the French city of Rouen. She was declared innocent 25 years after her death, and in 1920 the Pope made her a saint.

Moctezuma

971 **The Aztecs lived in the present-day country of Mexico.** They were fierce warriors who defeated rival tribes to become the strongest group in the region. The last Aztec emperor was called Moctezuma II (*c.*1480–1520). He became leader of the Aztecs in 1502. He was a powerful and ruthless leader who was feared and admired by his people.

▲ Moctezuma was regarded as a god by the Aztec people.

972 **The Aztecs were warriors.** Every able-bodied man was expected to fight in Moctezuma's army. They were taught to use weapons as children, and at 15 they were old enough to go to war. It was considered an honour to fight for the emperor. Warriors who did well were rewarded with gifts of land and slaves.

973 **The fiercest Aztec fighters were the Eagle and Jaguar warriors.** Eagle warriors wore suits made from feathers, and the Jaguars dressed in ocelot skins. They were full-time soldiers, while most of the army were part-time soldiers who returned to regular jobs after the fighting was over.

974 Fighters fought with slings, bows and spears launched from spear-throwers. The most dangerous Aztec weapon was the war-club, the edges of which were covered with blades of razor-sharp obsidian (a glass-like stone made inside volcanoes). It could slice an enemy's head off in one blow.

975 In 1519, an army of Spaniards landed in Mexico in search of gold. When the news reached Moctezuma, he thought they were gods and sent them gifts, and when they first arrived in the Aztec capital he treated them as guests. He soon realized his mistake. Fighting between the Aztecs and the Spaniards began in May 1520. Moctezuma was killed, and the Aztec city was looted and destroyed.

▼ The Aztecs outnumbered the Spaniards, but the Spaniards had much better weapons.

Babur

976 The founder of the Mughal Empire in northern India was known as Babur (1483–1531). His real name was Zahir ud-Din Muhammad, but as he rose to power he was given the nickname Babur, meaning 'tiger'. He was a powerful Muslim leader.

▲ The Battle of Khanwa (1527) gave Babur control of northern India.

◀ The extent of the Mughal empire in India.

979 In the Battle of Panipat, Babur's warriors used gunpowder weapons called arquebuses. They were an early type of bullet-firing gun, and were the most up-to-date weapons of the time. The traditional weapons of Mughal warriors were a sword with a curved blade (*talwar*) and a mace. They wore chainmail armour and carried a small round shield (*dahl*).

977 In 1504, Babur and a group of Muslim fighters captured Kabul, in Afghanistan. He established a small kingdom there, and began making raids into northern India. In 1525, he was asked to attack Ibrahim Lodi, the sultan (ruler) of Delhi, so Babur mounted a full-scale invasion of northern India.

978 Babur and Lodi's armies met at Panipat, India, in 1526. Babur had 25,000 troops, Lodi had 40,000. Lodi struck first, but failed to break through Babur's line of 700 carts tied together. After defeating Lodi's army, Babur marched to Delhi, which became the capital of the Mughal empire.

▼▶ Weapons of Babur's Mughal warriors.

Mace

Knife

980 The largest part of Babur's army was the cavalry. He could muster tens of thousands of horsemen, who served as archers, and were his elite troops. His foot soldiers were peasants who were forced to fight. Mughal armies also made use of war elephants, which acted as firing platforms for archers and spear-throwers. Because of their height, elephants were also used as command and observation posts.

INVESTIGATE

As well as being a warrior leader, Babur was also a poet, and his interest in nature led him to create magnificent gardens. Use books and the Internet to see if you can find out anything else about the founder of the Mughal Empire.

▶ War elephants were used by Mughal and other armies in India. Some elephants wore armour.

Napoleon Bonaparte

981 **French general Napoleon Bonaparte (1769–1821) trained as a soldier from the age of ten.** At 27 he was in charge of the French army in Italy. For a short time, he ruled a large part of Europe, creating the largest empire in Europe since the time of the Romans.

◄ Napoleon Bonaparte was a military genius, and one of the world's great generals.

982 **Napoleon fought by new rules.** He marched his army at night, attacked in the rain and on Sundays, and ordered his troops to attack the enemy at their weakest point. He was young, ambitious and ruthless. In 1799 he overthrew the government of France, and became the country's new leader. In 1804 he organized his own coronation and became Emperor Napoleon.

▼ The Battle of Austerlitz. After his victory, Napoleon said to his troops: "Soldiers! I am pleased with you!"

983 **Napoleon's greatest victory was the Battle of Austerlitz.** It was fought on 2 December, 1805, in the present-day Czech Republic. Napoleon had 70,000 troops. They faced a combined army of 80,000 Russians and Austrians. The victory was a turning point for Napoleon, who sensed he could be master of all Europe.

▲ The extent of Napoleon's French Empire across Europe.

984 **In 1812, Napoleon set his sights on Russia.** He invaded with an army of half a million men, and the Russians retreated. He reached Moscow, but the Russians refused to make peace. Far from home, and with supplies running low, Napoleon had no choice but to retreat. It was a bitterly cold winter, and thousands of soldiers froze to death on the march home.

985 **In 1814, Austria, Russia, Prussia and Britain attacked France.** They reached Paris, and Napoleon was banished to the island of Elba in the Mediterranean. He escaped and returned to France to gather a new army. His last battle was at Waterloo, on 18 June, 1815. He was defeated by an army of British and Prussians and sent to the island of St Helena in the Atlantic Ocean, where he died six years later.

I DON'T BELIEVE IT!

Napoleon was supposed to be crowned by the Pope, but when his coronation took place, Napoleon crowned himself instead.

Shaka

986 The first great chief of the Zulu nation in southern Africa was a warrior chieftain called Shaka (c. 1788–1828). He organized the army into regiments and gave his soldiers better weapons. Shaka made the Zulu nation the strongest in southern Africa.

987 Before Shaka, the Zulu people were relatively peaceful. Battles were often wars of words. Shaka changed all this, bringing in stabbing spears and training his warriors to destroy their enemies. He organized campaigns against neighbouring peoples, whom the Zulu either killed or forced to surrender.

988 Zulu boys practised fighting with sticks. At 18 they joined a regiment (*iButho*). Zulu warriors would sometimes fight duels with each other, swinging *iWisa* (clubs). It was seen as a way of making them tougher. In battle, they also used stabbing spears (*iklwa*), and throwing spears (*assegais*), and protected themselves with shields of cowhide.

▲ Shaka, the Zulu warrior chieftain. In the 1820s he ruled more than 50,000 people.

989 Zulu regiments came together in a 'buffalo horns' formation. New warriors formed the horns, experienced warriors made up the chest at the centre, and older fighters formed the body at the back. When they came within range, they threw their *assegais*. At close range, they used their stabbing spears.

990 Shaka was murdered in 1828, but the Zulu fighting spirit lived on. In 1879, the Zulu army fought the British in the Battle of Isandhlwana. The British had better weapons (rifles and bayonets), but the Zulu had more men, and they won a great victory.

▼ The British army was defeated by Zulus in the Battle of Isandhlwana (1879).

QUIZ

1. What did Zulu boys practise fighting with?
2. What were Zulu clubs called?
3. What was the Zulu battle formation called?

Answers:
1. Sticks 2. iWisa 3. Buffalo horns

Crazy Horse

991 Crazy Horse (c. 1840–1877) was a Native American warrior chief. He belonged to the Oglala Sioux people and was involved in a struggle with the US Army and white settlers. Crazy Horse wanted to stop them taking the Sioux land, and this led to a series of battles. He said he was 'hostile to the white man' and that the Sioux wanted 'peace and to be left alone'.

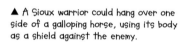
▲ A Sioux warrior could hang over one side of a galloping horse, using its body as a shield against the enemy.

◀ Crazy Horse was one of the greatest of all Native American war leaders.

992 The traditional weapons of Sioux warriors were bows, lances and knives. When they came into contact with white settlers, they began trading for rifles and pistols. However, weapons were not their most prized possessions – horses were. The Sioux used horses for hunting and for war. Their horses were small and very fast, and the Sioux were expert riders.

QUIZ

1. Which native American tribe did Crazy Horse belong to?
2. What was a Sioux warrior's most prized possession?
3. In what year was the Battle of Little Big Horn?

Answers:
1. The Sioux
2. His horse 3. 1876

994 From 1874, white settlers began moving into the Black Hills region of South Dakota, looking for gold. This was the ancestral homeland of the Sioux. The US government ordered the Sioux to leave the area, but many refused to go. Crazy Horse called for Sioux warriors to fight, and they were joined by allies from the Cheyenne and Arapaho nations.

993 As land was lost to white settlers, the Sioux began to act. Warbands of warriors began to make hit-and-run raids against US Army outposts and isolated settlements. Stagecoaches and wagon trains carrying supplies were ambushed, and telegraph wires were cut. The US Army found these tactics very difficult to fight. It was as if the Sioux were an invisible enemy.

▼ The Battle of the Little Bighorn is also known as Custer's Last Stand.

995 The US Army was sent to clear the area of Native Americans. Crazy Horse and other leaders brought more than 1000 warriors together to resist them. On 25 and 26 June, 1876, the Battle of the Little Bighorn was fought near the Little Bighorn River, Montana. A force of 700 soldiers of the US Seventh Cavalry, led by General George Custer, was wiped out. Custer and a group of his men fought to the last on a small hill.

Samurai

Come face to face with some of the finest
warriors ever to set foot on the battlefield.

Emperors • Bushido • Religion • Weapons • Castles
Rituals • Battles • Gempei War • Armies • Training
Taira Masakado • Minamoto Yoshiie • Armour
Food • Clothing • Flags • Oda Nobunaga

Warriors of Japan

996 **For hundreds of years, there was a group of warriors in Japan known as samurai.** Their name means 'someone who serves'. All samurai served a warlord (military leader) and battles were fought between armies of rival warlords. Samurai followed a set of rules called *bushido*. These rules told them how to behave, not just in battle, but in everyday life. Respected members of Japanese society, the bravest and fiercest samurai became well-known figures.

▼ Samurai armies fought at close range, on foot and on horseback. This scene shows the Battle of Kawanakajima in 1561, in the north of the main Japanese island of Honshu.

From emperor to shogun

997 Japan is an island country in the Pacific Ocean, located off the coast of mainland Asia. It is made up of four main islands (Hokkaido, Honshu, Shikoku and Kyushu) and nearly 4000 smaller ones. The islands are mountainous, with forested slopes and fast-flowing rivers. There are many active volcanoes, including the famous Mount Fuji.

◀ Jimmu, the first in a long line of emperors who ruled Japan.

Kyoto
Osaka
Nara
SHIKOKU
KYUSHU

▲ Japan is a nation of many islands that lie close together. It has had several capital cities over the years.

QUIZ

1. Which family took power away from the emperor?
2. Who was the first emperor of Japan?
3. What is the name of Japan's most famous volcano?
4. Which was the first permanent capital of Japan?

Answers:
1. The Fujiwara family
2. Jimmu 3. Mount Fuji 4. Nara

998 Japan was once ruled by emperors. Legend says that the first emperor was Jimmu, who reigned in 660 BC. Early emperors had great power. Then about AD 800 they became 'figurehead rulers'. This meant that they were still heads of state, but had little power.

HOKKAIDO

NSHU

▶ Japanese history is divided into several periods. These are often named after the most powerful family, or the site of the capital city at that time.

DATE	PERIOD	NOTABLE EVENTS
14,000–300 BC	Jomon	• Early people are hunter-gatherers and decorate clay pottery with distinctive patterns
300 BC–AD 300	Yayoi	• Farmers begin to grow rice in paddy fields
AD 300–710	Kofun	• Buddhism is introduced to Japan
AD 710–794	Nara	• Nara becomes the first permanent capital city
794–1185	Heian	• Kyoto becomes the capital city
1185–1333	Kamakura	• Battle of Dan-no-Ura • Minamoto Yoritomo becomes the first shogun
1333–1573	Muromachi	• Members of Ashikaga family become shoguns. They are finally driven out by the warlord Oda Nobunaga
1573–1603	Azuchi-Momoyama	• Oda Nobunaga is succeeded by Toyotomi Hideyoshie • Japan is reunited
1603–1868	Edo	• Japan isolates itself from the rest of the world • US Commodore Matthew Perry forces the Japanese government to open up ports for trade
1868–1912	Meiji	• Japan becomes modernized and grows to be a world power

999
In about AD 800, power was taken from the emperor. It fell into the hands of the Fujiwara clan. They were a noble family that had married into royalty, and for about 300 years they were the real rulers of Japan. However in the 1100s, the Fujiwaras lost control after a bitter war. From then on, power passed to military dictators called shoguns.

1000
Japan's first permanent capital city was Nara, on the island of Honshu. It became capital in AD 710 and the emperor lived there. In AD 794, Kyoto was made the new capital and home of the emperor. Tokyo, which was known as Edo until 1868, is now the present-day capital.

1001
Shogun means 'commander of the forces'. He was a military dictator – the person in control, with unlimited power. In 1192, Minamoto Yoritomo became the first shogun. He was known as the 'barbarian-conquering great general'.

▶ Minamoto Yoritomo, the first shogun. Shoguns controlled Japan until 1867.

Religion and ritual

1002 **Japanese society was divided between rich and poor.** A few rich families owned all the land and the poor owned none. The poorest people worked on the land, and had to pay taxes to the powerful landowners. This type of system is known as feudalism. Japan was a feudal society for hundreds of years.

▶ At the top of Japanese society was the emperor, even though he had no real power. Merchants were the lowest class.

Figurehead

Emperor

Shogun
(Political leader)

Daimyos
(Warlords)

Samurai
(Warriors)

Ronin
(Paid soldiers)

Warrior class

Peasants
(Farmers and fishermen)

90 percent of the population

Artisans
(Craftspeople)

Merchants
(Sales people)

Lowest class

▶ There are many statues of Buddha in Japan. This one is made of bronze and is 800 years old.

1003 **The two main Japanese religions are Shinto and Buddhism.** Shinto is an ancient religion in which the emperor is said to be a descendant of the Sun god. Its followers believe that spirits inhabit trees, waterfalls and other natural things. Buddhism is founded on the teachings of Siddhartha Gautama. He was called the Buddha and lived in India in the 4th or 5th century BC.

◀ Shinto priests bang drums during ceremonies. The sound is believed to attract the gods' attention.

1005 Before battle, a samurai warrior might visit a Shinto shrine.

A priest would give him a small cup of *sake* (rice wine) to drink, and the soldier would offer prayers to a god. In return for his prayers, the soldier hoped the god would protect him. Samurai had favourite gods to pray to, such as Taira Masakado (see pages 464–465). After he died, in AD 940, he was believed to have become a god.

◀ Shinto shrines were important places of worship. Samurai visited them to pray for good fortune.

1004 Ancestors were special.

If a samurai had heroes among his ancestors, he showed them great respect by displaying their names at his family altar. It was a way of keeping their memories alive, and the warrior hoped he would inherit their bravery and courage.

1006 Rituals were very important.

These were set ways of doing ordinary things. During the 1400s, samurai began to carry out the tea ceremony. This was an elaborate way of making and enjoying a cup of tea. The tea was made by carrying out steps in a precise order.

▼ Equipment used during the tea ceremony. The ritual is linked to Buddhist ideas of tranquility (calmness).

Hishaku (water ladle)

Kama (iron pot used to heat the water)

Mizusashi (container containing cold water)

Chashaku (tea scoop)

Chasen (bamboo whisk)

Chaki (dry tea leaf container)

Chawan (tea bowl, used for drinking)

The first samurai

1007 **The first samurai appeared in the AD 900s.** They were warriors who belonged to the private armies of Japan's noble families, or clans. The clans owned large amounts of land, which they needed to protect from their rivals. The best way to do that was to build up an army of soldiers in case of battle.

1008 **Samurai protected their bodies with armour.** The first samurai wore armour made from small iron or leather scales, laced together with silk or leather cords. The scales were arranged into separate sections, each of which was designed to protect a different part of the samurai's body.

1009 **In the early years of the samurai, the soldier on horseback was the elite warrior.** He was an archer, and fired arrows from a bow as his horse galloped along at speed. The mounted archer practised his archery techniques over and over again. In battle, when he had fired all his arrows, an archer fought with a sword.

Bow

Armoured
sleeve

Shin
guard

▶ A samurai warrior of the AD 900s. Mounted warriors were especially skilled at using the bow and arrow.

I DON'T BELIEVE IT!

One of the first types of armour worn in ancient Japan was made from iron. It was very heavy and awkward to move about in.

Shoulder guard

Arrows

Armoured kilt

Sword

1010 Infantry (foot soldiers) were lower class fighters. It was their job to hold up their shields to protect the mounted archers, who were seen as the main fighting force. As well as defending the horsemen, the infantry were also responsible for disrupting the enemy by setting fire to their property.

Minamoto clan mon, a flower

Taira clan mon, a butterfly

▲ ▶ Each clan had its own mon, or family crest. It was used on flags, and helped soldiers to identify their comrades.

1011 The two leading clans were the Minamoto (also called the Genji) and the Taira (also called the Heike). They were bitter rivals whose armies fought battles against each other to decide which was the leading clan.

Let battle begin!

▼ Battles began with archers firing a volley of whistling arrows.

1012 **An argument between rival clans would often lead to a battle.** When the two sides faced each other on the battlefield, the armies followed a strict sequence of events. The battle began with archers firing arrows that made a whistling sound. The noise was believed to be a sign to the gods, asking them to protect the samurai who were about to fight. It was also a scary sound for the enemy.

1013 *It was an honour to be first into battle.* A man was chosen from among the mounted warriors. He was picked because he was a champion fighter and came from a long line of warriors. Facing the enemy, he named his ancestors and listed his achievements in battle. It was a challenge to the other side to send out a warrior of equal status.

1014 **An opponent from the rival army would ride out to meet his enemy.** The two men then fought a duel on horseback, firing arrows at each other as they rode at speed around the battlefield. It was a contest to show who was the best rider and the best archer.

1015 **If the archery duel didn't produce a winner, the two men began hand-to-hand combat.** They dismounted from their horses, and fought until one of them was killed. The winner cut off his opponent's head and presented it to his commander as proof of his courage and skill. After the duel, fighting broke out. Men fought one to one, in groups, on horseback and on foot.

▲ In hand-to-hand fighting, samurai fought with swords that had long, curved blades.

I DON'T BELIEVE IT!

The mounted archer Minamoto Tametomo described how his arrow went straight through his opponent's saddle, passed through his body, then came out the other side!

1016 **The element of surprise was one of the most effective fighting tactics.** Soldiers would try to catch their enemies off-guard and ambush them, or creep up to their buildings and set them on fire.

Taira Masakado

1017 Born around AD 903, Taira Masakado is the first samurai commander that historians know much about. Part of the Taira clan, Masakado was the great-great grandson of Emperor Kammu. In his youth he served at the court of the Fujiwara clan in the capital Kyoto. The Fujiwaras were Japan's rulers at the time.

▼ Taira Masakado knocks a foot soldier to the ground. In old pictures such as this, he is always shown as a brave warrior.

1018 The Taira clan had its origins in AD 825, when the surname Taira was given to a branch of the royal family. The Taira settled in Hitachi, a district northwest of present-day Tokyo. They became the ruling family of the region, and built up a private army.

1019 Masakado wanted the Fujiwaras to appoint him as head of the national police. The Fujiwara clan refused to do this, so Masakado left their court and moved to the Kanto district of central Japan. From there, he led a war against the Fujiwara clan. In AD 939 he conquered districts in eastern Japan, and proclaimed himself to be the new emperor.

1021 In Kyoto, Masakado's head was put on a platform. Legend says the head flew back to Masakado's base in Kanto. From there it went on to Shibasaki, where it was buried with honour. Today, that place is known as Masakado Kubizuka (the Hill of Masakado's head), in Tokyo. Masakado is seen as a hero who fought the government for the rights of ordinary people.

1020 The government sent an army to defeat Masakado, who they regarded as a rebel. This army was led by Taira Sadamori. The two sides clashed at the Battle of Kojima, in AD 940, and Masakado was killed in the fighting. His head was cut off and sent to the emperor in Kyoto as proof of his death.

▼ At the Hill of Masakado's Head, there is a shrine in honour of Taira Masakado.

▼ The Battle of Kojima took place during a gale. Wooden shields erected by Masakado's army were blown down.

Minamoto Yoshiie

1022 The Minamoto clan was an offshoot of the Japanese royal family. But in the AD 800s it was decided that none of them would be emperor. They were given the surname Minamoto and moved from the capital at Kyoto to a new base at Osaka, in southern Japan. Here they became the district's ruling family.

1023 Minamoto Yoshiie was a samurai commander. He turned the Minamoto clan into a major fighting force. Born in 1039, at Kawachi, in the district of Osaka, his father was a samurai leader, and Yoshiie learned all the skills of the warrior from him.

◄ Minamoto Yoshiie was one of the greatest samurai commanders.

466

► Yoshiie earned the title *Hachiman-Taro*, meaning 'son of the god of war'.

1024 Yoshiie's first battles were against the Abe clan. He

fought alongside his father to defeat them in a war that raged for about nine years, and ended in 1062. The Minamoto clan took control of much of north Japan, with Yoshiie as ruler. Twenty years later, he defeated the Kiyowara clan, who had started to challenge him. The Minamotos were the undisputed rulers of north Japan.

I DON'T BELIEVE IT!

Once, Yoshiie guessed that his enemy was about to ambush him in a surprise attack because he saw a flock of geese suddenly fly out of a forest.

1025 After each battle, Yoshiie spoke to his troops. Men who had shown the most courage were invited to sit on a 'bravery' seat. All of them wanted this honour. No one wanted to sit on the other 'cowardice' seat. To be called a coward was a disgrace.

▼ A bronze statue of Minamoto Yoshiie in Fukushima, on the island of Honshu.

1026 Yoshiie's victories made him the greatest general in Japan. He

made Kyoto his home, and he hoped the government would reward him with a position of power, but they never did. Yoshiie spent his last years living quietly in the capital, where he died in 1106.

The Gempei War

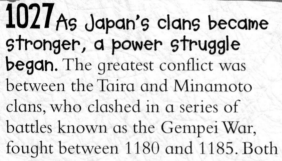

1027 As Japan's clans became stronger, a power struggle began. The greatest conflict was between the Taira and Minamoto clans, who clashed in a series of battles known as the Gempei War, fought between 1180 and 1185. Both clans were related to Japan's royal family, and they wanted to control it – and the rest of Japan.

1028 The Gempei War began when Taira Kiyomori ordered the death of Minamoto Yoritomo. Kiyomori and Yoritomo were the leaders of their respective clans. At first, the Taira forces were successful, and Yoritomo's army was heavily defeated. But the war was not over.

▶ Minamoto Yoritomo (1147–1199) led the Minamoto clan during the Gempei War.

▼ In 1180, Minamoto Yoritomo sent one of his men to kill an enemy from the Taira clan. This marked the start of the Gempei War.

1029 The Taira clan had a reputation for being harsh. As the war progressed, Taira troops started to defect and join the Minamoto army. It was now the Minamoto's turn for battle honours. In 1183, the Minamoto army seized the capital at Kyoto, then attacked the last strongholds of Taira resistance, which were in western Japan.

SAMURAI SYMBOLS

Every samurai clan had its own *mon* (see page 490). This was a symbol that was easy to recognize. *Mons* were usually based on plants or simple patterns made from dots, curves and lines. Some were based on animals, but these were less common. What *mon* would you design for your family? Look at the *mons* in the pictures in this book to give you some ideas.

1031 By 1192, the Minamoto clan controlled Japan. That year, Minamoto Yoritomo visited the emperor in Kyoto. The emperor appointed him as the first shogun (military dictator). From then on, Japan had two rulers – the god-like emperor (who had little power) and the shogun, the most powerful person in the land. It was a system that lasted until the mid–1800s.

1030 The final action of the Gempei War was the sea battle of Dan–no–ura, in 1185. Warships of the Taira and Minamoto clans fought in the narrow strip of water between the islands of Honshu and Kyushu. When it was clear the Minamoto would win, many of the Taira threw themselves into the sea.

▼ The Taira clan were defeated at the Battle of Dan-no-ura. This scene shows Taira Tomomori tied to an anchor, about to drown himself.

Bushido — the samurai code

1032 Samurai followed a code of behaviour known as *bushido*. It means 'the way of the warrior'. *Bushido* was a set of rules that governed all aspects of a samurai's lifestyle. It demonstrated that a samurai was an educated and refined man with knowledge of the arts and literature — as well as being a brutal killer who would slice off his enemy's head without hesitation.

▼ As well as being fierce warriors, samurai were required to be well dressed and educated.

1033 A samurai was expected to be a confident warrior. He had to believe he was strong, not just hope that he was. Self-belief was a key part of *bushido*. If warriors had doubts in themselves it meant they were weak, and weakness was not 'the way of the warrior'.

◄ A samurai was expected to show confidence at all times, and believe he was a worthy warrior.

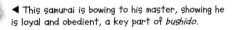
◀ This samurai is bowing to his master, showing he is loyal and obedient, a key part of *bushido*.

1035 **Courage was one of the most important rules of** *bushido*. To show courage, a samurai had to demonstrate that he was prepared to fight to the death. If he was outnumbered in battle, he had to carry on fighting. Running away was a sign of cowardice, which was punished.

1034 **Showing loyalty to the warlord was another rule of** *bushido*. The warlord gave orders, and samurai obeyed them without question. By obeying orders, a samurai showed obedience.

I DON'T BELIEVE IT!

Samurai were told to be careful when chasing their enemies. If an enemy got too far ahead, he could easily turn around and charge, putting the attacking samurai in danger.

1036 **If a samurai made a big mistake, he was punished under the rules of** *bushido*. In the most serious cases, he would kill himself. This was called *seppuku*, or *hara-kiri*. The samurai first ate a meal. After this he opened up his robes and plunged a dagger into his stomach. As he did this, another samurai cut his head off with a swing of his sword.

◀ A samurai about to commit *seppuku*, cutting open his own stomach.

Samurai armies

1037 By the 1550s, Japan was divided into many states, each of which was ruled by a *daimyo*. He was the warlord and head of a clan. Rival clans were almost constantly at war with each other. To protect their territory, warlords had large armies. As fighting increased, the armies grew more organized.

1039 Foot soldiers were called *ashigaru*. They made up a large part of a warlord's army, and there were always many more *ashigaru* than mounted samurai. *Ashigaru* fought with swords, spears, bows and *naginata* (see page 477). From the 1540s they began to use guns called arquebuses.

1038 Armies clashed during the fighting season, which lasted from spring until the end of summer. No fighting took place during the harvest season, which began in September, or in winter. Most foot soldiers were peasants from farming communities, and when it was harvest time they returned to their homes to gather crops.

1040 A samurai army was divided into units of men. The elite troops were always the men on horseback. The *ashigaru* were organized into groups of spearmen, archers and arquebusiers (soldiers with firearms). Other groups of *ashigaru* carried flags and banners, and some were given the job of carrying the army's baggage.

1041 On the battlefield, generals controlled troop movements by waving fans. The fans had swinging tassels on them, making the fan movements easy to see. Sound signals were another way of sending information to the troops, such as blowing on conch shells and beating on drums and gongs.

▼ A samurai army on the march. *Ashigaru* foot soldiers are flanked by mounted samurai. The most powerful clans had armies of over 100,000 men.

Warrior training

1042 **Boys were taught to be warriors.**
They began school at about the age of seven, and for the next five or six years were taught to read, write and play musical instruments. From about the age of ten, they were taught to fight. When a boy reached 13, he had a coming-of-age ceremony, and from then on he was ready to fight in battle.

▶ Boys were taught to fight using sticks, but these would eventually be replaced with swords.

1043 Some clans set up military training schools, or *dojo*. Here, boys were taught martial arts by trainers, or *sensei*. The *sensei* were skilled in the use of weapons, and had served in samurai armies. It was their job to pass these essential skills on.

1044 **Mounted warriors were the elite troops of a warlord's army.**
Their main weapon was the bow, and they had to fire arrows at moving targets as their horses raced at speed. They practised by firing arrows at running dogs. At the start of training, most arrows missed, but eventually they would learn when to release an arrow to hit a moving target.

I DON'T BELIEVE IT

Left-handed children born to samurai families had their left arms tied up, forcing them to become right-handed.

1046 Women married to samurai were trained to fight. Although their main work was to look after the family, there was always a chance that an enemy raiding party might attack the family home. To fight off attackers, women used daggers and *naginata* (see page 477). Some warlords had bands of armed women patrolling the grounds of their castles.

▲ When using dogs as target practice, the horsemen used blunt arrows. It was not their intention to kill the dogs.

1045 In another type of target practice, mounted samurai fired arrows at targets fixed to poles. They rode along a course, and as they moved past a small wooden board they fired an arrow. There were three targets, and the archer only had three arrows. The most skilful samurai made each arrow count and hit each target.

▶ Tomoe Gozen (c. 1157–1247) was a female warrior who fought on the side of the Minamoto clan during the Gempei War.

475

Weapons with edges

1047 Swords were the main edged weapons used by samurai. The blades were made of steel, in a process that involved heating and folding the metal several times. A sword was seen as the 'soul' of a samurai. The finest swords were made by master swordsmiths. They carved their own names, and the names of the owners, along with good luck verses on the sword handles.

Hilt or handle
(*tsuka*)

1048 New swords were tested for sharpness. They were tried out on sheaves of straw wrapped around bamboo, oak poles, copper plates and even metal helmets. Sometimes they were tested on people too, and were used to behead criminals. The best swords were so sharp they could cut through several bodies placed on top of one another.

▶ A master swordsmith at work. Each time the steel was reshaped, the sword became stronger.

Scabbard (*saya*)

Guard (*tsuba*)

Point of blade
(*kissaki*)

1049 The main fighting sword was called
a *katana*. It had a long, curving blade and was
mainly used for combat on foot. The samurai held
his sword in both hands as he moved it in a series
of attacking strokes, from zigzags and circles to up,
down and diagonal slashes. He could also use it
on horseback, holding it with one hand, not two.

▲ Each *katana* was highly prized. The best
swords were given names, such as 'The
Monster Cutter' or 'Little Dragon'.

▲ Guards at the end of the
hilt (handle) of a *katana*
stopped the swordsman's hand
from slipping onto the blade.

1050 Short swords called *tanto*
were used for fighting at close
quarters. Every samurai carried a
tanto. It was often the stabbing
thrust of a *tanto* that decided
the outcome of a duel.
The victorious
samurai then cut off
the loser's head.

▲ A short sword or *tanto* and its
scabbard. Like the *katana*, the
tanto was incredibly sharp.

◀ The curved blade at the
end of a *naginata*.

1051 Samurai used other
weapons with sharp edges.
The *naginata* was a long pole
with a curved metal blade at
the end. The blade was used for
slashing, and the pole for
beating. It was mainly a
weapon of the *ashigaru*, who
also used stabbing spears.

▶ Most spears had
pointed tips. Some
were hook-shaped
and used to drag
men from their
horses.

Missile weapons

1052 **The bow was as important to the samurai as the sword.** It was called a *yumi*, and was almost 2.5 metres in length. Made from strips of wood and bamboo, it fired arrows to a distance of about 380 metres, but its killing range was no more than about 80 metres.

► Arrowheads came in different shapes and sizes to carry out different functions.

Armour-piercing arrowheads

1053 Arrows were made of bamboo, and there were many types of arrowhead.

Some made whistling noises, some had armour-piercing tips, and some had forked heads to cut through ropes. One legend says a samurai archer sank an enemy ship by firing an arrow through its hull below the waterline.

Forked arrowhead

Whistling arrowhead

Match (rope for burning)

◄ The longbow was an effective weapon, and samurai archers were highly trained.

1054
In siege warfare (attacking a castle or city), samurai armies used machines to hurl stones. The first stone-throwers were giant crossbows but these were eventually replaced by trebuchets, a type of catapult. Trebuchets were used to bombard enemies with heavy rocks, which shattered when they hit the ground, causing casualties and damage.

▼ Samurai soldiers prepare to hurl a rock from a trebuchet.

▼ An *ashigaru* takes aim with an arquebus. Although these guns fired bullets in quick succession, they were less accurate than a skilled archer using a bow.

Barrel

1055
In the 1540s a new weapon arrived in Japan. It was the arquebus, a type of musket (a forerunner of the rifle). The Japanese called it a *teppo*, and it was carried by a foot soldier (*ashigaru*). The arquebus used gunpowder to fire a lead ball over a distance of about 500 metres, with a killing range of about 200 metres.

1056
Another gunpowder weapon was the cannon. However, unlike the arquebus, which was widely used, the cannon was not very popular with samurai armies. Any cannons that were used came from Dutch and English ships that visited Japan.

◄ This soldier is using a large bore arquebus, which fired a big lead ball.

Amazing armour

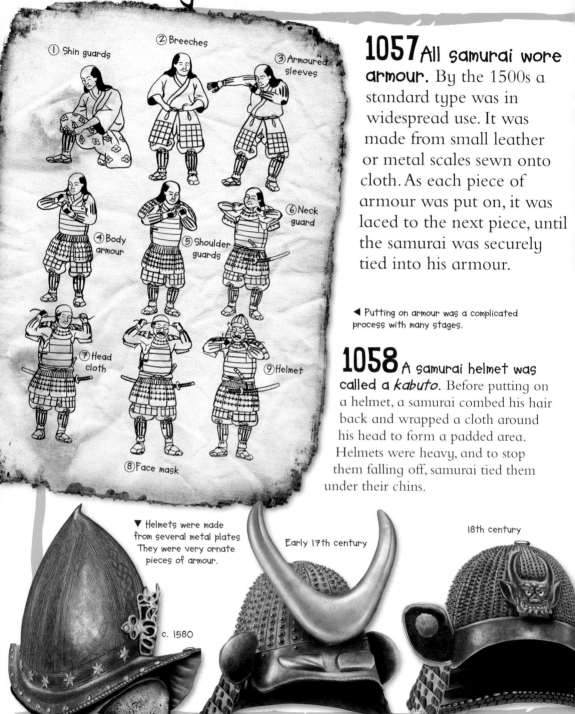

① Shin guards
② Breeches
③ Armoured sleeves
④ Body armour
⑤ Shoulder guards
⑥ Neck guard
⑦ Head cloth
⑧ Face mask
⑨ Helmet

◀ Putting on armour was a complicated process with many stages.

1057 **All samurai wore armour.** By the 1500s a standard type was in widespread use. It was made from small leather or metal scales sewn onto cloth. As each piece of armour was put on, it was laced to the next piece, until the samurai was securely tied into his armour.

1058 **A samurai helmet was called a *kabuto*.** Before putting on a helmet, a samurai combed his hair back and wrapped a cloth around his head to form a padded area. Helmets were heavy, and to stop them falling off, samurai tied them under their chins.

▼ Helmets were made from several metal plates. They were very ornate pieces of armour.

c. 1580

Early 17th century

18th century

1059 Most samurai went into battle barefaced, but some wore a face mask, or *mempo*. This could cover the whole of the face, or just the chin, cheeks, mouth and nose. The mask was usually painted, and the mouth was shaped like a grimace so the warrior looked as if he was snarling.

▲ Some masks had bristling fake moustaches to make the wearer seem even more terrifying.

1060 Samurai armour could be brightly coloured. Lacquer (varnish) was painted over each piece. It not only made the armour stand out, it also made it hard-wearing. The five 'lucky' colours were red, blue, yellow, black and white.

▶ Eighteenth century armour from the Edo Period.

1061 Samurai of the Li clan in the 1500s were known as the Red Devils. Their armour was coated with red lacquer, making them instantly recognizable. They chose red to make themselves appear more frightening, and because no other clan wore this colour.

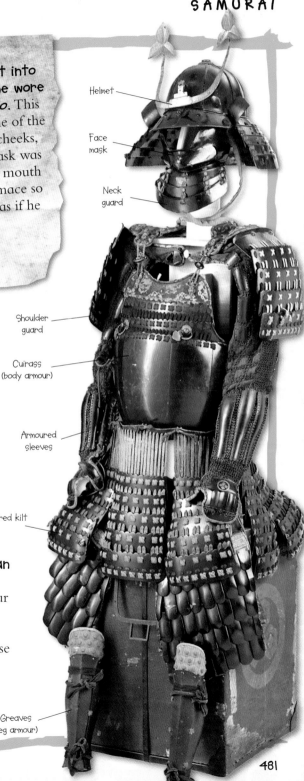

Helmet

Face mask

Neck guard

Shoulder guard

Cuirass (body armour)

Armoured sleeves

Armoured kilt

Greaves (leg armour)

481

Clothes and food

1062 For everyday clothing a samurai wore a *kimono*. This was a long, wide-sleeved gown that came down to below his knees and was kept in place by a belt wrapped around the waist. He wore a pair of *hakama* (wide trousers) under the *kimono* and socks and sandals on his feet. His *katana* (sword) was tucked into his belt.

Kimono

Katana

► A samurai in everyday dress. Even though he was not fighting, he still carried his sword.

Hakama

◄ A samurai with a typically shaven head. His remaining hair was tied in a bun at the back.

Socks and sandals

1063 Tidy hair was important. It was considered a disgrace if a man let his hair become untidy. In the 1500s, samurai began shaving the hair from the front part of their heads. This made it more comfortable to wear a helmet in battle. Hair at the sides and rear of the head was combed back and tied into a bun.

I DON'T BELIEVE IT!

Tokugawa Ieyasu, leader of the Tokugawa clan in the 1500s, didn't like shaved heads — he said it spoiled the look of a head when it was cut off!

1064 Rice was the staple food in Japan. It was eaten boiled and steamed, and as rice cakes and rice balls. Fish, pork, boar and rabbit were the main meats eaten. When samurai went to war, most warriors took portions of rice with them. If they raided an enemy camp or village, they took the enemy's food supplies.

◄ A local farmer offers a samurai commander baskets of melons for his troops. Fruit was popular with soldiers on campaign.

1065 Before a battle, samurai shared a meal together. It was a way of bringing the warriors closer to each other in the last few hours before fighting began.

1066 A helmet was not just for wearing. Some foot soldiers (*ashigaru*) used their metal helmets as cooking pots! They turned them upside down and boiled rice inside them over a fire. Small groups of men probably took it in turns to cook for their comrades.

▶ An *ashigaru's* metal helmet had two functions – protective armour and a cooking pot to boil rice.

Castle fortresses

1067 To protect their territory, samurai clans built castles. Some were built on flat plains, but most were built on mountains. Their purpose was to defend key areas such as bridges, river crossings, roads and mountain passes.

▶ A castle was surrounded by a strong wall. Inside were courtyards, each of which could be closed off if intruders broke through the main defences.

1068 Castles built in the 1500s were heavily defended. At the centre was the keep — the tallest and grandest building within the castle grounds, where the *daimyo* (warlord) lived. If intruders broke through the castle's outer line of defence, they were faced by a series of walls with gates that took them into open courtyards — where they could be easily attacked.

I DON'T BELIEVE IT!

Tottori Castle was besieged for 200 days. The occupants ran out of food and had to eat grass, dead horses, and possibly even each other.

③

④

484

1069 A clan's most important castle was the home of the *daimyo*. Around this castle were the homes of generals and family members. The more important the person was, the closer to the leader's castle they were allowed to live. A town grew up around the castle. Rice was grown in the surrounding fields to provide food for the townspeople.

1070 Matsumoto Castle is one of Japan's finest samurai castles. It was built in the late 1500s, on a flat plain in central Japan. Its location made it an easy target, but the builders protected it with three moats and strong ramparts. The castle complex was surrounded by an earth wall 3.5 kilometres in circumference. The only way to enter or leave was through two heavily fortified gates.

1071 Castles were difficult to attack. Armies besieged a castle until its occupants surrendered. When Takamatsu Castle was besieged in 1582, the attackers diverted a river until it formed a lake. As the lake grew, it flooded the castle, and the occupants gave in. The defeated leader rowed out on the lake and committed suicide (*seppuku*).

KEY

① Keep (where the *daimyo* lived)
② Moat
③ Outer wall
④ Inner wall
⑤ Gatehouse

The age of battles

1072 **Many battles took place all over Japan in the years 1450–1600.** This time is known as the Warring States Period. It was a time of civil war, when rival states attacked each other, trying to win territory. The battles were fought on a large scale, and from the mid–16th century arquebuses were used – the first time this deadly firearm was put into practise in a big way.

1073 **Armies fought in battle formations.** Generals decided which formation was best to use, and the troops moved into place. Formations had names such as 'birds in flight', 'keyhole' and 'half moon'. In the 'birds in flight' formation, the arquebusiers protected the archers, who fired arrows over the heads of the musketmen. The general was at the centre, surrounded by his warriors.

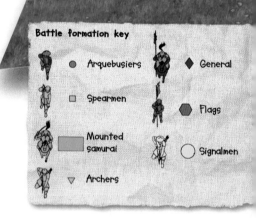

Battle formation key

- ● Arquebusiers
- □ Spearmen
- ▬ Mounted samurai
- ▽ Archers
- ◆ General
- ⬡ Flags
- ○ Signalmen

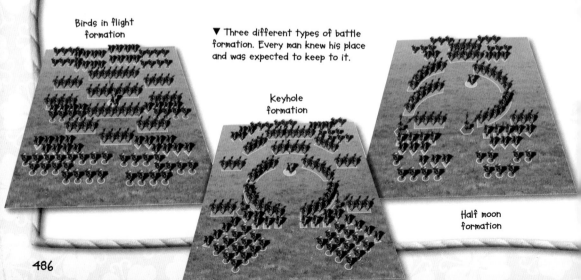

Birds in flight formation

▼ Three different types of battle formation. Every man knew his place and was expected to keep to it.

Keyhole formation

Half moon formation

1074 The 'arrowhead' formation was used to break through enemy lines. Arquebusiers fired their muskets, opening up gaps in the enemy's front ranks. When the gaps were big enough, samurai rushed past their gunmen, and through the gaps. Hand-to-hand fighting followed using swords, daggers, *naginata* and spears.

◄ The arrowhead formation takes its name from the pointed arrow-like position of the troops.

1075 The greatest prizes were the heads of the losers. They were cut off and presented to the general for him to inspect. First, the heads were washed, the hair was combed, and they were placed on spikes on boards. Labels attached to the hair gave the names of the dead, and the names of the men who had killed them.

1076 After the battle, the victors took the spoils. The dead of both sides were stripped of their weapons and armour. Scavengers from nearby villages helped themselves to whatever they could carry. Wounded warriors were of no use to anyone. They were killed by local villagers, who then took their belongings.

▼ The severed head of an enemy soldier being presented for inspection.

I DON'T BELIEVE IT!
If the eyes of a severed head were closed, it was a lucky sign. If they were open and looking upwards, it was an unlucky sign.

Oda Nobunaga

1077 One of greatest samurai commanders of the Warring States Period was Oda Nobunaga. He was born in 1534, and became *daimyo* (warlord) of the Oda clan when he was just 16. Because he was so young, rival clans thought they could easily overpower his army and take his land – but they were wrong. In a series of battles, Nobunaga's forces defeated his enemies.

1079 The Battle of Nagashino was fought in 1575. In this great battle, Nobunaga sent an army to the castle of Nagashino. The castle was besieged by an army from the Takeda clan. Nobunaga's plan was to end the siege by fighting the Takedas.

1078 Nobunaga's rise to power began in 1560. In that year, his territory was invaded by the Imagawa clan. The Imagawa army was 12 times the size of Nobunaga's, and they quickly took several of his fortresses. It looked as if Nobunaga would be defeated. But, during a thunderstorm, Nobunaga mounted a surprise attack. The Imagawa *daimyo* was killed, and Nobunaga's territory was saved.

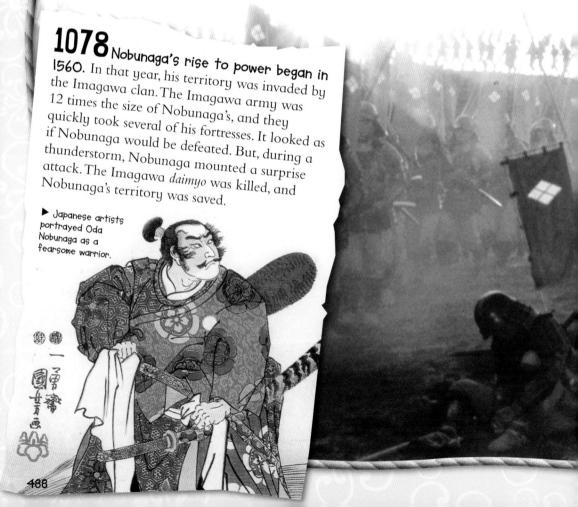

▶ Japanese artists portrayed Oda Nobunaga as a fearsome warrior.

1080 The Nobunaga and Takeda armies clashed on a plain near Nagashino Castle.
Mounted samurai from the Takeda clan charged at Nobunaga's forces, and were felled by shots from as many as 3000 arquebusiers. A second wave of Takeda horsemen swooped down, by which time the musketmen had reloaded. After hours of bitter fighting, the Takeda army withdrew.

QUIZ

1. How old was Nobunaga when he became leader of his clan?
2. What was the weather like when Nobunaga defeated the Imagawa daimyo?
3. How many arquebusiers did Nobunaga use against the Takedas?
4. When was the Battle of Nagashino?
5. In which city did Nobunaga die?

Answers:
1. 16 2. There was a thunderstorm
3. 3000 4. 1575 5. Kyoto

▼ A scene from *Kagemusha*, a film released in 1980. Set during the Warring States Period, it ends with the Battle of Nagashino.

1081 Oda Nobunaga died in 1582.
He had become the most powerful general in Japan, and acted as if he was the country's shogun. This made him many enemies. On a visit to Honnoji Temple, in Kyoto, he was attacked by his own men. Some accounts say he died in the attack, others say he was captured and forced to commit *seppuku*.

Flags and standards

1082 Samurai carried flags and standards into battle. There could be hundreds of flags fluttering in the wind on the battlefield, and each one had its own meaning. Some were decorated with family, clan or religious symbols, others had messages on them. It was the job of an army's foot soldiers to carry the flags.

1083 A battlefield could be a confusing place. In the rush of horses and the scattering of men, it was easy for a soldier to become separated from his fellow warriors, or lose sight of his *daimyo* (warlord). If this happened, all he had to do was look around for the flags of his own side, which he would recognize by their familiar symbols.

▲ The Soma-Nomaoi Festival is held each year in Haramachi City. Here, horsemen in traditional samurai armour parade with flags decorated with clan symbols, or *mons*.

▼ ▶ The red umbrella great standard of Oda Nobunaga and the golden bell great standard of Mukai Tadakatsu, leader of the Omura clan.

1084 In samurai battles of the late 1500s and 1600s, the *daimyo* had two standards. They were the 'great standard' and the 'lesser standard', both mounted on long poles. A standard was an important object to a clan. Not only was it instantly recognizable, it represented what the clan stood for, and was to be protected.

1085 Samurai could attach flags to their backs. These were called *sashimono*. The shaft of the flag slotted into a holder in the armour, leaving both hands free for weapons. *Sashimono* were often decorated with the clan's colours or symbols. Some samurai painted their flags with messages, giving the name of the wearer and the name of the man he hoped to kill in battle.

▶ A *sashimono* attached to the back of a samurai. 'Leader' is written on his flag in Japanese.

1086 It was a great honour to be a standard-bearer, but this honour brought danger. The enemy was drawn towards the other side's standard, so the standard-bearer was always in the thick of the fighting. The defending army would do everything they could to save the standard from being captured. If the standard-bearer fell, another man quickly took his place.

DESIGN A FLAG

Have a close look at the flags pictured in this book, then design one of your own. Note how the flags are long and thin, which made them easy to carry. Keep your design simple and bold, and use strong colours so that it really stands out.

Samurai in decline

► Tokugawa Ieyasu, the shogun who brought a long period of peace to Japan.

1087 **On 21 October 1600, the Battle of Sekigahara took place.** It was fought between the armies of Tokugawa Ieyasu (with 80,000 men) and Ishida Mitsunari (100,000 men). An estimated 30,000 men died on the battlefield. The Tokugawa clan won, and the battle brought an end to the Warring States Period.

1088 **Tokugawa Ieyasu became shogun in 1603.** It was the start of a relatively peaceful period in Japan's history that lasted for the next 250 years. In 1639, Japan became a 'closed country'. It was forbidden to have contact with foreigners, and Japanese people were not even allowed to leave the country.

▼ The arrival of the American navy in Tokyo harbour in 1853 caused great concern in Japan.

▼ Emperor Meiji ruled Japan from 1868 to 1912.

1089 The clans were now at peace with each other, and their armies were disbanded. The idea of going to war to steal another clan's territory became a thing of the past. Samurai traditions and rituals still carried on, but they were performed for peaceful purposes.

1090 In 1853 and 1854, a fleet of ships from the USA arrived in Tokyo Harbour. The American fleet was led by Commodore Matthew Perry. His aim was for Japan to stop being a closed country and to open up to foreign trade. The Tokugawa clan were still Japan's rulers, and the shogun Tokugawa Iesada decided to open up the country. Many Japanese thought this was a bad thing.

1091 Japan's system of an emperor sharing power with the shogun came to an end in 1867. It was a system that had lasted for 675 years. The last shogun, Tokugawa Yoshinobu, handed power back in 1867, and in 1868, Emperor Meiji became the sole ruler of Japan. For some people, these changes were too much to bear.

The last samurai

1092 The Satsuma Rebellion took place in 1877. Samurai were unhappy at the changes in Japan. For centuries they had been respected, and feared, members of society. Gradually their way of living had changed, and now they felt out of place as Japan began a process of modernization, bringing to an end centuries of feudal rule. When they were told to lay down their swords, it was the final insult, and a rebellion began.

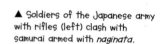

▲ Soldiers of the Japanese army with rifles (left) clash with samurai armed with *naginata*.

▶ Saigo Takamori (1828–1877), leader of the rebel forces during the Satsuma Rebellion, was the last samurai commander.

1093 Leader of the rebellion was Saigo Takamori. His army of 40,000 samurai fought against a larger government force. The samurai fought with their traditional weapons – the sword and the bow. The Japanese army fought with rifles.

1094 The rebellion lasted for about eight months. It ended at the Battle of Shiroyama, on 24 September 1877. Takamori's forces had been reduced to a few hundred men. He was heavily outnumbered, but refused to surrender as this was against the *bushido* code. Takamori was wounded, and then he committed *seppuku* rather than face being captured. His remaining men were cut down by gunfire.

1095 Many films have been made about the samurai. The most famous is *Seven Samurai*, made in Japan in 1954 and set in the Warring States Period. Another is *Kagemusha*, made in 1980. Both of these films were directed by Akira Kurosawa, who is regarded as the greatest samurai film-maker of all time. Hollywood has also made films about samurai, such as *The Last Samurai* in 2003 with Tom Cruise in the title role.

▼ In the 2003 Warner Brothers' film *The Last Samurai*, actor Tom Cruise plays the part of an American fighting on the side of the samurai during the Satsuma Rebellion.

I DON'T BELIEVE IT!

In the *Star Wars* movies, the costume of Darth Vader was inspired by samurai armour.

495

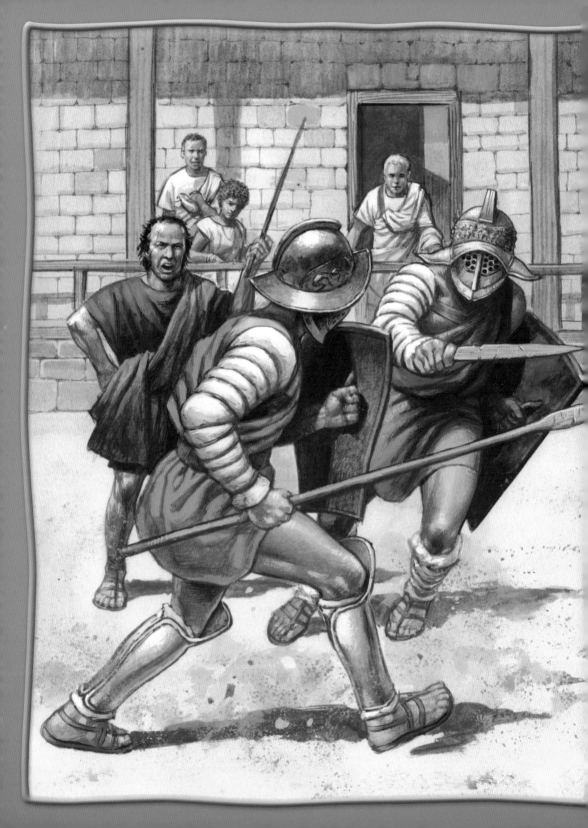

Index

Index

Entries in **bold** refer to main subject entries. Entries in *italics* refer to illustrations.

Index

Index

Index

Index

Index

Acknowledgements

All artworks are from the Miles Kelly Artwork Bank

The publishers would like to thank the following sources for the use of their photographs:
(t = top, b = bottom, l = left, r = right, c = centre, bg = background)

Alamy 54–55 M. Crame; 59(tr) Walter Rawlings; 80 Blaine Harrington III; 81(b) World Pictures; 137(br) Charles Stirling; 414(bc) Jim Cole; 423(tr) and 438(tr) North Wind Picture Archives; 457(b) Mary Evans Picture Library; 462 Photos 12; 469 V&A Images; 481(r) Interfoto; 488–489 Photos 12; 494(c) Tibor Bognar

The Art Archive 365(t); 459(t) Rijksmuseum voor Volkenkunde Leiden (Leyden)/Gianni Dagli Orti; 471(b) Bibliothèque des Arts Décoratifs Paris/Gianni Dagli Orti; 475(b); 477(t) and (c) Gunshots; 492–493(b) British Museum; 494–495(t) Private Collection/Granger Collection

Corbis 61(t) Roger Ressmeyer; 66–67 Richard T. Nowitz; 75 Benjamin Lowy; 81(t) Jeremy Horner; 94(b) Christophe Boisvieux; 118(b) Werner Forman Archive/The Greenland Museum; 120(b) Remigiusz Sikora/epa; 147(tr) The Art Archive; 159(t) Richard Cummins; 162–163 Jose Fuste Raga; 210–211 Bettmann; 242 Roger Wood; 244 K M Westermann; 354–355(b); 366–367 Robert Holmes; 437 Gianni Dagli Orti; 438–439 Barry Lewis; 440(bl) PoodlesRock; 450 Bettmann; 450–451(tc); 464; 467(t); 468(b) Asian Art & Archaeology, Inc.; 492(t) Sakamoto Photo Research Laboratory

Fotolia.com 20–21(bg) Maria Goncalves; 20(br) and 56(bg) Rafa Irusta; 106–107(bg); 129(t) felinda; 147(br) Svetlana Gatova; 480(tl) Kirsty Pargeter; 493(t) U.P.images

Getty Images 446–447 Bogdan Willewalde; 448–449 Rajesh Jantilal/AFP; 490–491(t) Hiroshi Higuchi

iStockphoto.com 59(b) Jakich; 79(c) Kelly Keely-Frost; 85(t); 128(b) maks dezman; 144(b) Keith Binns; 146(b) Andreas Karelias; 153(b) Vasiliki Varvaki; 157(b) Danilo Ascione; 198–199(bg) maks dezman; 442(tr) Constance McGuire; 446(tl) HultonArchive

The Kobal Collection 495(b) Warner Bros/James, David

Moviestore Collection Ltd 412–413 and 421(r) Warner Bros. Pictures; 433(b) Twentieth Century-Fox Film Corporation

Photolibrary 58–59 JTB Photo; 95(t); 465(c); 467(b) JTB Photo; 482(c) Corbis

Pictorial Press 243 Dreamworks/Universal; 245(b) Bryna/Universal; 246 Dreamworks/Universal

Rex Features 147(bl) Patrick Frilet; 161(b) KPA/Zuma

Shutterstock.com 52 holbox; 53 George Bailey; 166 Phant; 178–179(bg) Mark Carrel; 206–207(bg) Mark Carrel; 218(tr) Andrei Nekrassov; 288 Phillip Minnis; 329 PaulPaladin; 395(b) Alice Day; 404(bl) lrafael; 429(b) tovovan

Topfoto.co.uk 65(b) Werner Forman; 84–85(b) 2006 Alinari; 96 Topham Picturepoint; 98–99(t) The British Museum/HIP; 110(t); 111(t) Topham Picturepoint; 114(t) Topham Picturepoint; 118(b) Werner Forman Archive/The Greenland Museum; 121(t) Charles Walker, (b) Roger-Viollet; 122(b); 123(cr) John Malam, (b) TopFoto/Fotean; 134 Topham Picturepoint; 142–143 TopFoto; 422–423 Warner Bros. Pictures; 441 TopFoto/HIP; 443(b) Topham Picturepoint; 444(tr) The British Library /HIP; 448(tr) The British Library/HIP; 449(tl) The Granger Collection; 493(t) Print Collector/HIP

All other photographs are from:

Corel, digitalSTOCK, digitalvision, ImageState, John Foxx, PhotoAlto, PhotoDisc, PhotoEssentials, PhotoPro, Stockbyte

Every effort has been made to acknowledge the source and copyright holder of each picture. Miles Kelly Publishing apologises for any unintentional errors or omissions.